300 CROSSWORD PUZZLES

Amanda Darby

chartwell
books

INTRODUCTION

The first crosswords appeared in England during the 19th century, initially created for children. But in the United States, the crossword soon developed into a serious adult pastime. The first known published crossword appeared in the New York World newspaper in 1913 and was created by Arthur Wynne, a journalist from Liverpool, who since then has been credited as the inventor of the popular puzzle. During the early 1920s, other newspapers started running crosswords and within a decade the puzzles were featured in almost all American newspapers.

Going to work or school, grabbing a cup of coffee, taking out the trash—these are just a few parts of the average day-to-day. We form habits and do them without thinking. But what would we discover if we paid more attention to everyday norms?

In the following pages, you'll go on a journey through many moments from the random to familiar, solving crossword puzzles that deal with your gym routine, cleaning the house, a day at the beach, and many more general life experiences. There is beauty in the regular day-to-day, and actions or events that may seem simple or mundane or superfluous knowledge you have picked up over the years will actually hold the answers that will help you solve each puzzle!

The puzzles have been organized into three levels of difficulty and can be easily identified by their colors—yellow for easy, red for moderate, and teal for difficult.

PART 1: EASY

The puzzles in this section are a great warm-up round. The clues are straightforward and draw on generally understood facts and pop culture knowledge. Get through these to start off strong with a good foundation for what comes next.

PART 2: MODERATE

This section of puzzles is a bit more challenging as the themes center around more niche hobbies and knowledge that is more specific.

PART 3: DIFFICULT

You won't be able to breeze through these puzzles; they are real head scratchers! If you get stuck, you can always look to the name of the puzzle to remind you of the theme. All the clues and answers relate back to the title in some way.

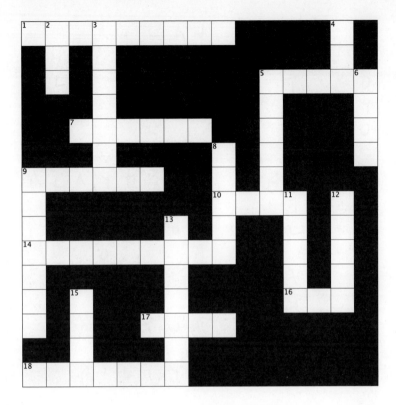

ACROSS

1. '_____ Young Woman'

5. 'The Trial of the Chicago _____'

7. Drama about an immigrant family in the 1980s

9. 'The _____', starring Anthony Hopkins

10. Film about the writing of 'Citizen Kane'

14. 2021 Best Picture winner

16. Language Ruben learns in 12-Down, for short

17. Chloe _____, director of 14-Across

18. David _____, director of 10-Across

DOWN

2. With 8-Down, star of 12-Down

3. 'Judas and the Black _____'

4. _____ Isaac Chung, director of 7-Across

5. Aaron _____, director of 5-Across

6. How many women of color had directed Best Picture winners before 8 See 2-Down

9. Emerald _____, director of 1-Across

11. Where the family in 7-Across is from

12. 'Sound of _____'

13. The Black _____ Party, subject of 3-Down

15. Part for Frances in 14-Across

Answer on page 303

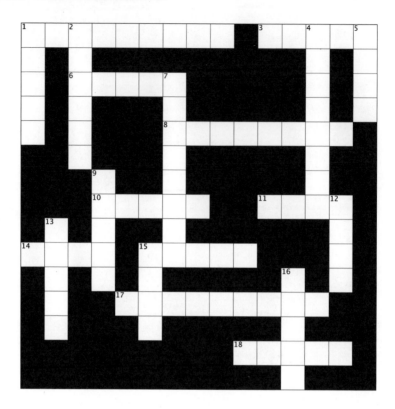

ACROSS

1. Coffee chain founded in Seattle
3. Coffee choice later in the day
6. Coffee drink made with 7-Down and 15-Down
8. Preparation in which 13-Down is run over coffee grounds and through a filter
10. French _____
11. Like cold brew
14. Coffee nickname with an island etymology
15. Coffee and chocolate drrink
17. 6-Down with a higher proportion of coffee to milk
18. Coffee preference

DOWN

1. Coffee sweetener
2. Cafe _____, popular in France
4. Stimulant in coffee
5. 6-Across topper
7. Concentrated coffee often served in shots
9. Coffee addition
12. Basic coffee preparation method
13. Liquid base for coffee
15. Dairy product often used in coffee
16. 13-Down, heated and vaporized and used to make 6-Across

Answer on page 303

ACROSS
1. Bird of prey
4. Medieval drink made from honey
7. Activity with lances
10. 'Here be ____'
13. Edward, Henry, and Charles
14. She presides over the faire
16. Magical man
17. Dishonest man
18. Live entertainment, perhaps
19. Messy spectacle

DOWN
2. Sharpened tool thrown at a target
3. State in which the first Renaissance festival was held
4. A polite term of address
5. Animal needed for 7-Across
6. Vessel for 4-Across, perhaps
8. Implement upon which much faire food is served
9. Art form demonstrated at many Renaissance faires
11. Sheep meat
12. '____ and well met!'
15. Quaint term for restrooms

Answer on page 303

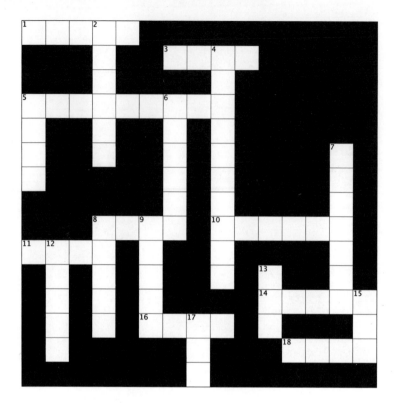

ACROSS

1. With 'the,' an energy that connects all things in the Star Wars galaxy

3. Diminutive Dagobah resident

5. Luke's surname

8. Enforcers of peace and justice in the galaxy

10. C-3PO, R2-D2, and BB-8, for example

11. Princess played by Carrie

14. Forest planet inhabited by 12-Down

16. Ice planet

18. Character played by John Boyega

DOWN

2. Affectionate nickname for 9-Down's Wookie sidekick

4. Luke's father

5. Enemy of the Jedis

6. Surname of Luke's first Jedi mentor

7. Harrison Ford role

8. _____ the Hutt

9. _____ Star, space station capable of destroying planets

12. Fuzzy residents of 14-Across

13. Character mentored by Luke in later episodes

15. Kylo _____, AKA Ben Solo

17. Standard starfighter used by the 5-Down

Answer on page 303

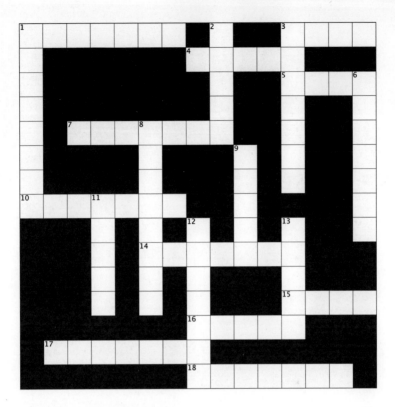

ACROSS

1. Light, airy fruit pie
3. Key ____ pie
4. Pie that is often delivered
5. Pie with an open top
7. Served with ice cream
10. Pie flavored with nutmeg and cinnamon
14. Rustic dessert sometimes made with apples
15. Traditional Filipino pie
16. Meat pie need
17. Despite the name, this sandwich cookie isn't actually a pie
18. Strawberry go-with in a pie

DOWN

1. Imitation whipped cream
2. Small British Christmas pie
3. Woven pie dough, usually placed on top of a pie
6. Type of British 5-Across with golden syrup and breadcrumbs
8. Lemon ____ pie
9. Pastry base
11. Thanksgiving pie
12. Elongated pie with one savory end and one sweet end
13. Chocolate pie from Kentucky

Answer on page 304

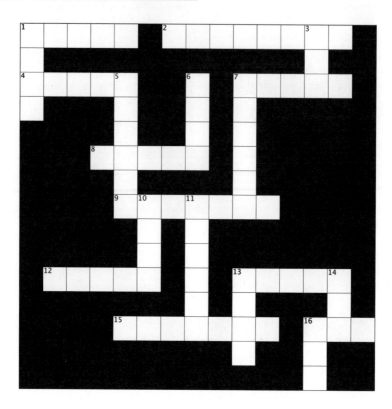

ACROSS

1. Person who carries a golfer's equipment
2. In casual golf, an uncounted extra shot
4. Area with uncut grass
7. Score that's one stroke over 14-Down
8. Score that's two strokes under 14-Down
9. Divots on a golf ball
12. Putting area
13. What a golfer does before the first stroke
15. Area where the grass is kept short
16. Someone who gets paid to play

DOWN

1. Vehicle on the course
3. Hole-in-one
5. Water or sand
6. What you're aiming for
7. Score that's one stroke under 14-Down
10. The most common type of golf club
11. Club used for short strokes
13. Sand-filled bunker
14. Predetermined number of strokes a hole or round should take
16. Professional golf org.

Answer on page 304

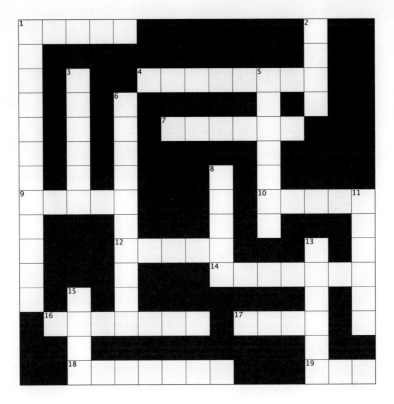

ACROSS

1. 'Four _____ and seven years ago...'
4. National conflict, 1860–1865
7. Lincoln boy who died age 11
9. Coin upon which Lincoln appears
10. Month in which Lincoln died, 1865
12. Prominent facial feature on Lincoln
14. Per Lincoln, 'if _____ is not wrong, nothing is wrong'
16. Lincoln's opponent in 1860
17. Lincoln's first political party
18. Series of seven public events in 1858
19. Youngest Lincoln son

DOWN

1. Lincoln's trademark headwear
2. With 15-Down, Lincoln's eventual wife
3. Lincoln's vice president
5. Poet who wrote several notable elegies after Lincoln's assassination
6. Site of a famous address
8. _____ Theatre, Washington DC
11. Lincoln's profession before politics
13. Notable physical attribute for Lincoln
15. See 2-Down

Answer on page 304

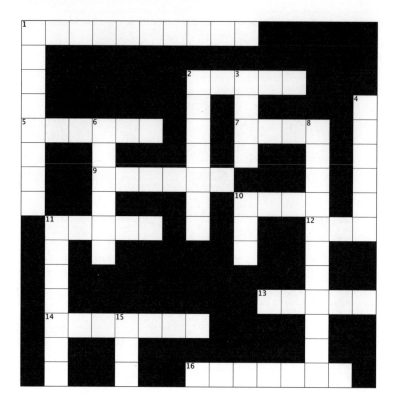

ACROSS
1. Prehistoric monument
2. Diana, Princess of _____
5. England's capital
7. British apartment
9. World's most famous clock
10. Baby carriage
11. Fish and _____
12. The London _____ (Ferris wheel)
13. '_____ Jack,' nickname for the British flag
14. Visit its green, rolling hills
16. National animal of 1-Down (really)

DOWN
1. Its capital is Edinburgh
2. London theater district
3. Elevator
4. Buckingham _____
6. Capital of 14-Across
8. It runs through London
10. Place for a pint
11. 2-Across's capital city
15. W.C.

Answer on page 304

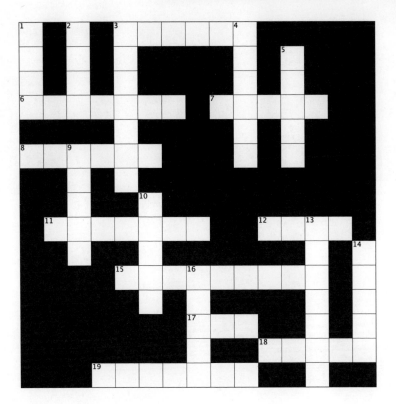

ACROSS

3. Chris (Col. Frank Fitts, 1999)
6. Justin (Kevin Garvey, 2014–2017)
7. Chris (Captain America, 2011–2019)
8. Heath (Patrick Verona, 1999)
11. Ryan (Lars Lindstrom, 2007)
12. Harrison (Han Solo, 1977–2019)
15. LaKeith (Snoop Dogg, 2015)
17. Jude (Dickie Greenleaf, 1999)
18. Tom (Bane, 2012)
19. Ben (Larry Gigli, 2003)

DOWN

1. Brad (Billy Beane, 2011)
2. Christian (Jack Kelly, 1992)
3. George (Michael Clayton, 2007)
4. Keanu (Neo, 1999–2003)
5. Tom (Forrest Gump, 1994)
9. Matt (Will Hunting, 1997)
10. Colin (Mark Darcy, 2001–2016)
13. Robert (Jay Gatsby, 1974)
14. Adrien (Wladyslaw Szpilman, 2002)
16. Nick (Kuill, 2019)

Answer on page 304

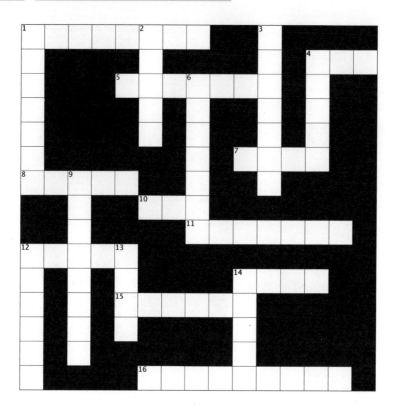

ACROSS

1. Emma ('Sense and Sensibility')
4. Brian ('Succession')
5. Alan ('Die Hard')
7. Sean ('Game of Thrones')
8. Hugh ('Love Actually')
10. Stephen ('QI')
11. Julie ('The Sound of Music')
12. Michael ('Alfie')
14. Florence ('Midsommar')
15. John ('Star Wars: Episode VII—The Force Awakens')
16. Daniel ('Harry Potter' series)

DOWN

1. Sandi ('The Great British Bake-Off')
2. Maggie ('Downton Abbey')
3. Kate ('Titanic')
4. Sacha Baron ('Borat')
6. Daniel ('Get Out')
9. Rowan ('The Lion King')
12. John ('Monty Python and the Holy Grail')
13. Idris ('The Wire')
14. Dev ('Slumdog Millionaire')

Answer on page 304

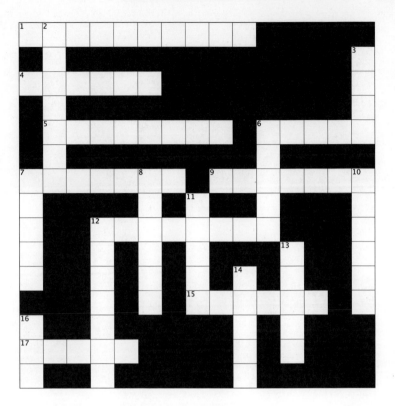

ACROSS

1. Kerry (Olivia Pope, 2012–2018)

4. Carrie (Leia, 1977–2019)

5. Emma (Professor Trelawney, 2004–2011)

6. Kathy (Annie Wilkes, 1990)

7. Julie (Maria von Trapp, 1965)

9. Natalie (Padme Amidala, 1999–2005)

12. Anne (Fantine, 2012)

15. Meryl (Joanna Kramer, 1979)

17. Catherine (Moira Rose, 2015–2020)

DOWN

2. Jennifer (Rachel Green, 1994–2004)

3. Elisabeth (Peggy Olson, 2007–2015)

6. Halle (Storm, 2000–2006)

7. Amy (Princess Giselle, 2007)

8. Emma (Hermione Granger, 2001–2011)

10. Thandiwe (Maeve Millay, 2016–2021)

11. Geena (Dottie Hinson, 1992)

12. Audrey (Holly Golightly, 1961)

13. Sally (Norma Rae, 1979)

14. Pam (Foxy Brown, 1974)

16. Laverne (Sophia Burset, 2013–2019)

Answer on page 305

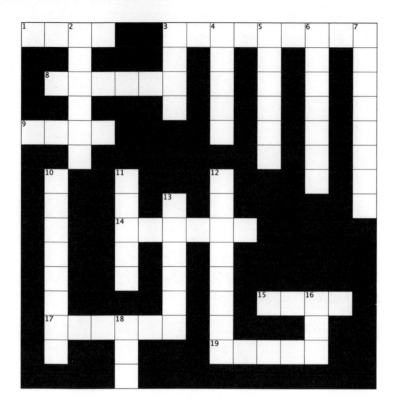

ACROSS

1. Dairy product sometimes added to tea
3. Bedtime drink
8. Product whose name means 'fine powder tea'
9. Summer tea choice
14. Per capita, world's largest consumer of tea
15. In Britain, a teapot's sweater
17. Type of tea also known as a tisane
19. Tea traditionally served in Chinese restaurants

DOWN

2. Tea source
3. Indian black tea with spices
4. Pleasant smell
5. Tea type in which the leaves are bruised and oxidized
6. Tool for brewing loose tea
7. Tea flavored with bergamot
10. Fizzy, fermented tea
11. Brewing necessity
12. Tea term for 'soaking'
13. British author who wrote the 1946 essay 'A Nice Cup of Tea'
16. On a hot day, you can brew tea using this
18. Tea sachet

Answer on page 305

ACROSS
1. Right, on a ship
5. Basic sailing maneuver
7. Onboard jail
8. Ship's steering wheel
10. Unit measuring six feet
12. Distress signal
14. Ship's left
15. Weight used to keep a ship in one place
16. Kitchen on a ship
18. Area used for embarking and disembarking

DOWN
1. Back of the boat
2. Sheltered from the wind
3. Boat's cockpit
4. Toward the rear of the ship
6. Enclosed space for sleeping
8. Where one does one's business
9. Steering device at the rear of the vessel
11. Tall pole on a ship
13. Fabric attached to 11-Down
17. Side-to-side movement of a ship

Answer on page 305

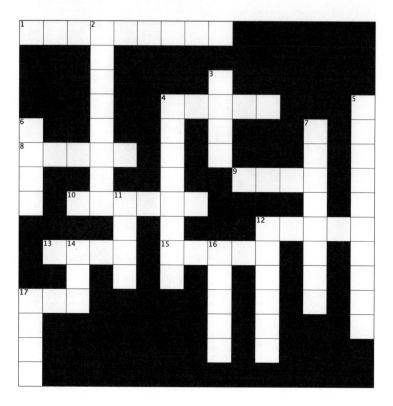

ACROSS

1. Alaska's most populous city
4. Indigenous group with a name that means 'the people'
8. Indigenous people with a namesake group of islands
9. Hawaiian city that sounds like two adjectives
10. Alaska's capital
12. Alaskan city with Russian heritage
13. Hormel product popular in Hawaii
15. US president who was born in Hawaii
17. Floral necklace

DOWN

2. Largest city in Hawaii
3. Polynesian dance form
4. Annual Alaskan race in which participants are both human and canine
5. First ruler of the Kingdom of Hawaii
6. Island that's home to Hawaii's capital
7. 'The Last _____'
11. Where 4-Down ends
12. State fish of Alaska
14. Mashed taro root
16. Hawaiian greeting
17. Traditional Hawaiian party

Answer on page 305

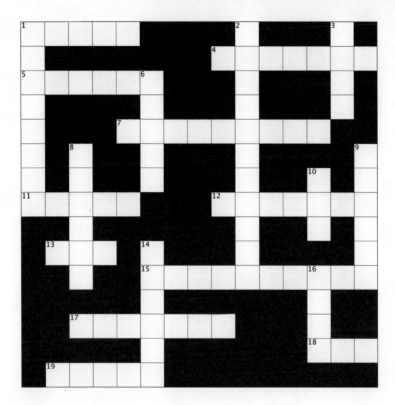

ACROSS

1. Alice's pet cat
4. Wonderland creator
5. Animal that Alice follows
7. Director of a live-action version of the story in 2010
11. Wonderland directive
12. Plants who sing to and insult Alice
13. Queen of Hearts's color
15. Holiday celebrated by 1-Down and 8-Down
17. 'Why is a raven like a _____ desk?'
18. '_____ with his head!'
19. Prominent feature of the Cheshire Cat

DOWN

1. 8-Down's small sidekick
2. Character whose seen smoking hookah
3. Prominent color of Alice's dress
6. Tweedledee and Tweedledum
8. Mad _____
9. Studio that produced the 1951 film version
10. Type of party Alice attends
14. Mock _____
16. Bird who tries to burn Alice's house down

Answer on page 305

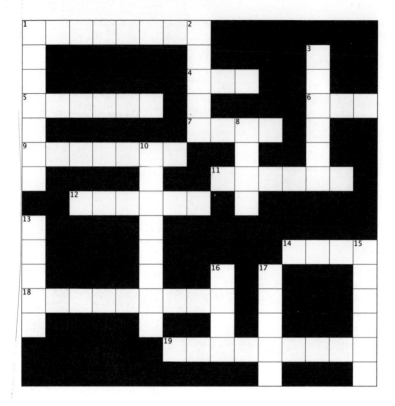

ACROSS

1. Long pass, usually made in desperation
4. Rule enforcer, informally
5. Two-pointer
6. Piece of protective equipment
7. When the QB is tackled before he can pass the ball
9. Change of play made after a 15-Down
11. Smallest player on the team, usually
12. Protective headgear
14. Any play that doesn't involve a pass
18. Play worth six points
19. NFL championship game

DOWN

1. Trophy awarded to the most outstanding college player
2. Units of measure for a football field
3. Name for a play and a player
8. It's flipped before a game
10. Namesake of the 19-Across trophy
13. High-risk defensive play
15. Meeting before 16-Down
16. Play starter
17. Former Packer Brett

Answer on page 305

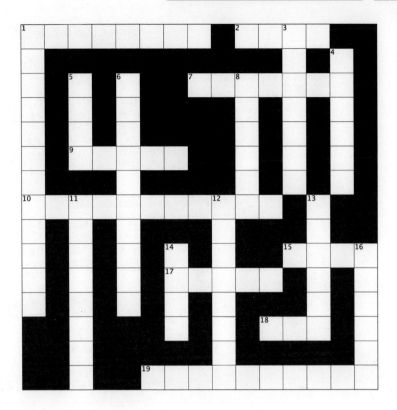

ACROSS

1. Old ____, Wyoming
2. Liberty ____, Pennsylvania
7. Fort ____, Maryland
9. ____ Hawk, North Carolina
10. Tourist spot in Manhattan, New York
15. Hollywood ____, California
17. Remember it, with 'the', Texas
18. Grand ____ Opry, Tennessee
19. ____ Memorial, mountain carving under construction in South Dakota

DOWN

1. Walking path in Boston, Massachusetts
3. ____ Memorial, DC
4. ____ Seaport, Connecticut
5. Plymouth ____, Massachusetts
6. Civil War battlefield in Pennsylvania
8. ____ Dam, Nevada
11. Washington ____, DC
12. Former prison in Californian waters
13. Golden Gate ____, California
14. National ____, DC
16. Space ____, Washington

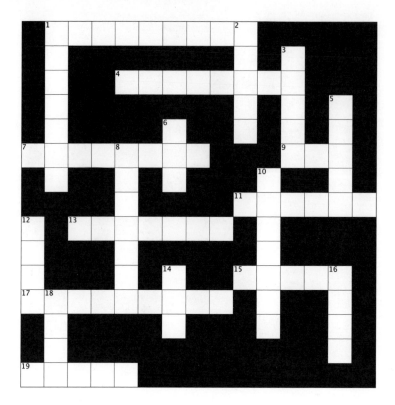

ACROSS

1. Fearsome river predator
4. Nocturnal primate that's named for the sound of its cries
7. Scaly anteater
9. Serpent in a Shakespeare play
11. Type of Old World monkey
13. Animal that falls six feet to the ground when born
15. Creature whose name means 'nose horn'
17. Social animals that travel in herds
19. Mamba or boomslang

DOWN

1. Fastest land mammal
2. Antelope with twisted horns
3. Animal that has a great laugh
5. Aggressive river dweller
6. Doubled, a type of small antelope
8. Animal that lays the largest eggs of any living bird
10. Pumbaa was one
12. Prominent feature on a male 18-Down
14. Wildebeest
16. Antelope genus
18. King of the jungle

Answer on page 306

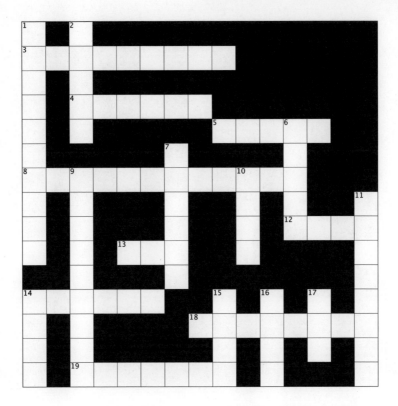

ACROSS

3. 1997 film inspired by the Russian revolution

4. 'My Neighbor _____' (1993)

5. Ogre voiced by Mike Myers

8. 2001 Miyazaki film

12. 'The Land Before _____' (1988)

13. '_____ Age' (2002)

14. 'The _____ of [6-Down]' (1998)

18. 2009 stop-motion film featuring the Other Mother

19. Brave little appliance

DOWN

1. With 'The,' 1994 film with Macaulay Culkin as the title character

2. 1995 film about a dog on a rescue mission

6. See 14-Across

7. Where all dogs go, in a 1989 film

9. With 'The,' 1999 film about a friendship between a boy and a robot

10. 'Fievel Goes _____' (1991)

11. 'Kiki's _____ Service' (1989)

14. 'South _____: Bigger, Longer, and Uncut' (1999)

15. 'How To Train _____ Dragon' (2010)

16. 'An American _____' (1986)

17. 2011 film named after the Brazilian city in which it's set

Answer on page 306

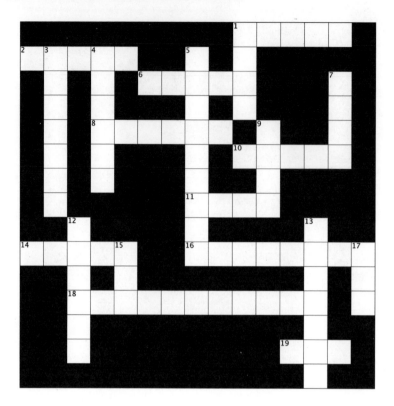

ACROSS

1. 17-Down's son, it's revealed

2. Teen who accidentally becomes a movie executive

6. Actress coveted by two Bluth brothers

8. Aspiring actor played by David

10. George's secretary

11. Shawkat who played 2-Across

14. With 19-Across, Bluth family vehicle

16. 'No ____!'

18. What there's always money in, with 'the'

19. See 14-Across

DOWN

1. Animal that bit off 4-Down's hand

3. …Her?

4. Youngest Bluth sibling

5. Possible answer to 'What have we always said is the most important thing?'

7. 4-Down's employer

9. British love interest played by Charlize

12. Jeffrey who played George Bluth

13. Michael's sister

15. Narrator Howard

17. Oldest Bluth sibling

Answer on page 306

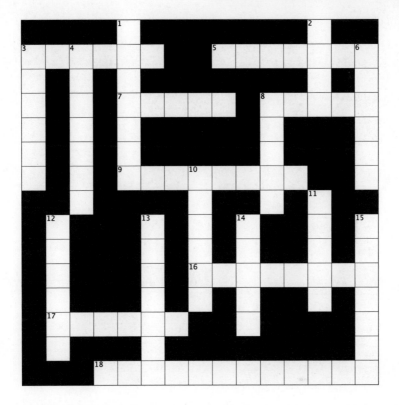

ACROSS

3. 'The Automat' (1927)
5. 'The Child's Bath' (1893)
7. 'Impression, Sunrise' (1872)
8. 'The Kiss' (1908)
9. 'Rosie the Riveter' (1943)
16. 'The Treachery of Images' (1929)

17. 'A Sunday Afternoon on the Island of La Grande Jatte' (1886)
18. 'Jim and Tom, Sausalito' (1977)

DOWN

1. 'Girl with a Pearl Earring' (1665)
2. 'The Persistence of Memory' (1931)

3. 'Ignorance = Fear' (1989)
4. 'Les Demoiselles d'Avignon' (1907)
6. 'Venus of Urbino' (1534)
8. 'Self-Portrait with Thorn Necklace and Hummingbird' (1940)
10. 'Infinity Room' series (1963)

11. 'Christina's World' (1948)
12. 'One Nation Under CCTV' (2007)
13. 'Fountain' (1917)
14. 'Little Dancer of Fourteen Years' (1880)
15. 'Cow's Skull: Red, White, and Blue' (1931)

Answer on page 306

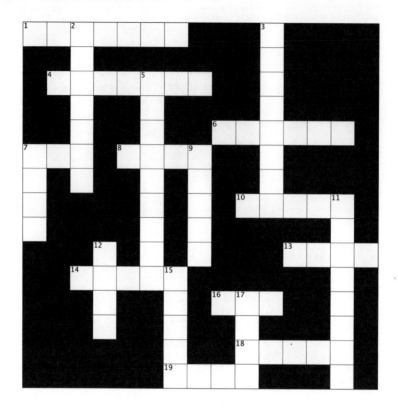

ACROSS

1. Dropping a line
4. Plastic disc for playing catch
6. Items that wash up on shore
7. Lie on the beach
8. Beach dweller that walks sideways
10. They may break near the shore
13. Go yachting
14. Alternative to 7-Down at some beaches
16. Sun protectant
18. Atlantic or Pacific, for example
19. Toy that works best in the wind

DOWN

2. Sport that might find you hanging ten
3. Sun protectant
5. 'Under the ____'
7. What many beaches are covered in
9. Vessels
11. Doing the backstroke
12. Pier
15. Predator at sea
17. Sunburn relief

Answer on page 306

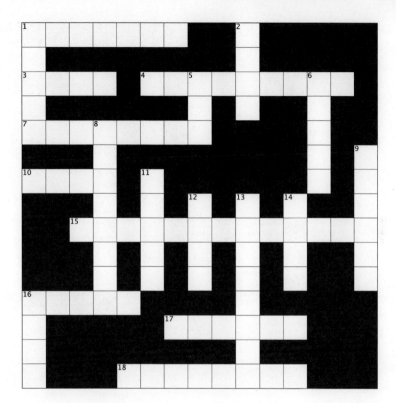

ACROSS

1. Casino floor authority
3. Casino game akin to the lottery
4. Game where the goal Is 21
7. Game with a ball and a wheel
10. Gambler's chances
15. What a casino newbie hopes for
16. It always wins, it's said
17. Term used for casino play
18. Favorite game of James Bond

DOWN

1. Game with variants like Texas Hold 'Em and Five-Card Draw
2. 13-Down's tool
5. Highest or lowest card in a deck
6. Dice game with a vulgar-sounding name
8. Gambling mecca
9. Person that accepts and pays off bets
11. They represent money
12. Opening stake in 1-Down
13. French term for a game manager
14. _____ machine
16. _____ roller

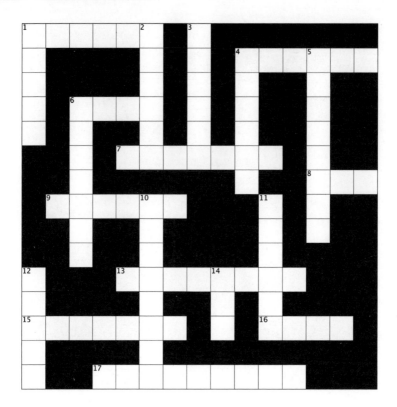

ACROSS

1. Like some Jewish delis
4. Muenster, swiss, or provolone
6. Sandwich with bacon and three pieces of bread
7. Turnovers with potatoes and onions
8. Bagel topper
9. Sweet filled crepe
13. Beef brined and smoked
15. Cucumbers soaked in vinegar and spices
16. Smoky type of 8-Across
17. Iconic deli soup

DOWN

1. Egg noodle casserole
2. Sandwich with beef, cheese, and sauerkraut
3. Potato pancakes
4. Beef preparation
5. Vegetarian (but not vegan) sandwich option
6. Sweet, braided bread
10. Grilled sandwich with fish and cheddar
11. Fish source for 8-Across and 16-Across
12. Brined berries sometimes served with 8-Across
14. Dark, dense bread

Answer on page 307

ACROSS

2. Biking class
5. It's good to break this
7. Exercise whose name derives from the Greek words for 'air' and 'life'
9. Where to go to lift
12. Jumping _____
13. Place to stash your keys and wallet
17. Rep in a pool
19. Free weight alternatives
20. Workout guide

DOWN

1. Popular equipment for 14-Down
3. Core exercise with a world record hold of over 8 hours
4. Exercise involving eagles, pigeons, and downward dogs
6. Squats work this part of the body
8. Exercise that can tone your abs
10. What you might need for 5-Across
11. How far you might go on a 1-Down
14. Exercise for heart health
15. A familiar figure in the locker room
16. Latin dance-based workout
18. Way to breathe while working out

Answer on page 307

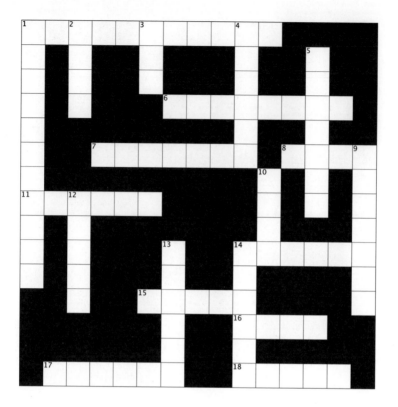

ACROSS
1. Florescent office supply
6. Two blades on a fulcrum, essentially
7. Epson or Brother product
8. Writing implements
11. Duplicates
14. Graphite writing tool
15. Paper fasteners
16. Organizers for 17-Across
17. Loose-leaf holder
18. Copier fluid

DOWN
1. Device used with 17-Across
2. Elmer's adhesive
3. Fluid that can be used with a quill, a brush, or 8-Across
4. The end of 14-Across
5. Colorful crayola products
9. 'Excuse me, I believe you have my ____'
10. Scotch or masking ____
12. Product sold in reams
13. Organizational tool
14. Sticky note

Answer on page 307

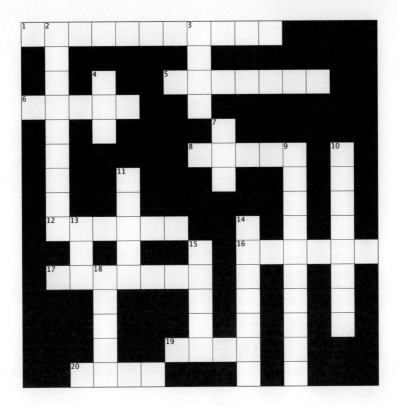

ACROSS

1. Traditional Chinese medicine
5. Tools for 1-Across
6. New Age or ambient, for example
8. Sweet exfoliant
12. Careful, they're hot!
16. Service provided for brows or legs
17. Rub
19. They're essential
20. Natural cleanser

DOWN

2. Plant slices traditionally placed on the eyes
3. Pedicure focus
4. Gratuity
7. Bath option
9. Goal of a spa visit
10. Soothing scent
11. Hand treatments, informally
13. Drink offered while you wait
14. Type of 17-Across
15. Energy healing
18. Small heated room

Answer on page 307

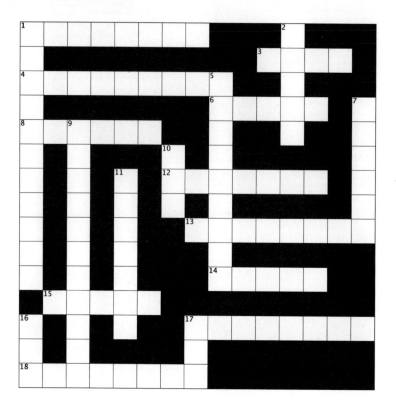

ACROSS

1. Birds dressed in black tie
3. King of the savannah
4. Formivores, familiarly
6. Playful river dweller
8. Animal whose name is from the Greek 'nose-horned'
12. Timon in 'The Lion King,' for one
13. Long-necked herbivores
14. Animal that moves so slowly, algae can grow in its fur
15. This picky eater consumes only eucalyptus leaves
17. Fastest land mammals
18. Largest land animal

DOWN

1. Burrowing desert rodents (not canines)
2. Striped feline
5. Things you can take home from the zoo
7. Highly aggressive, semiaquatic African mammals, briefly
9. Dark, humid space to see mantises and beetles
10. Flightless Australian bird
11. Animal that lives in a troop
16. The National Zoo doesn't charge one for entrance
17. Big _____ - 3-Across or 2-Down, for example

Answer on page 307

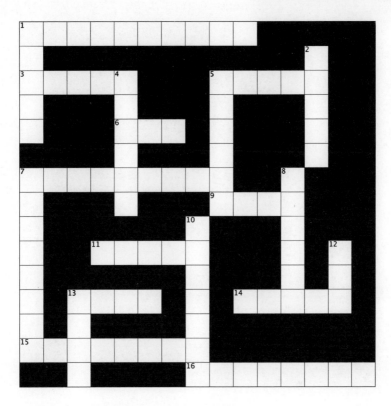

ACROSS
1. Passat or Jetta
3. RX or LS
5. 3 or S
6. M3 or i8
7. Corvette or Camaro
9. R8 or A4
11. Challenger or Durango
13. 124 Spider or 500X
14. Fit or CR-V
15. Voyager or Pacifica
16. Q50 or QX80

DOWN
1. S60 or XC40
2. Miata or CX-5
4. Outback or Forester
5. Corolla or Yaris
7. Escalade or XT5
8. Leaf or Rogue
10. Portofino or Roma
12. Sportage or Optima
13. Mustang or Bronco

Answer on page 308

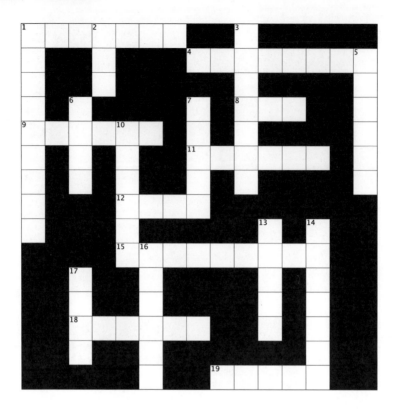

ACROSS

1. Tractor-drawn excursion
4. Autumn sport
8. Morning phenomenon, often
9. Color associated with 1-Down
11. Traditional Thanksgiving fare
12. Tool for an autumn chore
15. A literal strawman
18. Gala, Braeburn, and Granny Smith
19. Drink made with 18-Across

DOWN

1. October holiday
2. Color of 5-Down, maybe
3. Large open-air conflagration
5. They change color in autumn
6. Another name for autumn
7. Pumpkin spice _____
10. Pumpkins and calabashes
13. Gardeners dread the first one
14. Cardigan
16. Autumn weather, usually
17. Harvest

Answer on page 308

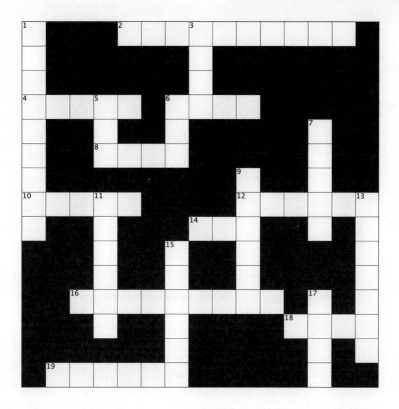

ACROSS
- **2.** Porcupines
- **4.** Cranes
- **6.** Deer
- **8.** Lemurs
- **10.** Cicadas
- **12.** Humans
- **14.** Newts
- **16.** Eagles
- **18.** Horses
- **19.** Swans

DOWN
- **1.** Turtles
- **3.** Llamas
- **5.** Bears
- **6.** Fish
- **7.** Pigeons
- **9.** Cats
- **11.** Platypuses
- **13.** Frogs
- **15.** Flies
- **17.** Kangaroos

Answer on page 308

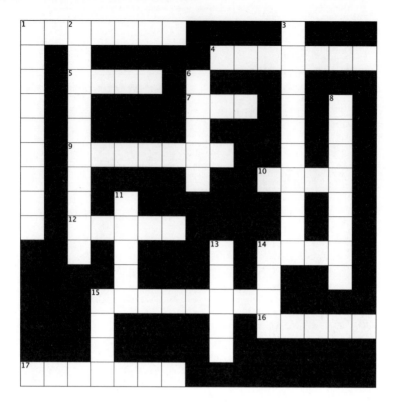

ACROSS

1. Director of the 1997 blockbuster film
4. Smokestacks
5. It can precede 'boat' or 'vest'
7. Actor who played Jack in the film
9. Irish city where the ship was built
10. Actor who played Rose

12. One of two groups of people asked to board lifeboats first
14. Titanic's downfall, briefly
15. The other of two groups
16. They included Boat, Saloon, Promenade, and Bridge

17. Researcher who discovered the wreckage in 1985

DOWN

1. Ship that came to Titanic's rescue
2. Colorful character later played by Kathy Bates

3. Adjective applied to Titanic before its voyage
6. First or third
8. Lowest tier on the ship
11. Titanic's captain
13. Month in which the disaster occurred
14. Heroic octet
15. Titanic's fuel

Answer on page 308

ACROSS

1. British teen wizard
4. With 18-Across, character created by Dav Pilkey
6. What Heather has two of in a 1989 picture book
7. How many shades of grey there are, per a 2011 novel
9. 'And ____ Makes Three,' picture book about a penguin family
12. Toni Morrison novel
14. Go ask her
15. Frequent reason for book challenges
18. See 4-Across

DOWN

1. He sails down the Mississippi on a raft
2. 'Daddy's ____,' 1990 picture book
3. 'Of ____ and Men' (1937)
5. 'Brave ____ World' (1932)
6. She talks to God in a 1970 Judy Blume novel
8. Author of 'I Am the Cheese' and 'The Chocolate War'
10. With 'the,' holy book in Christianity
11. With 13-Down, book series adapted for TV in 2007
13. See 11-Down
16. 'The ____ U Give' (2017)
17. '____ Home,' 2006 graphic memoir

Answer on page 308

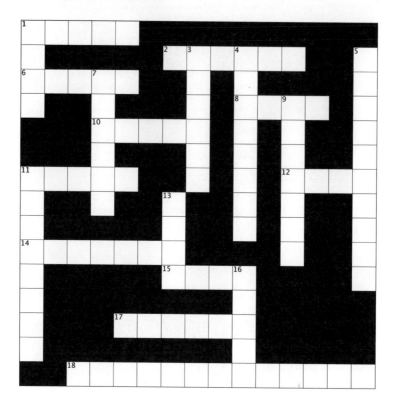

ACROSS

1. Obama's VP

2. '_____ from My Father,' 1995 Obama book

6. Younger Obama daughter

8. Immigration policy that created the Dreamers

10. 'Yes _____,' 2008 campaign slogan

11. Older Obama daughter

12. 'Crip _____,' 2020 film produced by the Obamas

14. Obama's middle name

15. Bo and 16-Down, for example

17. 2008 Obama opponent

18. '_____, we go high'

DOWN

1. Obama's predecessor

3. 2012 Obama opponent

4. 'The _____ of Hope,' Obama's second book

5. Obama won this Nobel award in 2009

7. Barack's birthplace

9. City in which Obama went to law school

11. Barack's First Lady

13. 'A Promised _____,' 2020 Obama memoir

16. Obama family pet

Answer on page 308

ACROSS
1. Pittsburgh
4. With 9-Across, Boston
7. Washington, D.C.
9. See 4-Across
10. Oakland, familiarly
11. Miami
14. Colorado
15. St. Louis
16. New York
17. Seattle

DOWN
1. San Diego
2. Texas
3. Minnesota
4. Tampa Bay
5. Baltimore
6. Arizona
8. Crosstown rivals of 16-Across
11. Org. to which all teams here belong
12. Kansas City
13. Detroit

Answer on page 309

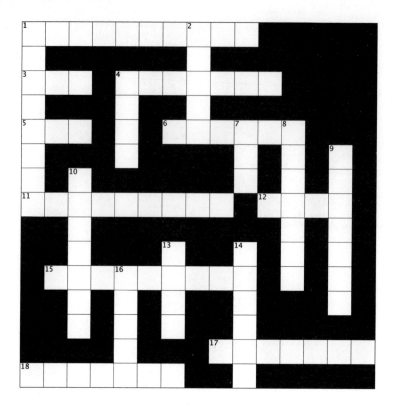

ACROSS

1. What one might do in Harvard Yard

3. _____ Sox, Boston's MLB team

4. Players at TD Garden

5. Type of 'party' once held in Boston Harbor

6. Boston _____, the city's central public park

11. Seasonal tourist attraction at 6-Across

12. Boston's public transit syst.

15. Town immediately north of Boston

17. Upper-crust Boston neighborhood

18. Isabella Stewart _____ Museum

DOWN

1. Group that founded Boston

2. Gas company whose logo is prominent in the Boston skyline

4. Ingredient in 'chowdah'

7. Private university focused on STEM

8. 'And to think that I saw it on _____ Street!'

9. River that runs through Boston

10. Ivy league school in 15-Across

13. 'Good _____ Hunting'

14. _____ Park, Boston's baseball stadium

16. Bostonian hockey player

Answer on page 309

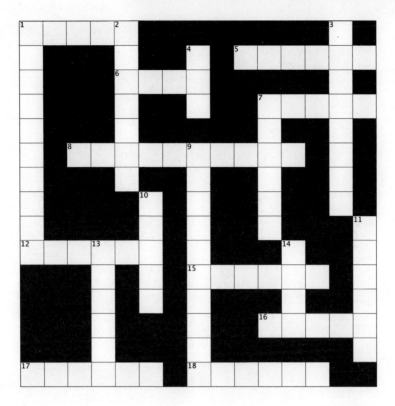

ACROSS

1. Most well-known Potter character
5. 'The Tale of Mr. Jeremy _____' (1906)
6. Color of 1-Across's jacket
7. Scientific interest of Potter's
8. Art form practiced by Potter
12. Surname for Tom in a 1907 tale
15. 'The Tale of Squirrel _____' (1903)
16. Zellweger who played Beatrix in a 2006 film
17. Area belonging to Mr. McGregor
18. 'The Tale of _____ Pig Robinson' (1930)

DOWN

1. Jemima's species
2. 1-Across, 7-Down, and 9-Down, for example
3. Mrs. Tiggy-Winkle's species
4. Nighttime drink for 1-Across
7. One of 1-Across's siblings
9. Another of 1-Across's siblings
10. Benjamin who is 1-Across's cousin
11. 'The Story of Miss _____' (1906)
13. With 14-Down, tale of a pair of household pests
14. See 13-Down

Answer on page 309

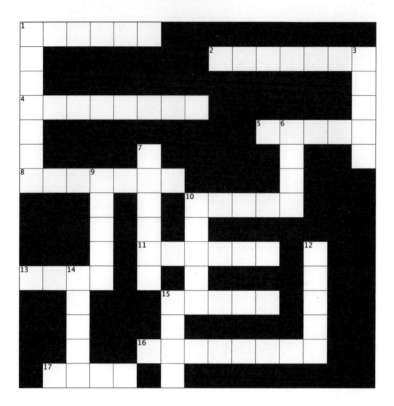

ACROSS

1. 1983, 'Tender Mercies'
2. 1984, 'Amadeus'
4. 1957, 'The Bridge on the River Kwai'
5. 2000, 'Gladiator'
8. 1940, 'The Philadelphia Story'
10. 2010, 'The King's Speech'
11. 1980, 'Raging Bull'
13. 1995, 'Leaving Las Vegas'
15. 1993, 'Philadelphia' & 1994, 'Forrest Gump'
16. 1977, 'The Goodbye Girl'
17. 2003, 'Mystic River' & 2008, 'Milk'

DOWN

1. 1987, 'Wall Street'
3. 2018, 'Bohemian Rhapsody'
6. 1996, 'Shine'
7. 1954, 'On the Waterfront' & 1972, 'The Godfather'
9. 1969, 'True Grit'
10. 1981, 'On Golden Pond'
12. 1990, 'Reversal of Fortune'
14. 1934, 'Mutiny on the Bounty'
15. 1985, 'Kiss of the Spider Woman'

Answer on page 309

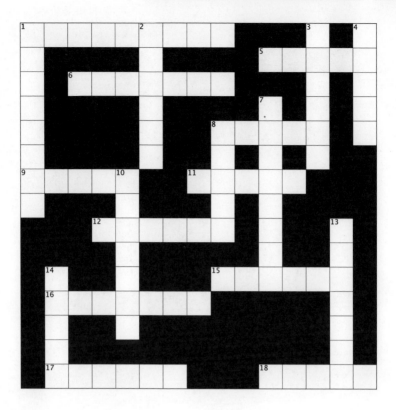

ACROSS

1. 1996, 'Fargo' & 2017, 'Three Billboards Outside Ebbing, Missouri' & 2021, 'Nomadland'
5. 2014, 'Still Alice'
6. 2010, 'Black Swan'
8. 2016, 'La La Land'
9. 1939, 'Gone with the Wind' & 1951, 'A Streetcar Named Desire'
11. 1989, 'Driving Miss Daisy'
12. 1980, 'Coal Miner's Daughter'
15. 2002, 'The Hours'
16. 1964, 'Mary Poppins'
17. 1982, 'Sophie's Choice' & 2011, 'The Iron Lady'
18. 1969, 'The Prime of Miss Jean Brodie'

DOWN

1. 1972, 'Cabaret'
2. 1986, 'Children of a Lesser God'
3. 1988, 'The Accused' & 1991, 'The Silence of the Lambs'
4. 2001, 'Monster's Ball'
7. 1957, 'The Three Faces of Eve'
8. 1999, 'Boys Don't Cry' & 2004, 'Million Dollar Baby'
10. 1932, 'Morning Glory' & 1967, 'Guess Who's Coming to Dinner' & 1968, 'The Lion in Winter' & 1981, 'On Golden Pond'
13. 2008, 'The Reader'
14. 1990, 'Misery'

Answer on page 309

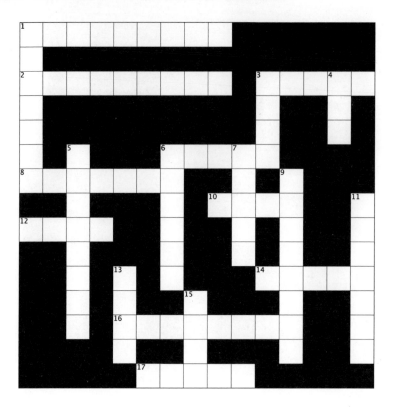

ACROSS

1. 1963 historical drama with Elizabeth Taylor in the title role
2. With 5-Down, Western romance
3. With 'The,' 2002 drama in which Virginia Woolf is a character
6. 1996 Coen Brothers black comedy
8. 1982 romcom with Dustin Hoffman
10. 2018 drama set in Mexico City
12. Quirky 2007 comedy starring Elliot Page
14. '_____ Swan,' 2010 psychological thriller
16. 2015 romantic period drama set in New York
17. 'Promising Young _____' (2020)

DOWN

1. 1972 musical featuring 'Maybe This Time'
3. 2011 fantasy about a boy living in a Paris train station
4. 2004 biopic with Jamie Foxx
5. See 2-Across
6. 2016 film based on an August Wilson play
7. 1990 film with a pottery wheel
9. 2016 film mistakenly announced as the winner
11. 2017 WWII drama
13. 1995 film with a talking pig
15. 2015 drama about a mother and child in captivity

Answer on page 309

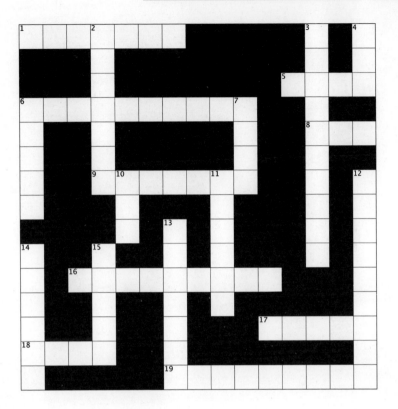

ACROSS

1. 1986 (Berenger, Sheen)

5. ,_____ Man,' 1988 (Hoffman, Cruise)

6. 1943 (Bogart, Bergman)

8. 'All About _____,' 1950 (Davis, Baxter)

9. 2002 (Zellweger, Zeta-Jones)

16. With 'The,' 1972 (Brando, Pacino)

17. With 'The,' 1973 (Newman, Redford)

18. 'My Fair _____,' 1964 (Hepburn, Harrison)

19. 2015 (Ruffalo, McAdams)

DOWN

2. 1997 (Winslet, DiCaprio)

3. 1995 (Gibson, Marceau)

4. With 10-Down, 1959 (Heston, Hawkins)

6. 2005 (Bullock, Newton)

7. 2012 (Affleck, Cranston)

10. See 4-Down

11. 1982 (Kingsley, Bergen)

12. 2016 (Rhodes, Ali)

13. 1984 (Abraham, Hulce)

14. 'Ordinary _____,' 1980 (Sutherland, Hutton)

15. 1976 (Stallone, Shire)

Answer on page 310

ACROSS
1. Poet Nikki
3. Author Chimamanda Ngozi
8. Poet Rita
9. Alex who wrote 'Roots'
10. Author and activist Frederick
16. Dystopian writer Octavia
17. Poet Langston
18. Fiction author Colson

DOWN
1. Writer Yaa
2. Alice who wrote 'The Color Purple'
4. Author Ta-Nehisi
5. 'Invisible Man' author
6. Author and activist bell
7. 'Native Son' and 'Black Boy' author Richard
9. Writer Zora Neale
11. Maya who wrote 'I Know Why the Caged Bird Sings'
12. Sociologist who wrote 'The Souls of Black Folk'
13. Ibram who wrote 'How to Be an Antiracist'
14. Poet Audre
15. Author of 'A Promised Land'… or 'Becoming'

Answer on page 310

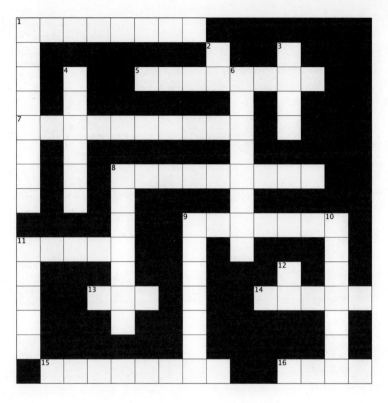

ACROSS

1. _____ of [11-Down], game involving territory and resources

5. Classic game with deeds and rents

7. Board game that originated in the middle east

8. Cross and circle board game that originated in India

9. With 8-Down, game with questions and answers

11. Game with queens, bishops, and castles

13. Six-sided game piece

14. _____ Land, easy game for children

15. In the UK, it's called draughts

16. Strategy game involving diplomacy

DOWN

1. Game with tiles and letters

2. Oldest board game played in present day

3. Mrs. Peacock's game

4. _____ to Ride

6. Cooperative game where players fight a plague

8. See 9-Across

9. Party game with a mat

10. It can be paired with snakes or chutes

11. See 1-Across

12. Game based on the Egyptian sun god

Answer on page 310

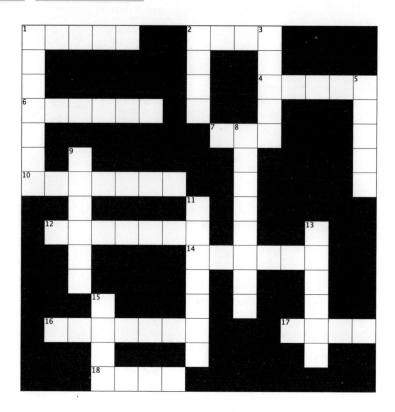

ACROSS

1. 'No ____ No Cry'
2. '____ It Up'
4. With 18-Across, percussion instrument
6. Bob Marley greatest hits album
7. Music genre precursor to 13-Down
10. Who got shot in a 1976 song
12. With 11-Down, person 'fighting on arrival, fighting for survival'
14. 'Three ____ Birds'
16. Song with the lyric 'Let's get together and feel all right'
17. Album with 'Is This Love'
18. See 4-Across

DOWN

1. Bob Marley's band
2. 'Redemption ____'
3. Adherent of a Jamaican folk religion
5. 'Could You Be ____'
8. City that's home to the Bob Marley Museum
9. Who didn't get shot in a 1976 song
11. See 12-Across
13. Marley's primary music genre
15. Drug associated with Bob Marley

Answer on page 310

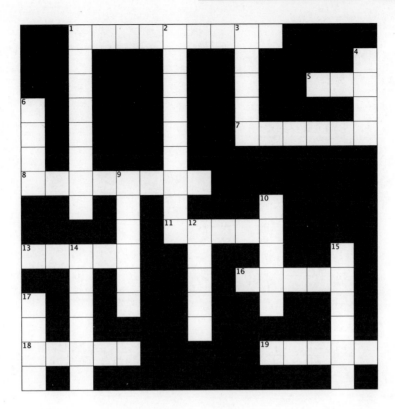

ACROSS

1. What happens when a stream meets a cliff
5. Caspian or Aral
7. Marshy areas
8. Temporary body of water at the beach
11. Yser or Danube
13. A parrot pines for one, in a Monty Python sketch
16. Water formation that shares its name with an airline
18. Manmade lane of transport, as in Venice
19. Southern term for an extremely slow-moving stream

DOWN

1. The Everglades, for example
2. Where large amounts of water can be stored
3. Titicaca and Champlain, for example
4. Biscayne and Chesapeake
6. Protective trench
9. Water in which a child might splash
10. Stream
12. Small indentation of a shoreline
14. The largest bodies of water on Earth
15. Sheltered area where boats can safely dock
17. Nessie's home

Answer on page 310

ACROSS

1. '_____ Russia with Love' (1963)
3. She sang the theme to 11-Down
5. Actor who portrayed Bond only once
8. Actor Roger
10. Actor Connery
13. Bond's profession
15. Last Bond film to star 6-Down (2002)
16. 'The Spy Who _____ Me' (1977)
17. 'Tomorrow _____ Dies' (1997)

DOWN

1. Bond's creator
2. Actor who portrayed Bond in 'GoldenEye'
4. First Bond film
5. 1973 Bond film
6. Actor Pierce
7. Double-oh _____
8. Bond's drink of choice
9. Maud Adams played her in 1983
11. 2012 Bond film featuring Javier Bardem
12. Preferred preparation method for 8-Down
14. 'For _____ Eyes Only' (1981)

Answer on page 310

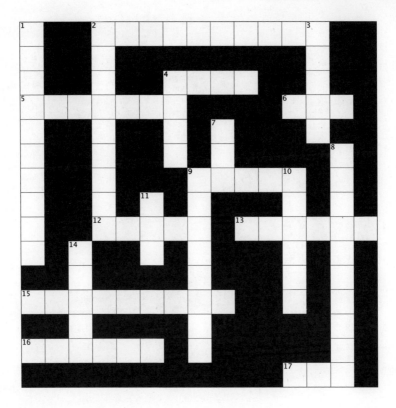

ACROSS

2. With 4-Across, band with Nick Carter and AJ McLean
4. See 2-Across
5. Irish boy band
6. With 15-Across, band with hits 'What Makes You Beautiful' and 'One Thing'
9. Nick, Joe, or Kevin
12. Band with 2000 album 'No Strings Attached'
13. Top hit by Hanson
15. See 6-Across
16. With 14-Down, artist whose solo work includes 'Watermelon Sugar'
17. K-pop boy band

DOWN

1. Justin of 12-Across
2. R&B group from Philadelphia
3. Primary boy band audience
4. 'It's Gonna ____' (2000)
7. Band who sings 10-Down
8. Proto-boy band with members Merrill, Jay, and Donny
9. Band with Jackie and Tito
10. '____ Girls,' song with refrain that starts 'New Kids on the Block had a bunch of hits...'
11. Tripled, top hit for 12-Across
14. See 16-Across

Answer on page 311

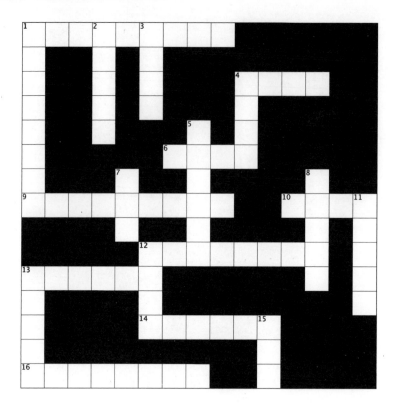

ACROSS

1. Subject taught by Mr. White
4. Communication tool used by Hector Salamanca
6. Sweet, doomed chemist
9. State in which the majority of the series takes place
10. Drug cooked by White and Pinkman
12. Los Pollos ____
13. Series finale title that's also an apt anagram
14. 'I am the one who ____'
16. Showrunner Vince

DOWN

1. He plays White
2. Walt's sister-in-law
3. Shady lawyer who got his own spinoff
4. Color of Walt's signature 10-Across
5. Diagnosis that serves as a catalyst
7. Org. for which 12-Down works
8. Role played by Aaron
11. Walt's infant daughter
12. First character to deduce that Walt is Heisenberg
13. Gustavo ____
15. Walt's wife and eventual partner in crime

Answer on page 311

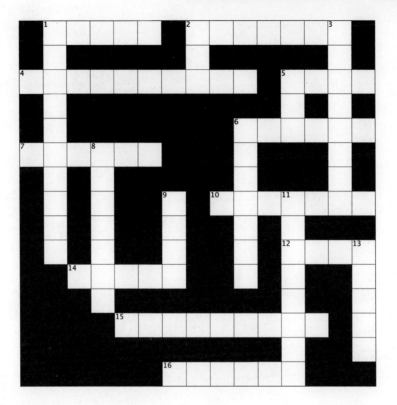

ACROSS
1. Disposable cleaning cloths
2. Formula containers
4. Nursery lamp
5. Post-feeding step
6. Hanging toy
7. Baby's attire
10. Nappies
12. Nursery furniture
14. Easily lost articles of clothing
15. Toddler's place at the table
16. Chair often found in a nursery

DOWN
1. Sound machine that aids sleep
2. Carrier
3. Baby carriage
5. Mealtime accessory
6. Device for watching a newborn from another room
8. Bath time need
9. Bonnets
11. Binky
13. Storytime essentials

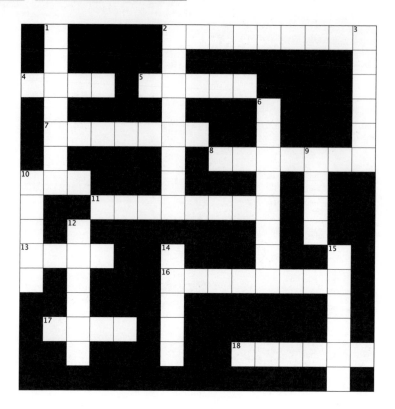

ACROSS

2. Popular spaghetti go-with
4. Meat found in salumi
5. Base for a white sauce
7. Folded over pizza
8. Leave the gun but take this
10. With 10-Down, fat used in many Italian dishes
11. Italian dessert flavored with 16-Across
13. _____ parmigiana
16. Coffee drink served in a small cup
17. Type of nut featured in 14-Down
18. Italian ice cream

DOWN

1. Dumplings traditionally made of potato
2. Red sauce
3. Type of cured meat
6. Long noodle that was also a surname in 'Ratatouille'
9. Rice-like pasta
10. See 10-Across
12. Staple seasoning
14. Basil-based green sauce
15. Beefsteak, heirloom, or cherry

Answer on page 311

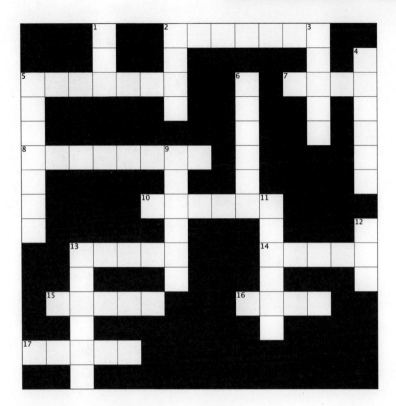

ACROSS

2. Bees that perform basic chores
5. Insects that build papery nests
7. Bee's home
8. Beekeeper
10. Bee collective
13. How bees communicate
14. Young bee
15. Sugary byproduct
16. Cell for protecting pupae
17. Royal bee

DOWN

1. Epi-____
2. Marvel superhero named for an insect, with 'the'
3. Wound from a bee
4. Sweet substance that attracts bees
5. Shape of a 16-Across
6. What bees collect
9. Tool for calming bees
11. Color associated with bees
12. Bee-made material
13. Mates for 17-Across

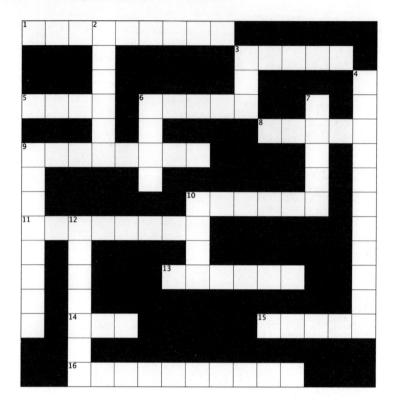

ACROSS

1. Skin protector
3. Firestarter
5. Camp invader
6. Portmanteau of 'glamour' and 'camp'
8. With 14-Across, a kit it's good to have in a pinch
9. Insect repellent
10. Small digging tool
11. Adhesive sold in rolls
13. They hold your 10-Down in place
14. See 8-Across
15. Sharp tool
16. Zigzag path for climbing a steep hill

DOWN

2. Snack with marshmallows and chocolate
3. Navigation aid
4. Canteen
6. Dried fruit and nuts
7. Path
9. Headwear or neckwear
10. Camp shelter
12. Tool with a magnetized needle

Answer on page 311

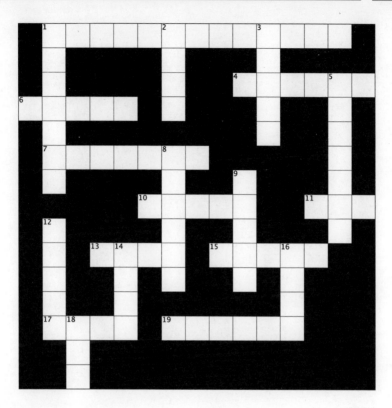

ACROSS

1. He began eating vegetables (only sometimes!) in 2007
4. Nickname for a mammoth-like Muppet
6. Human character played by Sonia Manzano
7. Yellow character who lives in a nest
10. Trashcan dweller
11. Best friend of 2-Down
13. Comic foil to 9-Down
15. Deaf librarian who moved to Sesame Street in 1972
17. With 1-Down, Muppet who loves magic
19. Jim _____, show creator

DOWN

1. See 17-Across
2. Red Muppet with his own spinoff show
3. First word of the show's theme song
5. He voices 1-Across and 13-Across
8. Bilingual blue Muppet
9. Singer of 'Rubber Duckie'
12. Muppet with autism introduced in 2017
14. Award won more than 180 times by 'Sesame Street'
16. Prairie _____
18. Actor McGrath who shares a name with his character

Answer on page 312

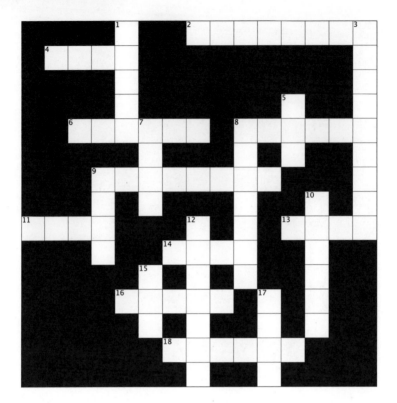

ACROSS

2. Cat's problem
4. Sound a happy cat makes
6. Newborn cat
8. Jump or leap on prey
9. Hairs that aid vision and navigation
11. What a cat in heat might do
13. Tailless cat breed
14. Fishy treat, perhaps
16. Striped cat
18. Cat with a tri-color coat

DOWN

1. Reward
3. Cat owner's necessity
5. Sign of affection
7. Cats uses this for balance
8. Cat breed with a 'grumpy' face and long fur
9. Cats can do this silently
10. Herb beloved by felines
12. Warm place for a cat nap
15. Cat's foot
17. Stereotypical prey for cats

Answer on page 312

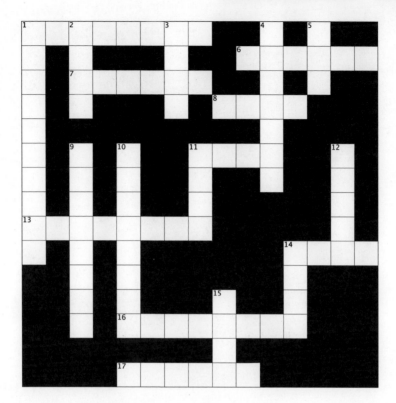

ACROSS

1. Its varieties include Honey Nut and Apple Cinnamon
6. _____ Pebbles
7. _____ Grahams
8. Tiger mascot who says 'They're grrrreat!'
11. Serving dish for cereal
13. _____ Toast Crunch
14. Frosted _____ Wheats
16. Cereal associated with dieting
17. They can be Frosted or Corn

DOWN

1. Cereal with a pirate mascot
2. Cereal you might waffle on
3. With 'O's,' cereal based on a cookie
4. Healthy cereal with oats and fruit
5. Its slogan is 'Kid Tested, Mother Approved'
9. Yellow cereal that used to have 'Sugar' in its name
10. Cereal with athletes on the box
11. Raisin _____
12. Silverware used for eating cereal
14. Cereal's go-with
15. _____ Krispies

Answer on page 312

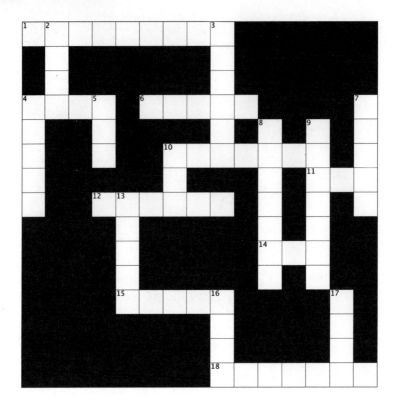

ACROSS

1. Martinis, mojitos, and margaritas
4. Any drink made with lemon or lime juice
6. Russian liquor
10. Olive, cherry, or orange
11. Frozen cubes
12. Liquor produced by distilling wine
14. Manhattan ingredient
15. Bar tool for stirring
18. Liquor made from agave

DOWN

2. Anise-flavored Greek liquor
3. Tool for James Bond's martinis
4. Drinks to throw back
5. Liquor distilled from sugar
7. Coke, maybe, or orange juice
8. Spirits sharply flavored with botanics
9. Types of this include Scotch, bourbon, and Irish
10. It's made with juniper berries
13. Bar lingo for 11-Across
16. Like a drink lacking 13-down
17. Term for cheaper liquor brands

Answer on page 312

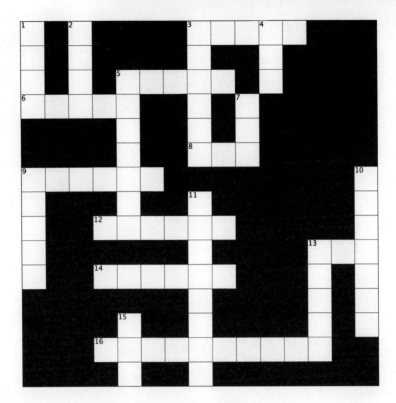

ACROSS

3. Sharon & Ozzy Osbourne

5. Demi Moore & Bruce Willis

6. With 8-Across, Christie Brinkley & Billy Joel

8. See 6-Across

9. Debbie Reynolds & Eddie Fisher

12. Angelina Jolie & Brad Pitt

13. Lisa Bonet & Lenny Kravitz

14. Jada Pinkett Smith & Will Smith

16. Alejandra Oaziaza & Jermaine Jackson

DOWN

1. Uma Thurman & Ethan Hawke

2. With 9-Down, Beyoncé and Jay-Z

3. Shirley Douglas & Donald Sutherland

4. Bebe Buell & Steven Tyler

5. Peggy Lipton & Quincy Jones

7. See 2-Down

9. Rita Wilson & Tom Hanks

10. Gail & Frank Zappa

11. Mariah Carey & Nick Cannon

13. Rita & Bob Marley

15. Anne Meara & Jerry Stiller

Answer on page 312

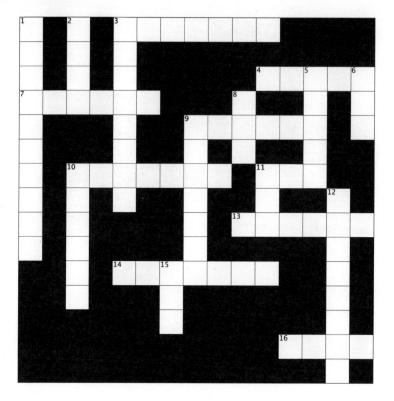

ACROSS

3. Game played with tiles

4. With 12-Down, lighting source used in festivals

7. Tiered tower

9. Mythical creature symbolic of strength and power

10. China's capital

11. Green _____

13. Twelve-year cycle

14. Important Chinese holidays

16. _____ fu

DOWN

1. Utensils that come in pairs

2. Yin's counterpart

3. Language with nearly a billion speakers

5. Symbol of China

6. Color that's considered lucky

8. Author of 'The Little Red Book'

9. Examples include Qin, Ming, and Han

10. Hardy grass eaten by 5-Down

11. Chinese word meaning 'way' or 'principle'

12. See 4-Across

15. Round-bottomed cooking pot

Answer on page 312

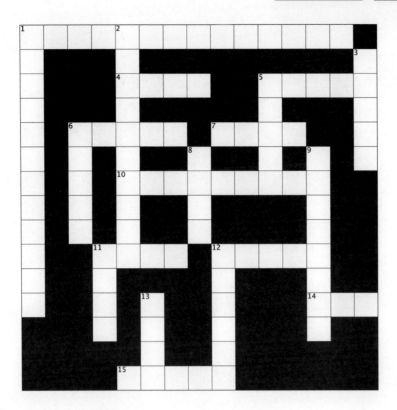

ACROSS

1. Chicago expressway
4. Chicago's county
5. Airport serving Chicago
6. The _____ City
7. With 'The,' landmark where you might do some reflecting
10. Proper name for 7-Across
11. With 'Park,' a Chicago neighborhood
12. Chicago's natural history museum
14. With 6-Down, Chicago's AL MLB team
15. Chicago NFL team

DOWN

1. Body of water adjacent to Chicago
2. Improv troupe based in Chicago
3. Original namesake for the Willis Tower
5. President with ties to Chicago
6. See 14-Across
8. Wrigley Field team
9. Chicago pizza
11. '_____ Alone,' 1990 film
12. He spent a day on the town in a 1986 John Hughes film
13. 1871 Chicago disaster

Answer on page 313

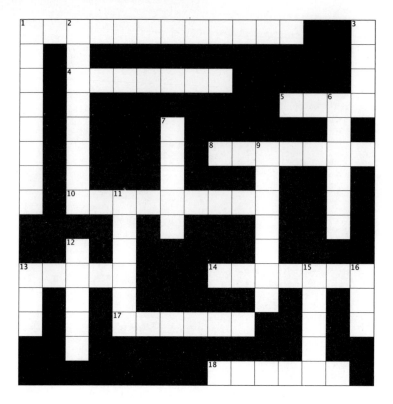

ACROSS

1. Film in which Hugh Grant plays the Prime Minister
4. 'A ____ [13-Across] Christmas,' in which Linus tells the Nativity Story
5. '____ Alone'
8. Reindeer who originally appeared in a stop motion 1964 TV special
10. 'The ____ Before Christmas,' spooky animated musical
13. See 4-Across
14. '____ on 34th Street'
17. 'A Very ____ and Kumar Christmas'
18. '____ All the Way,' film with Schwarzenegger and Hartman

DOWN

1. 'National ____ Christmas [2-Down]'
2. See 1-Down
3. 'It's a Wonderful ____'
6. 'A ____ Christmas [15-Down],' film in which Charles Dickens is played by Gonzo
7. With 13-Down, film with Billy Bob Thornton
9. Movie that takes place in and around Nakatomi Plaza
11. He hadn't stopped Christmas from coming! It came! Somehow or other, it came just the same!
12. 'The ____ Express,' train taken to the North Pole
13. See 7-Down
15. See 6-Down
16. Film in which Will Ferrell's character brings the Christmas spirit back to New York

Answer on page 313

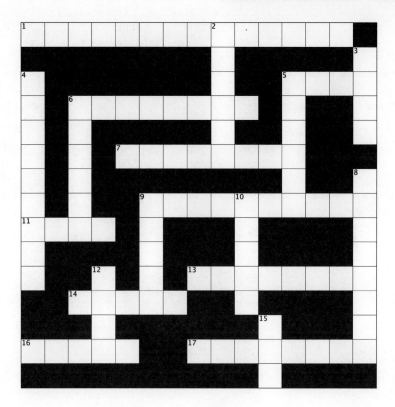

ACROSS

1. Las Vegas staple
5. _____ of Death, dangerous motorcycle stunt
6. Circus that refrains from using animal acts
7. Part of a circus that's now largely out of fashion
9. The person running the show
11. Speechless performer
13. Vehicle that might prompt a wag to ask 'Where's the other wheel?'
14. One might be ridden bareback
16. Black-and-orange feline
17. Performers with incredible balance and agility

DOWN

2. They boost a performer up
3. Circus enclosure
4. Cat person?
5. They have red noses, often
6. Bailey's partner
8. Aerial apparatuses
9. A circus generally has three
10. Tricks and illusions
12. A 17-Across might walk across one of these stretched taut
15. Big _____

Answer on page 313

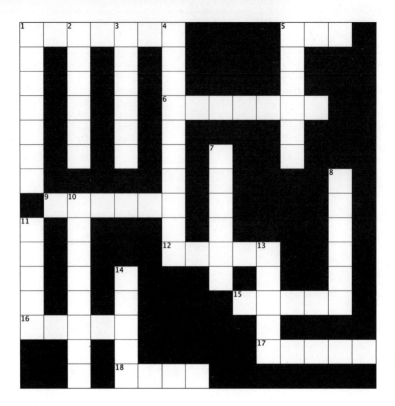

ACROSS

1. Body of laws that enforced racial segregation
5. Decentralized org. founded in 2013
6. Activist Fred killed in 1969
9. Till murdered in 1955
12. Org. for Black rights
15. Plaintiff in a 1954 case
16. Alabama town where 5-Down took place
17. Nonviolent form of protest
18. Activist with a dream

DOWN

1. President who signed the Civil Rights Act
2. Trayvon murdered in 2012
3. Freedom _____
4. Site of a major 1963 march
5. With 7-Down, event in which peaceful marchers were beaten and gassed
7. See 5-Down
8. Activist Bayard
10. Activist born with the surname Little
11. Activist and politician John
13. She played a key role in the Montgomery bus boycotts
14. _____ Panthers

Answer on page 313

ACROSS

1. Alec who would go on to play Obi-Wan
4. Katharine who said, 'If you obey all the rules, you miss all the fun'
5. 'Gone with the Wind' star
8. Western staple
9. Grace or Gene
10. He married 14-Down...twice
11. He coulda been a contender
13. Montgomery who starred in 'Judgment at Nuremberg'
15. Doris who frequently costarred with Rock Hudson
16. Debbie who died a day after her daughter in 2016

DOWN

1. 'Gone with the Wind' star
2. He played Mr. Smith in 1939
3. 'The blonde bombshell'
6. 'Bringing Up Baby' costar (with 4-Across)
7. Noted WWII pin-up girl
10. Noir star Lauren
11. 10-Down's husband and frequent costar
12. 'Vertigo' star Kim
14. She played Cleopatra in 1963
15. First actor to receive a posthumous Oscar nom

Answer on page 313

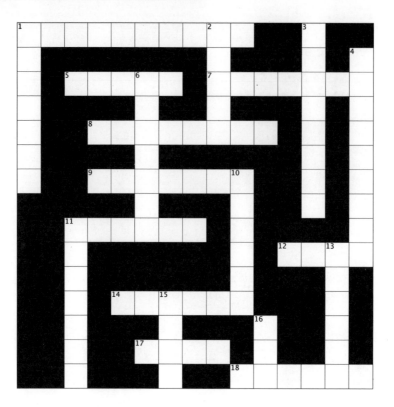

ACROSS
1. Bumpy air, so to speak
5. Option for a large suitcase
7. _____ claim
8. Area past security
9. Time between flights
11. Flight attendant's offerings
12. Waiting area
14. Bridge at an airport
17. Row with more leg room
18. Subject of a pre-flight briefing

DOWN
1. First stage of a flight
2. 'You are now free to move about the _____'
3. Safety harness
4. The D in ETD
6. Aptly-named type of luggage
10. Landing site
11. Security canine
13. Boarding pass
15. Movement after landing
16. Org. in charge of security

Answer on page 313

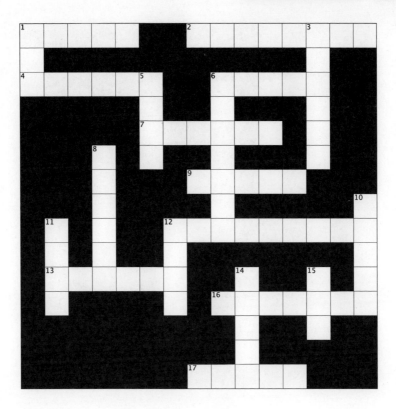

ACROSS

1. David who played Tobias Funke
2. Jim with a Hot Pockets bit
4. John with an HBO show
6. Larry with an HBO show
7. George with seven words you can't say on TV
9. Richard who frequently collaborated with Gene Wilder
12. Dave with an eponymous show
13. Tig whose most famous set centered on her cancer
16. Mitch with one-liners
17. Bill who only lived to age 32

DOWN

1. Margaret whose Korean mother often features in her sets
3. Hannah whose comedy is 'bigger than comedy'
5. Chris who got his start on 'Saturday Night Live'
6. Lea who was the first openly gay comic to appear on American TV
8. Patton who voiced Remy
10. Ken who's a judge on 'The Masked Singer'
11. Ali who has filmed specials while pregnant
12. Dane who played 'The Waffler' in 'Mystery Men'
14. Wyatt who's a 'Daily Show' alumnus
15. Tina who wrote 'Mean Girls'

Answer on page 314

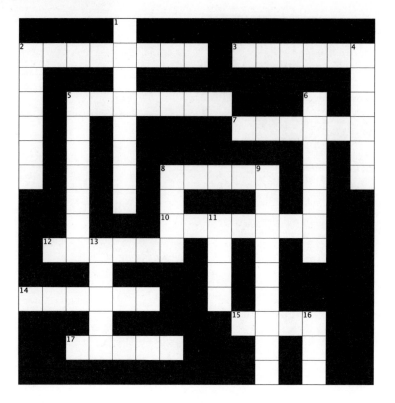

ACROSS

2. Cruise line whose name sounds like a party

3. All-you-can-eat dining option

5. Area to see live entertainment

7. Jamaica or Bermuda, for example

8. Promenade and Lido, among others

10. The person at the helm

12. Board

14. Cruise line with Mickey and Minnie

15. Left on a ship

17. Key ingredient in piña coladas and Bahama mamas

DOWN

1. You want it to be aboard, but you don't want to need it

2. Gambling locale on board

4. Small boat that ferries passengers from the ship to land

5. Cruising is part of this industry

6. Your 9-Down might have one of these amenities

8. Structure to which ships can be tied

9. Your living quarters on the ship

11. Place to swim

13. Game involving a 5×5 card

16. Sunbathe

Answer on page 314

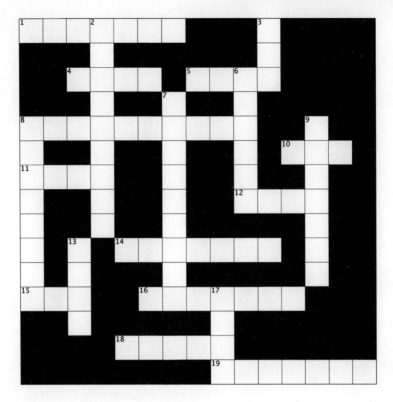

ACROSS

1. Shy, enormous, ape-like creature

4. With 12-Across and 9-Down, famous Scottish legend

5. Unreal, like the creatures in this puzzle

8. Its name comes from the Spanish for 'goat sucker'

10. What the Scottish legend of 4-Across turned out to be

11. Himalayan version of 1-Across

12. See 4-Across

14. Flying West Virginian creature with red eyes

15. Where you might meet a 6-Down… if it were real

16. Creature whose name is a portmanteau of 'Chesapeake' and 'Nessie'

18. Purported evidence for 1-Across

19. Mythical medieval figure that may have given rise to 1-Across

DOWN

2. Impression left behind by 1-Across, supposedly

3. 1-Across is said to be half-man, half-this

6. Giant cephalopod of Norse legend

7. Alternate name for 1-Across

8. Class of 'animal' for the creatures in this puzzle

9. See 4-Across

13. Fraud or trick

17. Abominable _____ Man

Answer on page 314

ACROSS

1. Sweet chocolate drink with ice cream
3. Process used to make chocolate smooth and shiny
5. Piece of cacao bean
6. Liquid chocolate poured over ice cream
9. With 10-Across, fat present in cacao beans
10. See 9-Across
11. Chocolate with no cocoa solids
14. Type of bitter chocolate used in desserts
15. Sweetner
17. Tree from which chocolate is derived
18. Ice cream topping also called jimmies

DOWN

1. Group first known to make chocolate
2. Type of chips often found in chocolate chip cookies
4. Chocolate glaze made with cream
7. Chocolate snack served in a cup
8. Coffee drink with chocolate
12. Headquarters of the largest chocolate manufacturer in North America
13. Sound of a chocolate eater
14. It takers around 400 of these to make one pound of chocolate
16. Like some bitter chocolate

Answer on page 314

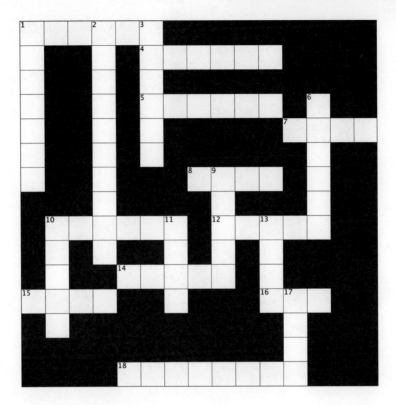

ACROSS
1. Largest desert in the world
4. Landscape feature caused by erosion
5. Desert dog
7. Sound made by 5-Across
8. Asian desert
10. Spiny plant
12. 'There's a ____ in my boot!'
14. Formations made by wind and 11-Down
15. What animals go underground to escape
16. Lacking moisture
18. Predatory arachnid

DOWN
1. Tall, imposing 10-Across
2. Southernmost desert
3. Tree found in Australia and Africa
6. Southwestern US desert
9. Haven in the desert
10. Animal with a hump
11. Granular material
13. 16-Across synonym
17. Precipitation that deserts lack

Answer on page 314

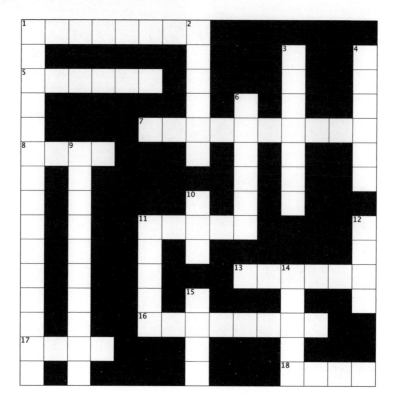

ACROSS

1. One who preys on smaller creatures
5. English translation of Greek 'saur' or 'saurus'
7. Tracks left behind
8. Prominent feature on an Apatosaurus
11. Living relatives of dinosaurs
13. Its arrival meant lights out for the dinosaurs
16. It's comprised of 11-Down
17. King dino
18. One of three on a Triceratops

DOWN

1. Scientists who study dinosaurs
2. Dinosaur whose name means 'swift seizer,' familiarly
3. No longer in existence
4. Preserved remains
6. Feature at the end of a Stegosaurus tail
9. Fossilized poo
10. Mesozoic, for example
11. Femur, vertebra, and skull, for example
12. 'Jurassic ____'
14. On a 17-Across, this could grow up to a foot long
15. What a carnivore eats

Answer on page 314

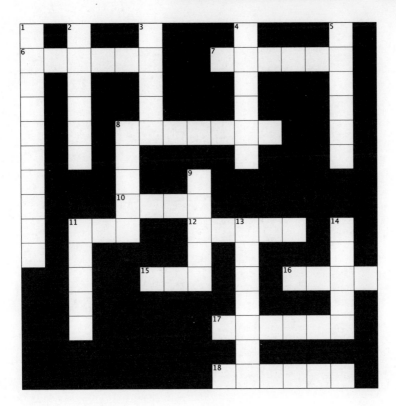

ACROSS

6. Enchanted maiden (1959)
7. Hound dog (1981)
8. Friendly rabbit (1942)
10. Lioness (1994)
11. Evil snake (1967)
12. Dwarf who's not very smart (1937)
15. Rotund mouse (1950)
16. Hook's first mate (1953)
17. Geppetto's cat (1940)
18. Burly he-man (1991)

DOWN

1. Foxy love interest, so to speak (1973)
2. Sea witch (1989)
3. Pet tiger (1992)
4. Streetwise dog (1988)
5. Murderous French captor (1996)
8. New Orleans waitress (2009)
9. God of the underworld (1997)
11. Human-turned-llama (2000)
13. Mama to 101 (1961)
14. Mischievous raccoon (1995)

Answer on page 315

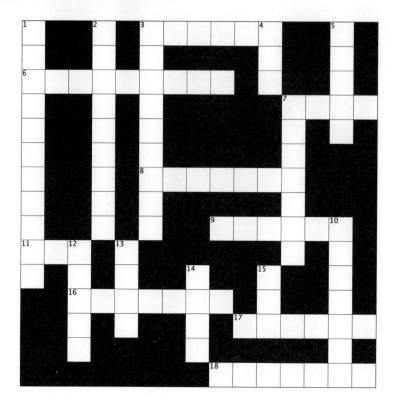

ACROSS
3. Type of insect that shares its name with a Volkswagen model
6. Large, hairy spider
7. They start life as nits
8. Lightning bugs
9. Biblical plague insect
11. Member of a colony
16. They emerge from the ground every 17 years and make a lot of noise
17. Crop-destroying pest
18. Chirper that shares its name with a British sport

DOWN
1. Larval stage of 3-Down
2. Flying insect often found near water
3. Viceroy, monarch, or queen, for example
4. Beginning stage of life for most insects
5. Household pest, familiarly
7. Garden dweller that eats aphids
10. Wood-eater
12. Hiker's concerns
13. Type of 'worm' named for the way it moves
14. Its nest is made of paper
15. Hive dweller

Answer on page 315

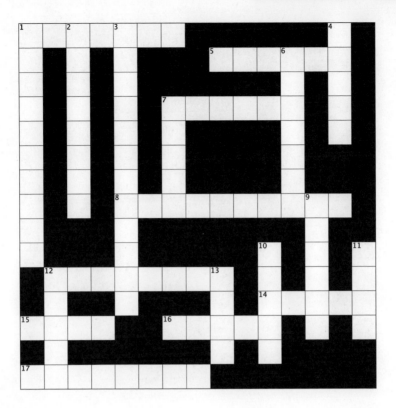

ACROSS
1. Vast, arid area
5. 'Put another shrimp on the ____!'
7. Harbour ____
8. Daintree or Kuranda, for example
12. Big hopper
14. Coral formations
15. Australian buddy
16. Sunshine ____
17. Australia's capital

DOWN
1. Famed 9-Down landmark
2. Island home to devils and tigers
3. Isolated town that's passed through on the way to Uluru
4. Australian outlaw Ned
6. First meal of the day
7. ____ Beach, surfing destination
9. Capital of New South Wales
10. Southwestern Australian city
11. Any non-urban area, colloquially
12. Eucalyptus eater
13. National gemstone

Answer on page 315

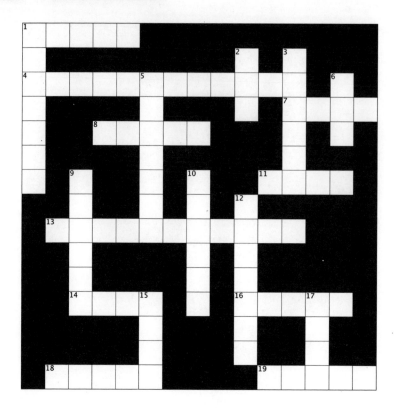

ACROSS
1. Slow down or stop
4. It can be manual or automatic
7. First or fifth, for example
8. Most cars have four
11. Wintertime must-have
13. Blinkers
14. Traffic warning
16. It provides the jams
18. Wheel shafts
19. Radar gun measurement

DOWN
1. It might need a jump
2. Lubricant for 3-Down
3. It converts power into motion
5. They can be side or rearview
6. What you get at the pump
9. Third pedal in some cars
10. Helpful at night or in fog
12. Traffic signals
15. Unfortunate things to lock in the car
17. What you might do at a drawbridge or railroad crossing

Answer on page 315

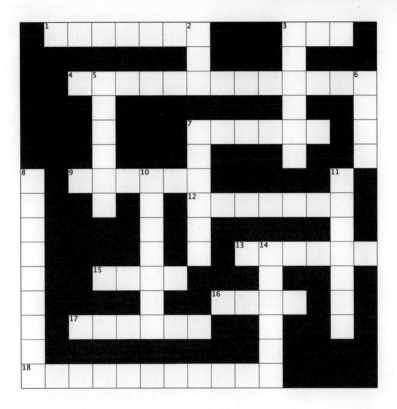

ACROSS

1. With 3-Across, character that's watching you

3. See 1-Across

4. The temperature at which books burn

7. 'The _____ Games,' young adult series set in Panem

9. With 'The,' film that added 'red pill' to the lexicon

12. 'Never _____,' Ishiguro novel with clones

13. Author of 6-Down

15. Author of 'Do Androids Dream of Electric Sheep?'

16. 'Atlas Shrugged' author

17. Dystopia's antithesis

18. Bong Joon-ho film set on a train

DOWN

2. 'Logan's _____' (1967)

3. She wrote 'Parable of the Sower'

5. '_____ Farm,' novel with Snowball and Napoleon

6. Quintessential dystopian novel

7. 'Brave New World' author

8. With 'The,' HBO series in which 2% of the world's population has vanished

10. 1987 film in which a murdered police officer comes back as a cyborg

11. '_____ Green is people!'

14. 'Blade _____' (1982)

Answer on page 315

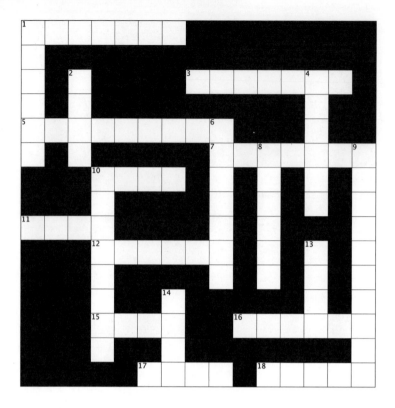

ACROSS

1. Popeye's favorite vegetable
3. Base of many salads
5. Spring onions
7. They may be green, red, or yellow
10. Dwight Schrute famously grew this crop
11. Pacific root vegetable
12. Bugs Bunny's favorite treat
15. Vegetable that sounds like a plumbing problem
16. Curly, bitter green
17. Ingredient in a trendy smoothie, maybe
18. Vegetable that might make you cry

DOWN

1. Delicata _____
2. Snap or snow
4. Vegetable for making 'ants on a log'
6. Brussels _____
8. Starchy vegetable
9. A vegetable...or a tall, thin person
10. Vegetable abhorred by toddlers
13. Relatives of sweet potatoes
14. Vegetable common in Southern cooking

Answer on page 315

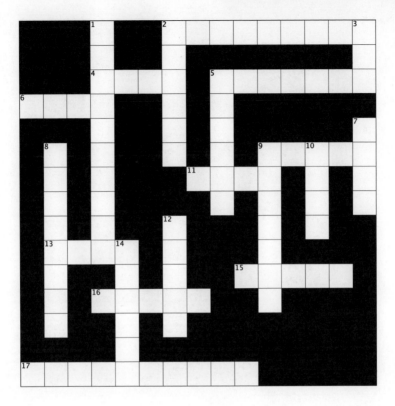

ACROSS
2. Elvis's estate
4. With 9-Across, Elvis's daughter
5. Nickname for Elvis
6. 'A Little ____ Conversation' (1968)
9. See 4-Across
11. Word before 'Hawaii' or 'Suede shoes'
13. Body part associated with Elvis
15. 'Suspicious ____' (1968)
16. Subject with Elvis in the most requested photo in the U.S. National Archives
17. TV host who initially declared Elvis 'unfit for family viewing'

DOWN
1. Song that contains the line 'I'm itchin' like a man on a fuzzy tree'
2. Elvis's mom
3. 'Hound ____' (1956)
5. Birthplace of Elvis
7. 'Elvis has ____ the building'
8. '____ Falling in Love' (1961)
9. Tennessee locale of 2-Across
10. 'Jailhouse ____' (1957 film)
12. Elvis's middle name
14. Gyrate

Answer on page 316

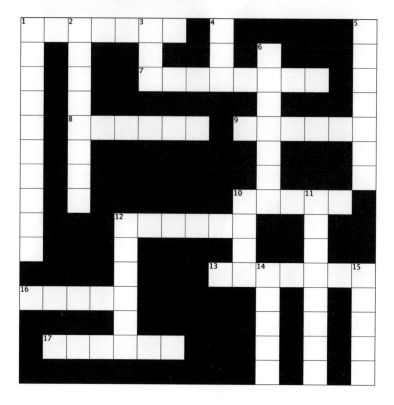

ACROSS

1. Type of 15-Down created at a noted hotel

7. Candy bar named for a Yankees player

8. With 17-Across, drink with lemonade and iced tea

9. Grilled sandwich with sauerkraut and corned beef

10. It can precede toast or follow peach

12. Cherry _____, Ben and Jerry's ice cream flavor

13. _____ Rockefeller

16. Toffee candy bar

17. See 8-Across

DOWN

1. Beef and mushroom dish wrapped in pastry

2. Quiche in a B-52s song

3. With 4-Down, cocktail named for a Scotsman

4. See 3-Down

5. _____ Foster, flambe dessert with ice cream and rum

6. Flaming crepe dessert

10. With 'bloody,' tomato cocktail

11. Eggs served with ham and Hollandaise

12. Crackers called 'digestive biscuits' in Britain

14. Granny _____ apple

15. Cobb or Caesar

Answer on page 316

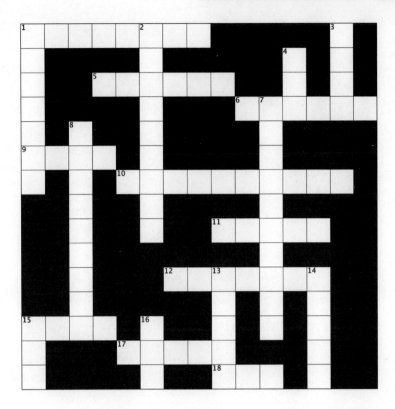

ACROSS

1. Large mammal with fur and tusks
5. Bird that became extinct in the wild in 1987 but has since recovered
6. Steller's _____
9. Golden _____
10. Not quite 7-Down
11. Tasmanian _____
12. Taxon name for animals once thought to be extinct but which have 'come back to life'
15. Type of wolf not only in 'Game of Thrones'
17. _____-toothed 16-Down
18. This bird resembled the penguin

DOWN

1. Woolly _____
2. Dimetrodon and Parasaurolophus
3. Extinct bird with a stupid-sounding name
4. Flightless New Zealand bird
7. Animal coming close to extinction
8. _____ pigeon
13. The quagga was a type of this striped mammal
14. Slow ground mammal
15. Thylacine or Alpine Mastiff
16. See 17-Across

Answer on page 316

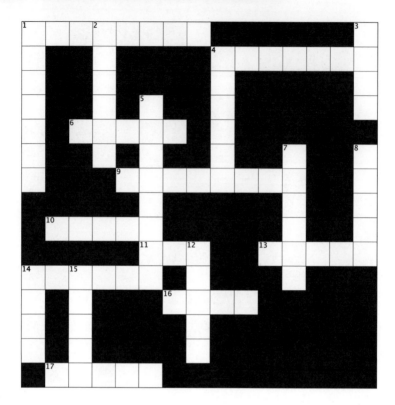

ACROSS

1. Puerto Rican Pirate
4. Ken Senior or Junior
6. Hammerin' Hank
9. Joltin' Joe
10. Player with the most career home runs
11. Master Melvin
13. Mr. Cub / Mr. Sunshine
14. Player with the most consecutive games started
16. Player with the most career RBIs
17. Catcher prone to malapropisms

DOWN

1. Winner of seven Cy Young awards
2. Stan the Man
3. All-time strikeout leader
4. The Iron Horse
5. First Black MLB player
7. Youngest player ever elected to the Hall of Fame
8. Third baseman for the Red Sox
12. Gregarious player and active philanthropist
14. The Great Bambino
15. His career lasted until he was 59 years old

Answer on page 316

ACROSS
1. He had 'No Reservations'
2. Alice of Chez Panisse
6. British baker Mary
7. French chef and author
9. Rachael who popularized 'EVOO'
10. Paula with gooey butter cake
11. Bobby of 'Iron Chef'
15. Author of 'Garlic and Sapphires'
16. Irma who wrote 'The Joy of Cooking'
17. British organic chef

DOWN
1. Mark with 'How to Cook Everything'
3. World Central Kitchen humanitarian
4. Chef from 'Hell's Kitchen'
5. His catchphrase is 'Bam!'
6. James with a cooking school and foundation
8. Author of 'Salt Fat Acid Heat'
11. Guy in Flavortown
12. The Barefoot Contessa
13. Julia with a distinctive voice
14. With Hollywood, current 'Great British Bake-Off' judge

Answer on page 316

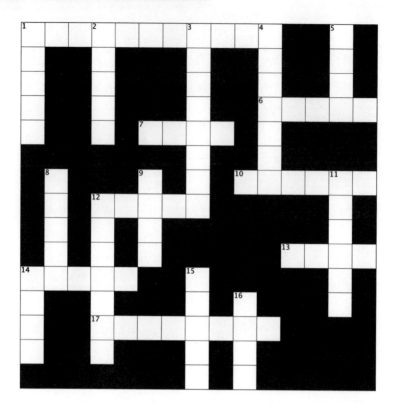

ACROSS

1. Swimmer Johnny who also played Tarzan

6. Legendary track and field athlete who competed in Berlin, 1936

7. Boxer who was later known by a different name

10. First Native American to win a gold medal at the Olympics

12. Sprinter and long jumper Carl

13. Usain with name determinism

14. Gymnast Simone

17. Figure skater Nancy

DOWN

1. Snowboarder Shaun

2. 'Magnificent Seven' member Kerri

3. Diver Greg

4. First American woman to win three gold medals in a single Olympics

5. Alpine skiier Lindsey

8. The 'Flying Finn'

9. Most decorated figure skater in US history

11. Most decorated Olympian of all time

12. American swimmer Katie

14. Larry on the 'Dream Team'

15. Swimmer who won seven golds in Munich

16. Soccer player Mia

Answer on page 316

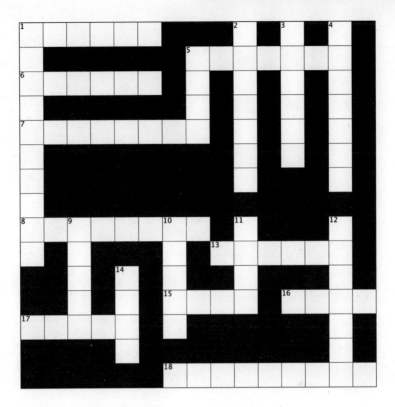

ACROSS

1. Peaches and plums
5. Harvest
6. Crop that can make you cry
7. Key ingredient in marinara sauce
8. Sweet fermented tea
13. Grab a bag or a cup
15. They're sold by the dozn
16. _____ and crafts
17. 'Think global, buy _____'
18. Jams or jellies

DOWN

1. Dining option at a farmers' market, maybe
2. Reusable sack
3. Dairy product often sold by the stick
4. Ingredient in 5-Down, often
5. They could be cherry or pecan
9. Live entertainment at a larger market, perhaps
10. Bee byproduct
11. These guests are welcome if leashed
12. Salad base
14. It can be skim, 2%, or whole

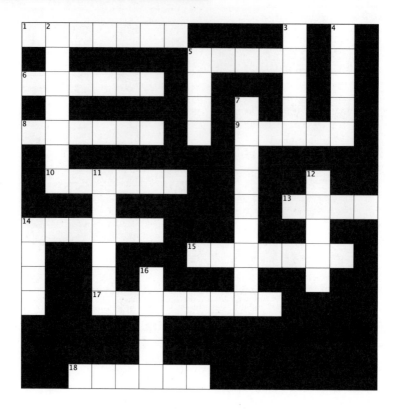

ACROSS

1. Burger King's signature sandwich
5. Drive-in fast food chain
6. Chocolatey dessert at Wendy's
8. Type of 'burger' becoming more popular as a vegan offering
9. Chain noted for its roast beef
10. Most popular fast food chain in America
13. Fried chicken bits, familiarly
14. Beef between buns
15. Pick one up at Auntie Anne's
17. Wear tinfoil clothing here on Halloween to get a free burrito
18. Clown mascot who shares his surname with the restaurant he represents

DOWN

2. Southern chain with a star logo
3. Controversial pork product
4. Dunk these in your 6-Across for a treat
5. Coke or Pepsi, for example
7. Child's combo served in a box
11. 'Two all-beef patties, special sauce, lettuce, cheese, pickles, onions on a sesame seed bun'
12. Dairy _____, home of the Blizzard
14. Taco _____
16. Mainstay of Domino's and Sbarro

Answer on page 317

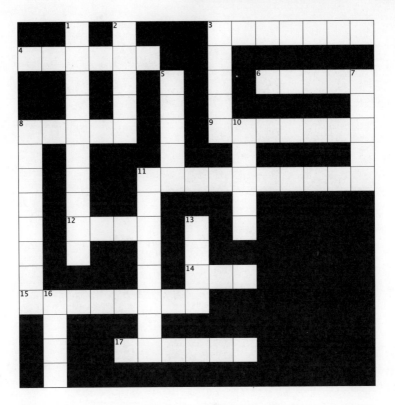

ACROSS

3. It might be red-necked, rock, or nail-tail
4. Diet of choice for 7-Down
6. Great 3-Down ____, ocean predator
8. Distinctive feature of 1-Down
9. Spiny anteater
11. Bird with a laughing call
12. With 'ant,' fiercely predatory insect species
14. Flightless bird
15. Sadly, one was Steve Irwin's cause of death in 2006
17. The only known animal that poops cubes

DOWN

1. Examples of this class of mammals include possums and potoroos
2. Tasmanian devils have prominent, sharp ones
3. See 6-Across
5. It probably didn't steal your baby
7. Arboreal creature with fluffy ears and a round behind
8. Venomous, egg-laying mammal whose existence was once thought to be a hoax
10. Cassowaries have two of these so sharp they've been compared to daggers
11. Leaping animal with a prominent tail
13. Baby 11-Down
16. In an old rhyme, 11-Across sits in one

Answer on page 317

ACROSS

1. Hiccup ('How to Train Your Dragon')
3. Kristoff ('Frozen')
5. Aladdin ('Aladdin')
7. Pocahontas ('Pocahontas')
8. Jack Skellington ('The Nightmare Before Christmas')
11. Wallace ('Wallace and ____')
12. Peter ('Homeward Bound')
14. Alice ('Alice in Wonderland')
16. Peter Griffin ('Family Guy')
17. Spongebob ('Spongebob Squarepants')

DOWN

1. Dorothy ('The Wizard of Oz')
2. Sabrina ('Sabrina the Teenage Witch')
3. Charlie Brown ('Peanuts')
4. Jon Arbuckle ('____')
6. Harry ('Harry Potter' series)
9. Joe Talbot ('____')
10. Jon Snow ('Game of Thrones')
13. Fern Arable ('Charlotte's Web')
14. Fred Flintstone ('The Flintstones')
15. Carl ('Up')

Answer on page 317

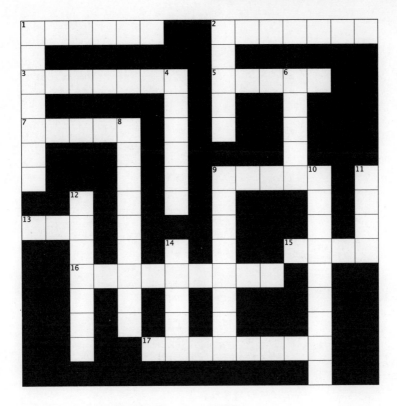

ACROSS

1. 'Beetlejuice' and 'Edward Scissorhands'
2. 'The Virgin Suicides' and 'Lost in Translation'
3. 'Brazil' and 'Fear and Loathing in Las Vegas'
5. 'Get Out' and 'Us'
7. 'Eraserhead' and 'Mulholland Drive'
9. 'Alien' and 'The Martian'
13. 'Do the Right Thing' and 'Chi-Raq'
15. 'Metropolis' and 'M'
16. 'Requiem for a Dream' and 'Black Swan'
17. 'The Grand Budapest Hotel' and 'Rushmore'

DOWN

1. 'The Hurt Locker' and 'Zero Dark Thirty'
2. 'It's a Wonderful Life' and 'It Happened One Night'
4. 'American Beauty' and 'Skyfall'
6. '12 Angry Men' and 'Murder on the Orient Express'
8. 'Vertigo' and 'Rope'
9. 'Shutter Island' and 'The Wolf of Wall Street'
10. 'Reservoir Dogs' and 'Kill Bill'
11. 'Parasite' and 'Snowpiercer'
12. 'Carrie' and 'Mission: Impossible'
14. 'The Dark Knight' and 'Inception'

Answer on page 317

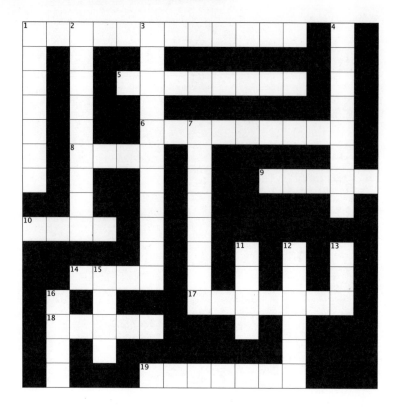

ACROSS

1. 1984 film with Gozer and Zuul

5. 1989 dark comedy about a high school clique

6. 1986 fantasy film with Bowie

8. 1984 sci-fi film with Sting

9. '_____ and Deliver'

10. '_____ Times at Ridgemont High'

14. Film with three different endings

17. 'Dead Poets _____' (1989)

18. '_____ 7-Down' (1983), Tom Cruise breakout film

19. Where we spent a weekend in 1989

DOWN

1. With 'The,' 1985 adventure comedy film with Sean Astin

2. With 'The,' 1983 film with Soda and Ponyboy

3. Say his name three times to manifest him

4. 'Say _____,' in which John Cusack holds up a boom box

7. See 18-Across

11. '_____ to the Future' (1985)

12. 'Field of _____' (1989)

13. With 'The,' remake in which Jeff Goldblum becomes an insect

15. 'The _____ Boys,' teen vampire drama

16. Many 1980s actors were in this 'pack'

Answer on page 317

ACROSS

1. Fictional Swedish cult harga
4. '_____ thou like to live deliciously?'
5. 'The _____ Day,' 2020 HBO series
6. Black Phillip's species
7. 1922 silent film about witchcraft
9. Animal at the climax of 8D
11. 'The _____ Man' (1973)
13. Setting for 16-Across
14. Star of 11-Across
15. Director Ari
16. 'The Blair Witch _____' (1999)
17. Nebraska town in 12-Down

DOWN

1. 2018 film involving the god Paimon
2. 2017 Jordan Peele film
3. Actress Florence of 8-Down
4. 'The _____,' 2015 Anya Taylor-Joy film
8. 2019 film about a pagan cult
9. Oft-derided line in the 2006 remake of 11-Across
10. Setting for 8-Down
12. '_____ of the Corn' (1984)

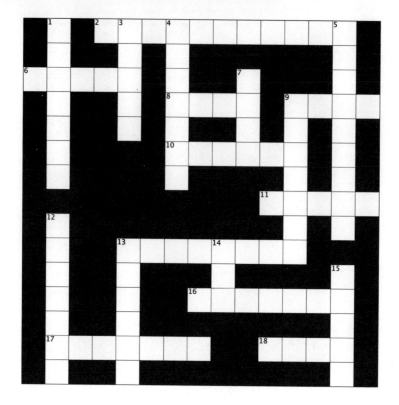

ACROSS

2. Vietnamese appetizers in rice paper
6. South American cornmeal cake
8. Japanese soybean paste
9. Hawaiian dish with raw fish
10. Mesoamerican meal in a corn husk
11. Japanese chocolate-coated biscuit sticks
13. Spicy sauce with roots in Portugal and Africa
16. Canadian food with cheese, fries, and gravy
17. National dish of Hungary
18. Middle Eastern 'pocket bread'

DOWN

1. Ukrainian beet soup
3. Japanese freshwater eel
4. British malt spread
5. Maghrebi dish with eggs and tomatoes
7. South Indian savory crepe
9. Polish potato dumpling
12. Korean for 'fire meat'
13. Spanish seafood dish
14. Vietnamese noodle soup
15. Middle Eastern grilled meat dish

Answer on page 318

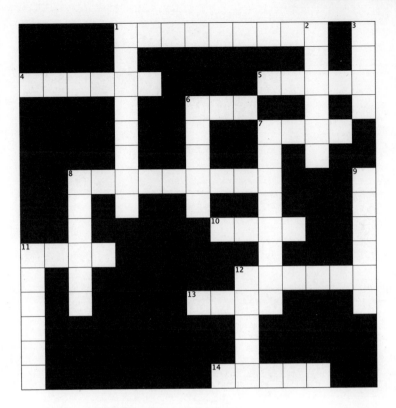

ACROSS
1. Edible substance
4. Bitter cold
5. Aspect
6. Dandy
7. Muppet material
8. Intense, destructive blaze
10. Refrain from eating
11. In British slang, to fuss over something unimportant
12. Weak or ineffective
13. Fight
14. Young female horse

DOWN
1. Showy or gaudy clothing
2. Hot and cold
3. Gala
6. Belief
7. Starving
8. Apt name for a long-haired cat
9. Aesop's tales
11. Farmland left unsown
12. Yeast and mushrooms, for example

Answer on page 318

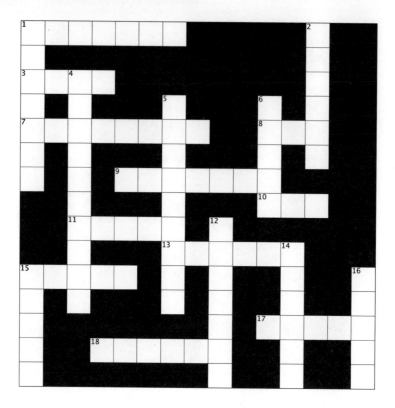

ACROSS

1. Night's Watch commander who was raised at Winterfell and
3. 'A Song of 8-Across and _____,' book series on which the TV show is based
7. Appellation for Melisandre
8. See 3-Across
9. With 6-Down, capital of Westeros
10. Honorific in Westeros
11. 'A 5-Down always pays his _____'
13. He drinks and he knows things
15. Eldest daughter of Ned & Catelyn
17. Brother of 2-Down
18. George R. R. _____

DOWN

1. He's poisoned at his own wedding
2. Mother of 1-Down
4. Ill-fated marriage celebration
5. Surname of Tywin
6. See 9-Across
12. She's portrayed by 6'3" Gwendoline Christie
14. 'A girl has _____'
15. Arya and Bran's surname
16. _____ Greyjoy, Ned's ward

Answer on page 318

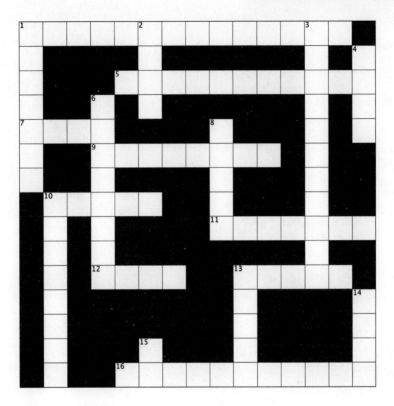

ACROSS

1. A: This game show requires that you answer in the form of a question

5. 'Who Wants to Be a _____'

7. 'You Bet Your _____,' game show hosted by Groucho Marx

9. 'The _____ Game,' in which spouses are pitted against each other

10. 'The _____ Is Right'

11. Regis who hosted 5-Across

12. '_____ You!,' NPR quiz show

13. Potential 1-Down purchase

16. 11-Across question

DOWN

1. '_____ Fortune'

2. 1-Down action

3. Chance to earn - or lose - significant money in 1-Across

4. '_____ or No _____,' show hosted by Howie Mandel

6. Highest-earning American game show contestant of all time

8. 'Supermarket _____'

10. Game with mystery words

13. White, who described her job as 'touching letters and wearing pretty clothes'

14. '_____ Factor,' show that involved eating bugs

15. British trivia show originally hosted by Stephen Fry

Answer on page 318

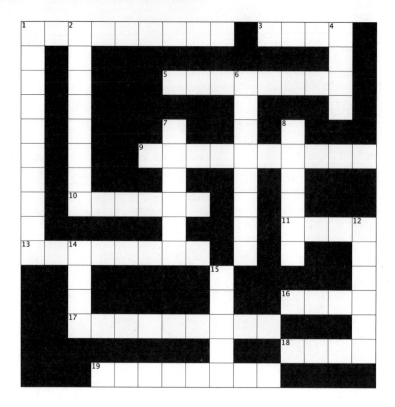

ACROSS

1. With 'The,' film with the quote 'Leave the gun. Take the cannoli.'

3. 'Gangs of New ____'

5. With 'The,' De Niro played him in 2019

9. 'On the ____,' film with 'I coulda been a contender!'

10. '____ Brasco'

11. 'Reservoir ____'

13. With 'The,' TV series with Tony and Carmela

16. 'Once ____ a Time in America'

17. 'Road to ____'

18. 'Black ____'

19. Black comedy set in Belgium

DOWN

1. Scorsese film with Liotta, Pesci, and Bracco

2. With 'The,' 2006 film about moles in Boston

4. '____ of New York'

6. 1932 film with a 1983 remake

7. Scorsese film with De Niro, Pesci, and Stone

8. He played Corleone and Malloy

12. 'Boondock ____'

14. '____ Fiction'

15. With 'The,' 1974 Best Picture winner

Answer on page 318

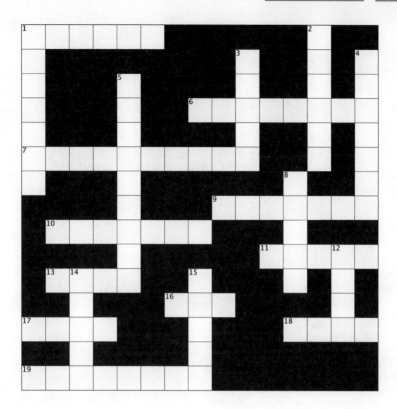

ACROSS

1. Opaque variety of silica
6. Blue gemstone
7. Pale pink crystal
9. A girl's best friend, it's said
10. Green mineral that's the birthstone for August
11. Gem from an oyster
13. Ornamental material that's also a woman's name
16. Location where an increasing number of gems are grown
17. Iridescent stone found in Australia
18. Black mineral
19. Purple gemstone

DOWN

1. Accessories that often have gemstones
2. It's also known as fool's gold
3. Golden-brown or yellow gemstone
4. Green gemstone
5. Mineral found in the Southwestern United States
8. Fossilized resin
12. Like Dorothy's slippers
14. Mineral with curved bands
15. Flat, polished side of a cut gemstone

Answer on page 319

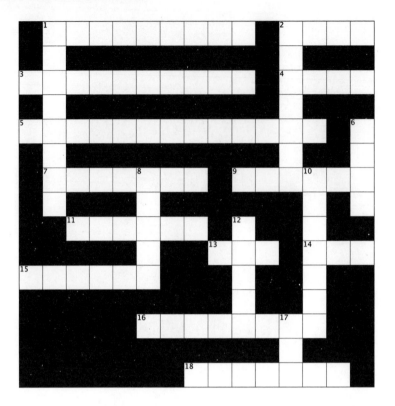

ACROSS

1. Hip-hop group from Queens
2. Part of Emma Bunton's nickname
3. British girl group from the '90s
4. 'Say My ____' (2000)
5. Group that included Beyoncé
7. R&B group with 'Hold On'
9. #1 hit for 1-Across
11. Part of Geri Halliwell's nickname
13. ____ Ketchup, 'Asereje' band
14. Little ____, British group
15. Guys that can't get no love from 17-Down
16. 17-Down song that begins 'I wish I could tie you up in my shoes'
18. 2005 hit from the Pussycat Dolls

DOWN

1. 1960s Motown group with Diana Ross
2. Band with hits 'Walk Like an Egyptian' and 'Manic Monday'
6. Russian pop dup
8. Belinda Carlisle's girl group, with 'The'
10. Fifth ____
12. 'C'est ____,' 1998 hit from B*Witched
17. Group with Chilli, T-Boz, and Left Eye

Answer on page 319

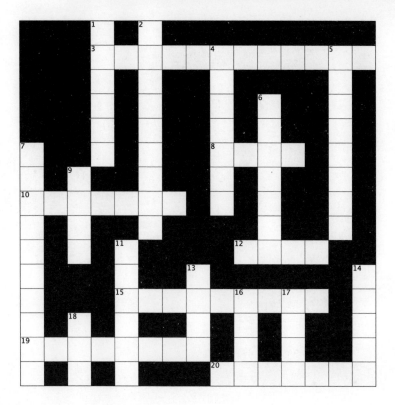

ACROSS

3. Break between acts

8. Behind-the-scenes folks

10. 'The _____ of the Opera,' longest-running Broadway show

12. Actor's accessory

15. It might be sought by a fan

19. 'The Great _____,' Broadway nickname

20. City where Broadway can be found

DOWN

1. The last number in a show

2. Where a fan may wait for a 15-Across

4. 'Annie' or 'Cats,' for example

5. Number played before the curtain rises

6. Play place

7. A show's status before opening night

9. Playbill listing

11. Cue for actors that the show will begin shortly

13. Coveted award

14. For luck, do this to your leg (figuratively)

16. Actor's part

17. The thing, in 'Hamlet'

18. Orchestra locale

Answer on page 319

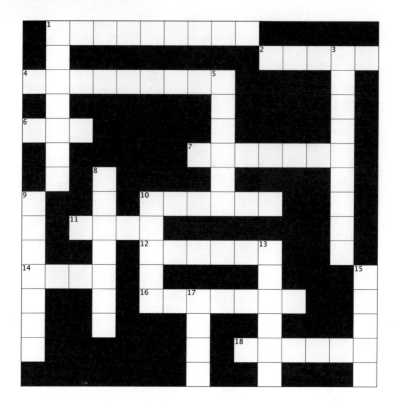

ACROSS

1. Nut that can be red, green, or white
2. Nuts found inside pods with burrs
4. Nut associated with Hawaii
6. Liquid extracted from nuts
7. Sweet white fruit that's technically not a nut, despite its name
10. Candy bar with nougat and peanuts
11. Nut found in pesto
12. Nut with a characteristic curve
14. Flavor enhancer
16. Hazelnut and chocolate spread
18. The B in PB&J

DOWN

1. Sugared nuts
3. Nuts associated with Christmas
5. Dieter's nut
8. Confection often made with peanuts
9. Common nut preparation
10. You might find it in a Thanksgiving pie
13. They might be candied
15. Oak nut
17. _____ nut allergy

Answer on page 319

ACROSS
1. Breed associated with France
3. It has claws, pads, and toes
5. Undesirable dinnertime behavior, perhaps
7. Sled dog
9. If you're happy and you know it, wag your _____
11. Small breed with a 'smushed' face
12. Cairn, Skye, or Airedale
13. Classic dog name
16. Lassie, for one
17. They can be yellow, black, or chocolate

DOWN
1. Dog that gets its name from its trademark hunting stance
2. You'll need one of these for a 4-Down
3. Young dog
4. A dog's absolute favorite activity, maybe
5. Dog sound
6. Breed that shares its name with a bus company
8. What a dog might do after swimming
10. Canine warning sound
14. Command while on a 4-Down
15. _____ Inu

Answer on page 319

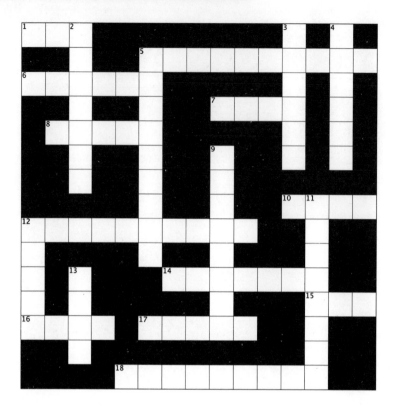

ACROSS

1. Big League Chew or Doublemint
5. Now-standard antibiotic
6. With 8-Across, salty, crispy snack
7. _____ Flakes
8. See 6-Across
10. Microwave _____
12. Packing material that can be cathartic to destroy
14. Malaria preventive
15. Acid
16. Detector of broken bones or contraband in carry-ons
17. Post-it _____
18. A bit of bubbly

DOWN

2. Contents of some books
3. Coiled toy
4. The "little blue pill"
5. Cool treat on a stick
9. Explosive patented in 1867
11. Petroleum jelly brand
12. Paralytic used in cosmetic dermatology
13. _____-Doh

Answer on page 319

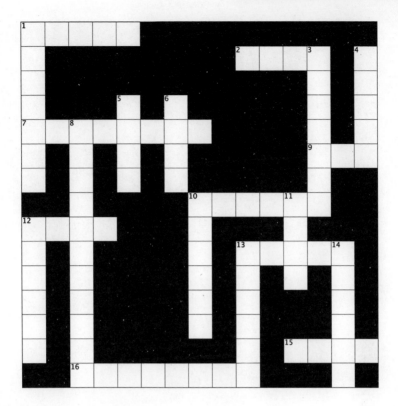

ACROSS

1. Boat for lake fishing, maybe
2. Rod's partner
7. Legally established time for a given species to be fished
9. Trawler's trap
10. Fishing gear
12. Fish's temptation
13. Popular 12-Across option
15. What's at the end of the line
16. Avian beggars

DOWN

1. Bottom feeder
3. Paperwork needed to fish, in some spots
4. Varieties include lake, brook, and rainbow
5. Throw one's line into the water
6. Natural material for 12-Down
8. Sailing ailment
10. Atlantic game fish
11. Artificial type of 12-Across
12. In the UK, it's called a float
13. Protective clothes for an angler
14. Alaskan catch

Answer on page 320

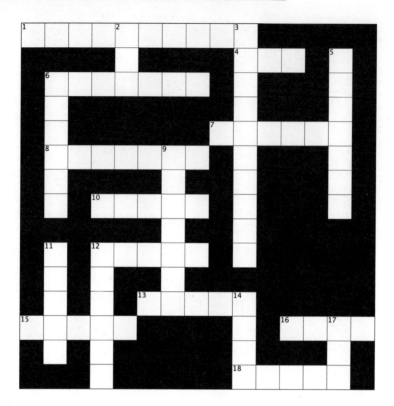

ACROSS

1. Bedroom accessory for one scared of the dark
4. Diffuser filler
6. Bedtime clothes
7. Place to get clean
8. Calming song
10. 'To sleep, perchance to ____'
12. Toe warmers
13. Bedtime reading
15. End of an evening routine
16. Cozy
18. Don't forget to set it!

DOWN

2. Sleepytime ____
3. Canine cleaner
5. Write your emotions down in this
6. Head rest
9. Bed covering
11. A heavy 9-Down
12. Bed coverings
14. Stretching exercise
17. Nighttime cycle (abbr.)

Answer on page 320

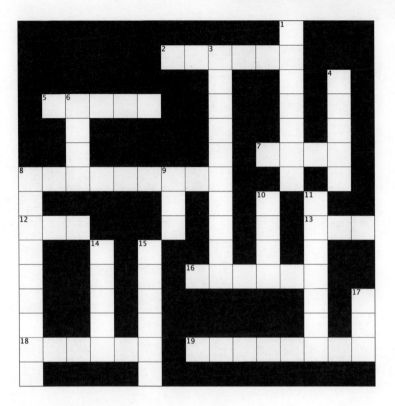

ACROSS

2. Key red sauce ingredient
5. Pizza foundation
7. What you might do to your 5-Across to shape it
8. Much-maligned tropical pizza topping
12. Pizza unit
13. Pizza _____, chain with a distinctive roof shape
16. Allium used to enhance flavor
18. Italian birthplace of pizza
19. Pizza topping that's a fungus

DOWN

1. Pizza chain with a game piece as its logo
3. Pizza representing the colors of the Italian flag
4. Pizza's edge
6. Cooking apparatus
8. Spicy cured meat
9. Deep-dish pizza holder
10. Shovel-like tool used by bakers
11. City known for deep-dish pizza
14. Green herb that's also a man's name
15. Mozzarella, for example
17. Pair this with 8-Across for a Hawaiian pizza

Answer on page 320

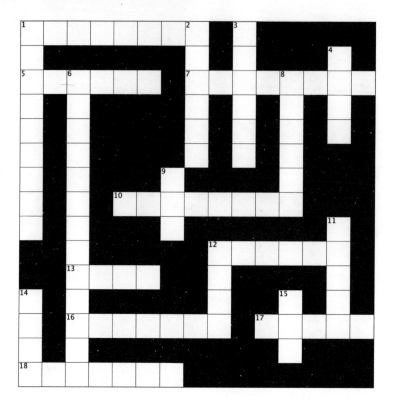

ACROSS

1. Food of the gods
5. Sun god
7. Hero with twelve labors
10. God of wine
12. God of archery and music
13. The Earth mother
16. Mountain home to the pantheon
17. He abducted Persephone
18. Goddess of the hunt

DOWN

1. Goddess of love and beauty
2. Goddess symbolized by an owl
3. God with wings on his heels
4. King of the gods
6. Weapon of choice for 4-Down
8. 4-Down's father
9. Goddess of the dawn
11. Hephaestus, god of the ____
12. God of war
14. Wife of 4-Down
15. Satyr god of the wild

Answer on page 320

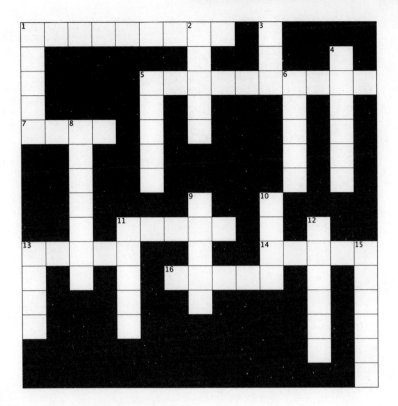

ACROSS

1. What bears do in winter
5. Fictional bear fond of marmalade
7. Cartoon bear who lives in Jellystone Park
11. Mowgli's friend in 'The Jungle Book'
13. White Arctic bear
14. Common North American bear
16. Look out for this part of the bear!

DOWN

1. Substance produced by bees and desired by bears
2. Child's toy named after Theodore Roosevelt
3. Southeast Asian bear
4. Joke-telling Muppet bear
5. Black-and-white bamboo-eater
6. Multicolored candy bears
8. Northwestern American bear
9. Contrary to popular belief, not a bear
10. Baby bears
11. Color of an 8-Down
12. Preferred food source of 8-Down
13. Winnie-the-_____
15. Bear found in Alaska

Answer on page 320

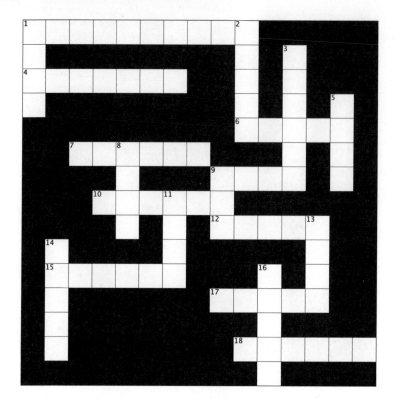

ACROSS
1. Owls
4. Cats
6. Lions
7. Rats
9. Quail
10. Geese
12. Pigs
15. Magpies
17. Bees
18. Fish

DOWN
1. Dogs
2. Kangaroos
3. Otters
5. Snakes
8. Leopards
9. Sloths
11. Elk
13. Oxen
14. Flamingos
16. Nightingales

Answer on page 320

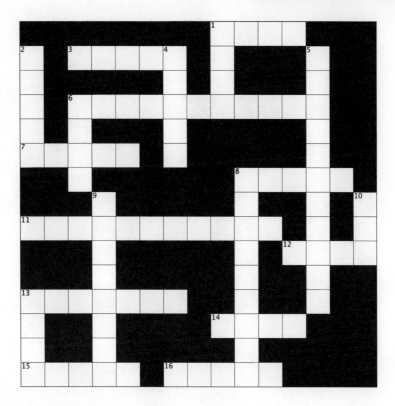

ACROSS
1. Pike, tuck, or aerial, for example
3. Event that involves a choreographed routine
6. Narrow tumbling platform
7. Kerri of the 1996 Olympics
8. Mineral used to decrease slipperiness
11. Equipment used for 16-Across
12. Hand protector
13. McKayla whose face became a meme
14. Aerial jump
15. Gymnastics term for a somersault
16. Event involving a runway

DOWN
1. The Final _____, 2016 women's Olympic team
2. Simone who is the most decorated American gymnast of all time
4. Gymnastics event requiring extreme upper body strength
5. Equipment with handles
6. They might be uneven or parallel
8. Sideways handspring
9. Gymnasts finale
10. Friction injury to the palms
13. Protective padding

Answer on page 321

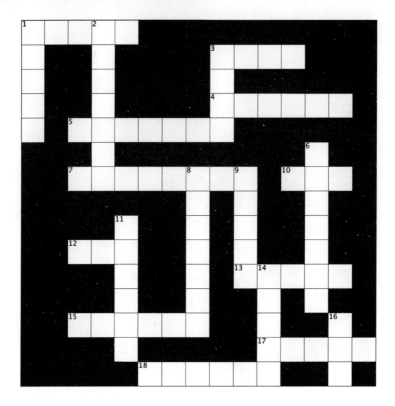

ACROSS

1. Halloween option with 1-Down
3. Eerie effect similar to fog
4. With black, traditional Halloween color
5. Jack-o-Lantern gourd
7. Lycanthrope
10. A black one of these is a bad omen
12. Halloween exclamation
13. Frightening
15. Eight-legged insect
17. Get-up with horns and a tail
18. Sinister or ghostly

DOWN

1. See 1-Across
2. Halloween outfit
3. What a 7-Across howls at
6. Bloodsucking being
8. Halloween's month
9. Dracula's prominent teeth
11. Undead being
14. Halloween haul
16. Inscription on a tombstone, maybe

Answer on page 321

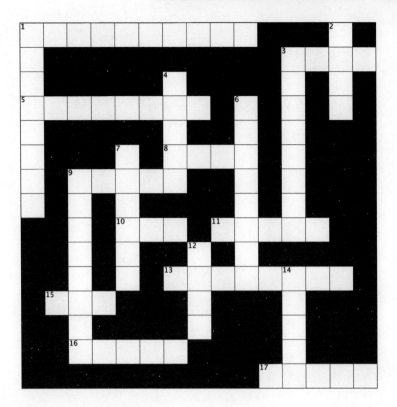

ACROSS

1. In French, they're 'haricot verts'
3. With 2-Down, sluggishness after a big meal
5. Day of the week on which Thanksgiving falls
8. Sweet potatoes
9. Potatoes
10. Thanksgiving guests, often
11. Single-serve breads
13. Thanksgiving month
15. It could be apple or pumpkin
16. Sauce made from meat juice
17. Nutty type of 15-Across

DOWN

1. Thankful
2. See 3-Across
3. Thanksgiving sport
4. Parade sponsor
6. Lucky part of 7-Down
7. Traditional Thanksgiving bird
9. 7-Down filling
12. It may be served on the cob
14. Moisten

Answer on page 321

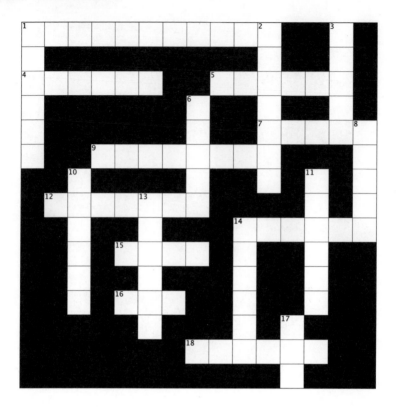

ACROSS

1. Hat worn to a Rays or an Orioles game
4. 1920s hat from the French for 'bell'
5. Head protector for many sports
7. Military or French hat
9. Wide-brimmed Mexican hat
12. 1920s cap
14. Close fitting hat
15. Protective type of hat, as in construction
16. Hat associated with Shriners
18. Headwear created from wound cloth

DOWN

1. Denim or canvas hat with a downturned brim
2. Hat type famously worn by Jackie Kennedy
3. Ceremonial Catholic headwear
6. Celebratory hat typically made out of paper
8. Chef's hat
10. Indiana Jones wears one
11. It's worn at the beach or in the garden
13. Summer hat made from straw
14. Hat associated with Charlie Chaplin
17. _____ o'shanter

Answer on page 321

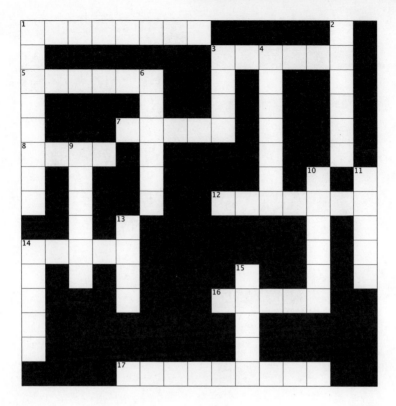

ACROSS

1. Soapy-tasting herb, to some
3. Seeds used in Asian cooking
5. Key spice in pumpkin pie
7. Licorice-flavored spice
8. Spice derived from 5-Across
12. Sweet spice made into an extract
14. Spice available as powder or flakes
16. Indian spice blend
17. 1-Across, across the pond

DOWN

1. _____ Toast Crunch
2. Common spice that can make you sneeze
3. Earthy spice often included in sausage
4. Expensive yellow spice
6. Spice from an oddly-shaped root
9. Fluffy's favorite spice
10. Seafood spice blend popular in the Mid-Atlantic
11. Main component of pesto
13. Spice often used in pickling
14. Spice used in chai
15. Spice often found in Tex-Mex blends

Answer on page 321

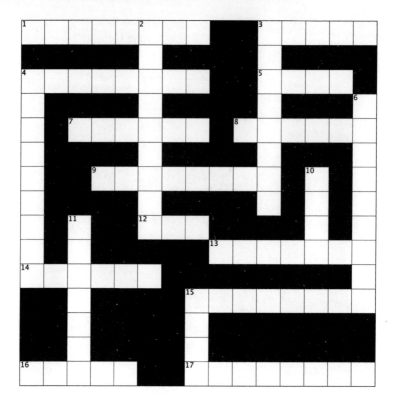

ACROSS

1. 2007 film with 'McLovin'

3. '_____ and Confused' (1993)

4. 1998 Wes Anderson film

5. TV series set at McKinley High

7. James Van Der Beek character

8. Sissy Spacek part

9. 1989 black comedy with Winona Ryder

12. '_____ [14-Across] I Hate About You'

13. Broderick played him in 1986

14. See 12-Across

15. 1995 film based on an Austen novel

16. Holmes who played Joey

17. '_____ World' (1993-2000)

DOWN

2. 2019 buddy comedy film with Beanie Feldstein

3. Canadian drama franchise

4. 'Fast Times at _____ High' (1982)

6. On Wednesdays, they wear pink

10. 'Saved by the _____,'

11. '_____ On,' cheerleading movie franchise

15. 'The Breakfast _____,'

Answer on page 321

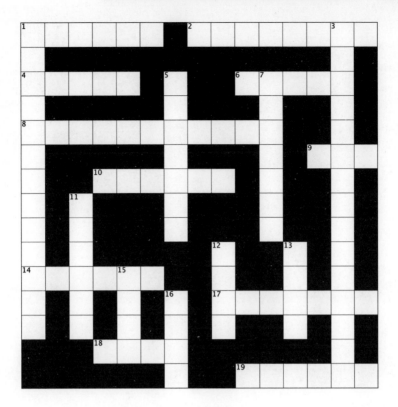

ACROSS

1. Shakespeare play with Ophelia and Laertes
2. Archetypal man vs. nature novel
4. Holocaust memoir
6. Title character in a Beckett play who never actually shows up
8. Woolf novel that spans one day
9. 'To Kill a Mockingbird' author
10. '____ of Grass'
14. Author with six major books
17. With 19-Across, mark of shame worn by Hester Prynne
18. With 13-Down, titular governess
19. See 17-Across

DOWN

1. With 'The,' dystopian novel with Offred and Serena Joy
3. With 'The,' famous Salinger work
5. 1987 Morrison novel
7. Homeric epic
11. Titular millionaire in a Fitzgerald novel
12. '____ of [16-Down],' Steinbeck's magnum opus
13. See 18-Across
15. Novel that was later adapted for the screen as 'Clueless'
16. See 12-Down

Answer on page 322

117

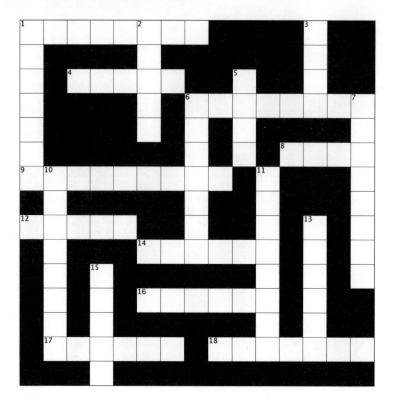

ACROSS

1. First person to circumnavigate the globe
4. First woman to win a Nobel Prize
6. First Black woman in Congress
8. First woman to be Israel's Prime Minister
9. First man on the moon
12. First Black president of the US
14. First woman to hold federal office in the US
16. First woman to be Vice President of the US
17. First sherpa to summit Mt. Everest
18. First Catholic president

DOWN

1. First Black president of South Africa
2. First dog in space
3. First woman to be US Attorney General
5. First American woman in space
6. First woman to run for president on a major party ticket
7. First Black Supreme Court justice
10. First Black player in Major League Baseball
11. First explorer to reach the South Pole
13. First test-tube baby
15. First explorer to reach the North Pole

Answer on page 322

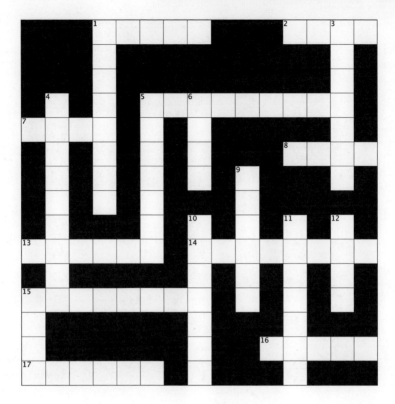

ACROSS

1. A 5-Down has three

2. Horn with the lowest range

5. There were 76 of them in a song from 'The Music Man'

7. Improvisational music genre

8. Natural material from which winds can be made

13. Brass instrument similar to 5-Down

14. Instrument played by Goodman and Shaw

15. Elementary school instrument

16. Ron Burgundy played one in 'Anchorman'

17. Type of 15-Down with two strips

DOWN

1. Simple instrument associated with football matches

3. It represents the grandfather in 'Peter and the Wolf'

4. Instrument that may be alto or tenor

5. Traditional 'Taps' instrument

6. Instrument an orchestra tunes to

9. What a musician uses to produce sound on a wind instrument

10. Ancient wind instrument with finger holes

11. Smallest wind instrument

12. A 16-Across, fittingly, has sixteen

15. Thin strip of vibrating material often attached to a mouthpiece

Answer on page 322

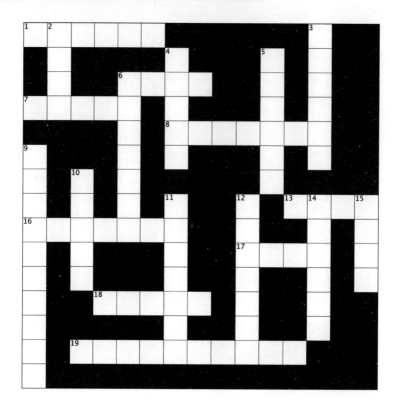

ACROSS

1. Old Faithful, for example

6. Center of the Earth

7. Molten rock beneath Earth's surface

8. Adjective describing 9-Down

13. What 1-Across or 12-Down might do

16. Destructive tidal event

17. 7-Across after surfacing

18. Metamorphic rock often used with chalk

19. It might follow a large 9-Down

DOWN

2. 12-Down on the island of Sicily

3. Rock that floats

4. Surface of the Earth

5. Small vibration

6. Volcanic crater

9. Event caused by a sudden tectonic shift

10. Blow, like a 12-Down

11. Scale used to measure the strength of a 9-Down

12. Active mountain

14. Sections of Earth's 4-Down

15. 16-Across is an enormous one, essentially

Answer on page 322

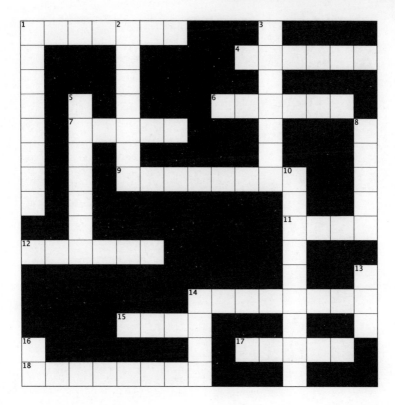

ACROSS

1. With 2-Down, hero whose sidekick is Bucky Barnes
4. 'Universe' for Thor and Thanos
6. Protector of Gotham
7. Harley ____
9. Team of heroes assembled by Nick Fury
11. ____ Man, AKA Tony Stark
12. ____ Woman
14. It's a bird! It's a plane!
15. 1980s team of sewer-dwelling, pizza-eating heroes (abbr.)
17. With 3-Down, alter ego of T'Challa
18. Opportunity to cosplay, maybe

DOWN

1. Batman's foil and love interest
2. See 1-Across
3. See 17-Across
5. Hero played by Jason Momoa
8. ____ Lantern
10. His origin story involves a radioactive arachnid
13. '____-Man and the Wasp' (2018)
14. Marvel legend Lee
16. 'Universe' for Lex Luthor and the Joker

Answer on page 322

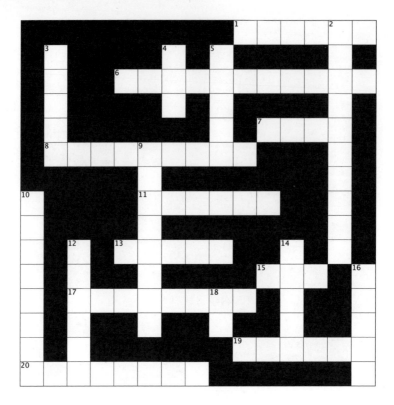

ACROSS

1. You can get there through a wardrobe
6. Home to Bart and Lisa
7. In 'The Matrix,' last human city on Earth
8. Home to Butters and Cartman
11. Dystopia in 'The Handmaid's Tale'
13. With 14-Down, inn run by Norman
15. _____ Eisley, Star Wars spaceport
17. Central kingdom in 'Game of Thrones'
19. Spock's home planet
20. _____ Hotel, secluded resort in Colorado

DOWN

2. Home to a dinosaur park
3. Twin _____, town prone to supernatural happenings
4. Mork's home planet
5. Forest moon in the Star Wars universe
9. School for witches and wizards
10. South American city of gold
12. Indiana town in 'Parks and Recreation'
14. See 13-Across
16. Hometown of the Martells in 'Game of Thrones'
18. It's over the rainbow

Answer on page 322

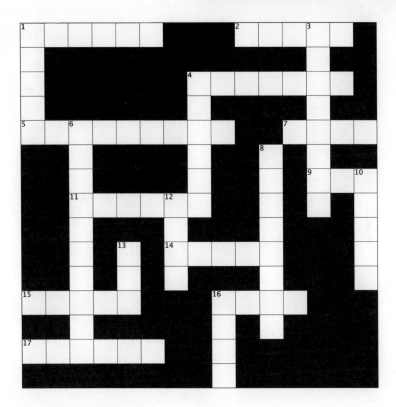

ACROSS
1. Silver
2. Black's opposite
4. Color designation for 9-Across, 16-Across, and 17-Across
5. Color designation for 11-Across, 15-Across, and 4-Down
7. Magenta
9. Scarlet
11. Tangerine
14. It consists of different-colored wavelengths
15. Chartreuse
16. Cerulean
17. Citrine

DOWN
1. Rods counterpart, in the eye
3. Color designation made by mixing one 4-Across and one 5-Across
4. Lilac
6. Round tool for visualizing different hues
8. Full range of all colors in existence
10. The color of jeans, maybe
12. Color that shares its name with a metal
13. Color that's also a beach activity
16. Ivory

Answer on page 323

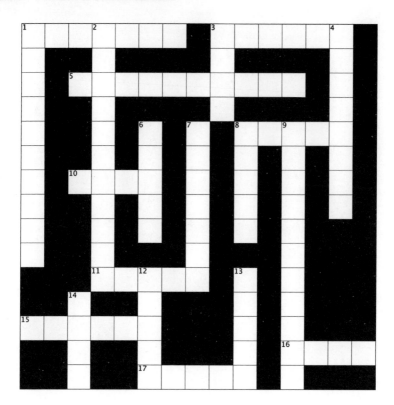

ACROSS

1. Lilies, daffodils, or zinnias
3. Bushes
5. Plants that grow year after year
8. You might push it or ride it
10. Tool for collecting dead leaves and detritus
11. They come up when it rains
15. 12-Down's defenses
16. Covering for 18-Across
17. Nursery purchases

DOWN

1. Plant supplement made with manure
2. Device for transporting loads of dirt
3. Where plants take root
4. Gardener's faunal bane
6. Gardener's floral bane
7. Plants that only grow once
8. Organic material applied to garden beds
9. Tool to hydrate plants
12. They may be English or climbing
13. Basil, chives, or cilantro
14. Garden vessels

Answer on page 323

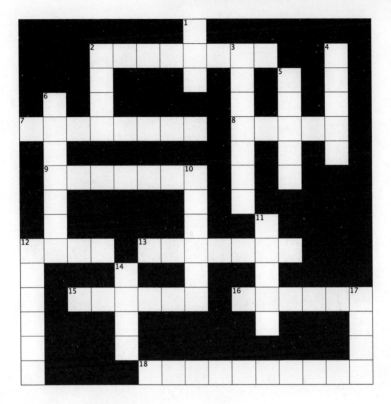

ACROSS

2. Wrist ornament
7. String of pearls
8. Jewelry worn on the fingers
9. Military identification
12. 3-Down that doesn't dangle
13. Stacked adornments that share their name with an '80s band
15. Good luck charm
16. Decorative pin
18. Type of 2-Across made at summer camp

DOWN

1. Precious stone
2. Easily lost fastener for 3-Down
3. It can be worn in the rook, the lobe, or the tragus
4. Fastener for 2-Across
5. With 14-Down, jewelry for dress shirts
6. Locket or charm
10. Seal used to make an impression in wax
11. Natural 'jewel' produced by an oyster
12. Jewelry metal with the chemical symbol Ag
14. See 5-Down
17. Round 3-Down

Answer on page 323

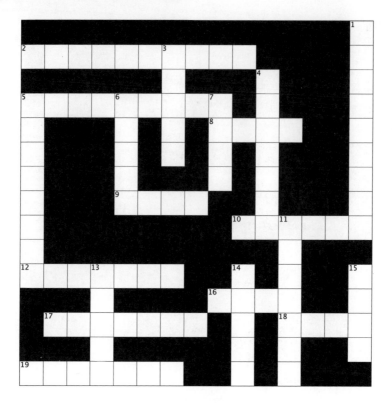

ACROSS

2. It has a cycle
5. Inspiration for dinner, maybe
8. The hot zone
9. Where the washing-up happens
10. Appliance that prevents spoilage, briefly
12. Cooking implement
16. Glove to prevent burns
17. Bread-burner
18. They're helpful for a spill
19. 10-Across part for produce

DOWN

1. Putting metal in this will break it
3. It might be gas or electric
4. Compartment with ice cream, perhaps
5. Kitchen surfaces
6. Deep dishes for Fido's food and water
7. 9-Across need
11. Where to get rocks for cocktails
13. Devices for catching kitchen pests
14. Equipment with a head and beaters
15. Grocery ____

Answer on page 323

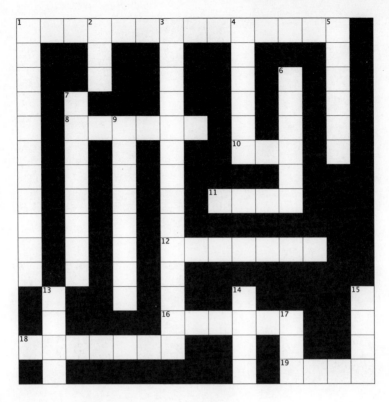

ACROSS

1. Seasonal blooms popular in Japan
8. Tropical fruit with small spines
10. Wilbur or Porky
11. Pinkish color and flower
12. Diamond sought by Clouseau
16. Crunchy salad vegetable
18. Adornments worn for breast cancer awareness
19. Food eaten by carnivores

DOWN

1. Treat at the ballpark or circus
2. Dye brand
3. Shoes worn by some dancers
4. Sea crustaceans
5. Fish whose Japanese name is 'sake'
6. Home to the taste buds
7. Bird often found standing on one leg
9. Car in a Springsteen song
13. Paper bearing bad news at work
14. Kissers
15. Himalayan food flavoring
17. The flesh of a pig

Answer on page 323

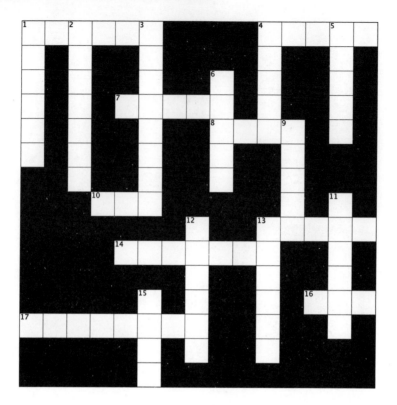

ACROSS

1. Big rainforest feline
4. Neither plants nor animals
7. Scaly slitherer
8. These plants grow in mats on the ground or tree trunks
10. Shocking fish
13. Intelligent rainforest primate
14. Carnivorous fish
16. 7-Across that squeezes its prey
17. Pest that can carry malaria

DOWN

1. 'The ____ Book'
2. Largest primate
3. Precipitation
4. Little jumpers
5. Primary color in a rainforest
6. Rainforest dwellers found only in Madagascar
9. Slow-moving creature
11. World's largest rainforest
12. Colorful bird
13. Rainforest layer made up of overlapping branches
15. What Tarzan swings on

Answer on page 323

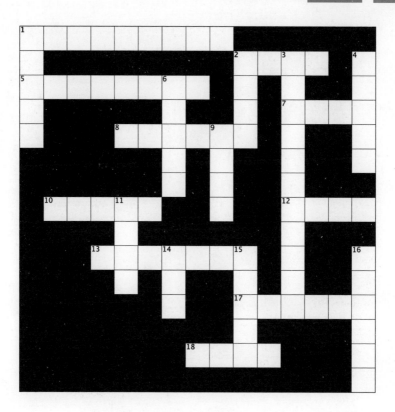

ACROSS

1. Indian film industry
2. In Indian food, it's commonly basmati
5. India's capital
7. Clothing whose name means 'strip of cloth' in Sanskrit
8. Nonviolent leader Mahatma
10. Taj ____
12. Spiritual practice involving asanas
13. India's most popular sport
17. City formerly known as Bombay
18. Savory rice cake

DOWN

1. Forehead adornment that may represent the third eye
2. Indian flatbread
3. Indian societal structure
4. Supreme being in 6-Down
6. World's third-largest religion
9. Ancient festival with colored powder
11. It's home to 10-Across
14. Animal regarded as sacred
15. ____ Nadu, Indian state
16. The 'Pink City'

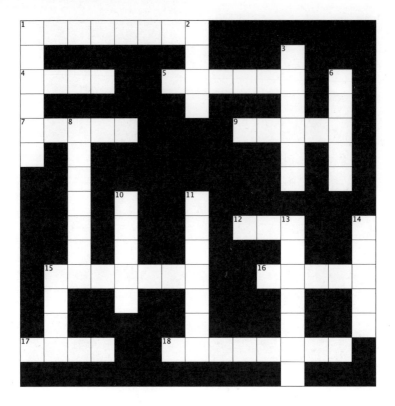

ACROSS

1. Type of 6-Down with peanuts, potatoes, and coconut, originating in Thailand
4. Mulligatawny, for example
5. Savory food whose name means 'triangular pastry'
7. Yogurt drink
9. Dessert made with rice, milk, and sugar
12. Any dish with 13-Down as the main ingredient
15. Condiment made with tomato, mango, or cucumber, to name a few
16. Type of 15-Down that might make your eyes water
17. Grain grown in a paddy
18. Based on a Portuguese dish, it's particularly fiery

DOWN

1. Mixture of ground spices
2. Type of Indian flatbread
3. Fresh cheese
6. Both a spice and a dish
8. Green known as 'palak' in Hindi
10. Yogurt sauce
11. Mixed rice dish flavored with saffron or turmeric
13. Small legumes that can be black, brown, or green
14. Fruit you might find in a 7-Across
15. Spiced tea

Answer on page 324

ACROSS

1. Peruvians who built Machu Picchu in the 1400s
6. Sydney skyline sight
8. Colosseum locale
9. Hollywood _____, Los Angeles
10. Designer of Paris's most famous attraction
12. With 13-Down, tomb in India
15. _____ Wat, Cambodia
17. Island that's home to the Moai statues
18. _____ Gate Bridge, San Francisco
19. Sacred Australian monolith

DOWN

2. Figure who sits near the Pyramids at Giza
3. Landmark that's also a Ferris wheel
4. Like the Tower of Pisa
5. Prehistoric monument in England
7. Big _____, famed clock on the Thames
9. _____ Chapel, Vatican City
11. _____State Building, New York City
13. See 12-Across
14. _____ of Liberty, New York City
16. Home to Christ the Redeemer, in short

Answer on page 324

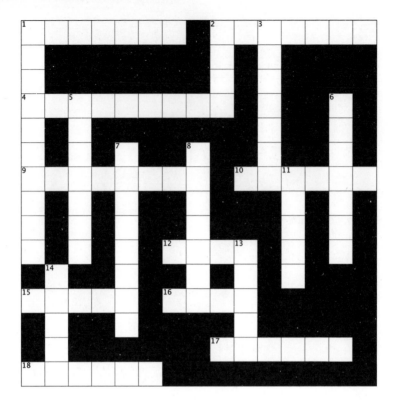

ACROSS
1. Palma's Island
2. Island that lends it's name type of shorts
4. Largest island in the world
9. Island off the tip of India
10. Largest island in the Mediterranean
12. Island country with a water brand named after it
15. Country that shares its island with the Dominican Republic
16. Indonesian province
17. Only US state made up entirely of islands
18. Largest island in Canada

DOWN
1. Only island where lemurs live
2. Doubled, tourist destination in French Polynesia
3. Indigenous name for Easter Island
5. Florida island noted for its seashells
6. Lush, green island in the North Atlantic
7. Devils' home
8. Bob Marley's home country
11. Resort island in Italy
13. Spanish island famous for its nightlife
14. Southern European island country

Answer on page 324

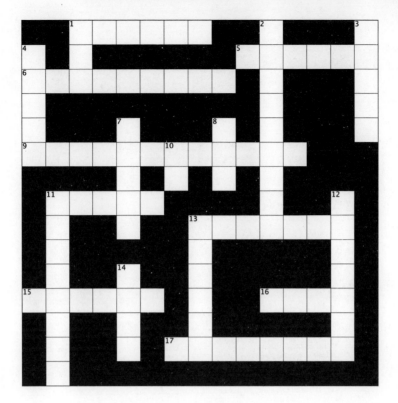

ACROSS
1. Attend without a date
5. Pre-prom date option
6. Prom vehicle
9. Elected figureheads
11. It might be spiked
13. Flower arrangement that worn on the wrist
15. Deadline for returning home
16. Coif requiring spray and pins
17. Chaperones, maybe

DOWN
1. School room big enough for prom
2. Stilettos or pumps
3. Important prom purchase
4. More daring students might sneak one in
7. 'Would you like to _____?'
8. Garb that's typically rented
10. Music maker, briefly
11. Mementos of the evening
12. Prom attendees, typically
13. 1976 horror film with a climactic prom scene
14. Quaint term for a prom date, maybe

Answer on page 324

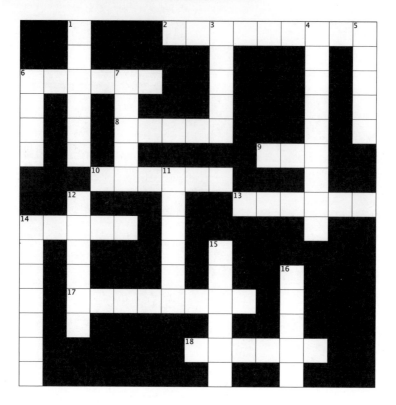

ACROSS

2. 'A Muppet _____ Carol' (1992)
6. Nerdy scientist
8. Blue Muppet with a curved nose
9. Type of animal that 3-Down is
10. 6-Across's long-suffering assistant
13. 'Muppet Treasure _____' (1996)

14. Muppet said to be the most similar to his creator
17. Dr. Teeth and the _____ [18-Across]
18. See 17-Across

DOWN

1. Muppet creator and visionary
3. Gonzo's rodent sidekick

4. 'The Muppets Take _____' (1984)
5. Actor Jason in 'The Muppets' (2011)
6. Fozzie _____
7. Type of bird Sam is
11. He's often the straight man

12. Home country of a Muppet chef
14. 'The _____ Connection'
15. Muppet who communicates mostly by saying his own name
16. 'The Great Muppet _____' (1981)

Answer on page 324

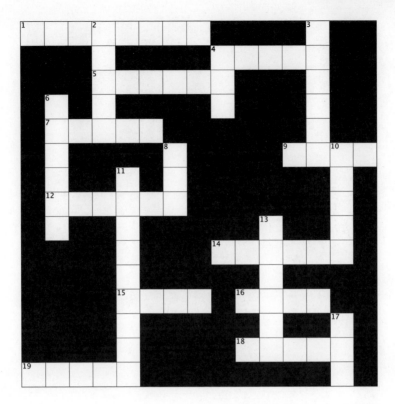

ACROSS

1. Cherry _____
4. Former capital of Japan
5. Religious majority in Japan
7. Japanese cartoon style
9. Sport in a ring
12. Japanese for 'cute' or 'lovely'
14. Female entertainers and artists
15. Mountain that's also an active volcano
16. Traditional Japanese sandals
18. Japan's capital
19. Background color of the Japanese flag

DOWN

2. Raw fish and rice
3. Largest Japanese island
4. Fish for a decorative pond
6. Heavily stylized theatrical genre
8. Sash for tying 13-Down
10. Japanese comics
11. _____ Rising Sun
13. National dress of Japan
17. Classical dance-drama

Answer on page 325

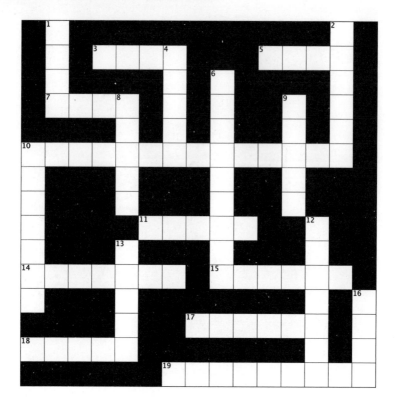

ACROSS

3. Actor Alan who played Cameron Fry

5. '____ Alone' (1990)

7. With 16-Down, young Gen X actors who often appeared in '80s films

10. Hughes' directorial debut

11. Girlfriend of 2-Down

14. City beloved by Hughes

15. 'Planes, ____, and Automobiles' (1987)

17. '____ in Pink' (1986)

18. '____ Sue,' final film directed by Hughes (1991)

19. 1989 film about a bachelor babysitting his niece and nephew

DOWN

1. See 6-Down

2. Matthew played him in 1986

4. 5-Across protagonist

6. With 1-Down, film that takes place in detention

8. Like many characters in Hughes films

9. Actress Ringwald

10. 'Weird ____' (1985)

12. '____ (Forget About Me)'

13. Frequent Hughes collaborator

16. See 7-Across

Answer on page 325

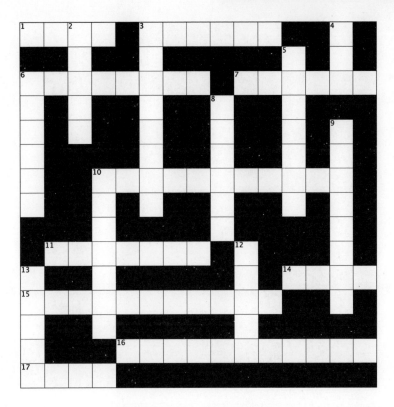

ACROSS

1. Citrus found in a Floridian pie
3. Type of cream pie or doughnut
6. French sandwich cookie made with almonds
7. Campfire dessert
10. Desert with a name that literally means 'burnt cream'
11. Middle Eastern sweet pastry
14. Spanish custard
15. Dessert known has kheer in India
16. UK dessert similar to cannoli
17. Black-and-white cookie

DOWN

2. Sweet Japanese rice cake
3. Fudgy treats
4. Dessert with a pastry base and a fruit or cream filling
5. Dessert baked in a ramekin
6. Airy dessert made with whipped egg whites
8. Italian ice
9. Chubby Hubby, Phish Food, or Half Baked, for example
10. In Britain, these are called biscuits…
12. …and these are called sweets or lollies
13. Self-serve dessert fad, familiarly

Answer on page 325

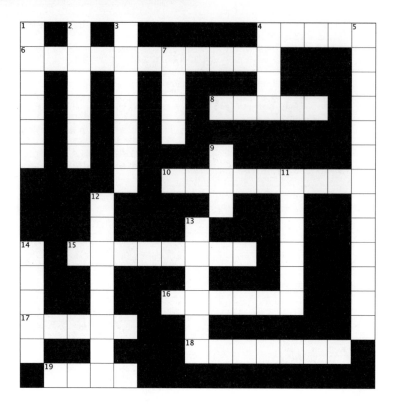

ACROSS

4. Manacles
6. Magic incantation
8. Hex
10. Magician's aid whose often described as lovely
15. Animal that 18-Across famously disappeared
16. Reflective surface that might trick the eye
17. Blaine or Copperfield
18. Hungarian escapologist
19. Magician's stick

DOWN

1. Creature pulled out of a hat
2. 'Voila!'
3. Lightweight pieces of fabric
4. Dramatic garb
5. Fine motor skills used in magic
7. Bird associated with magic shows
9. Mental magic, briefly
11. Penn & _____
12. Magic trick
13. Disappear
14. Items that can be used for magic tricks, games, or fortune telling

Answer on page 325

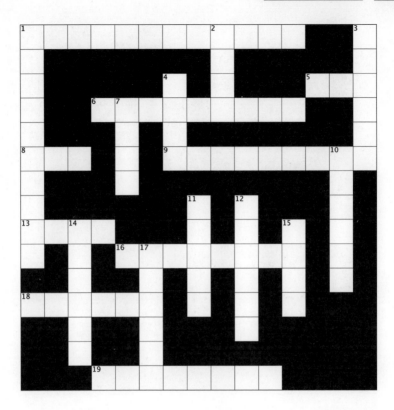

ACROSS

1. Animation studio that produced 'The Jetsons' and 'The Yogi Bear Show'
5. Peppa's species
6. Magic vehicle in the '90s
8. _____ McStuffins
9. Teacher voiced by Lily Tomlin
13. Explorer with a backpack
16. Captain who's friends with Mr. Green Jeans
18. '_____ Babies,' show created by Jim Henson
19. Kids' host who was also a Presbyterian minister

DOWN

1. '50s show with marionettes
2. Nye with a science show
3. Thomas the Tank _____
4. Variety show that originally aired in the '70s
7. 'Mickey Mouse _____'
10. Yellow Teletubby
11. Species for Daniel
12. Criminal mastermind Sandiego
14. With 15-Down, '50s show for preschoolers
15. See 14-Down
17. Animated series with Buster, D.W., and Binky Barnes

Answer on page 325

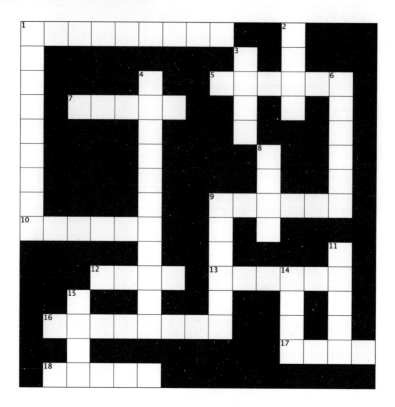

ACROSS
1. They might get tucked inside a mesh bag
5. Dyed items
7. Laundry phase
9. Items that can be bleached
10. They might be mildewed
12. Phase with centrifugal force
13. Laundry basket
16. Fabric _____
17. Separate laundry
18. Business-casual item

DOWN
1. Laundry soap
2. Press with heat
3. Finish the laundry
4. Outdoor rack, maybe
6. Bedding
8. One of 1-Across, perhaps
9. Laundry's first stop
11. Next stop
14. Clothing fasteners
15. It might lose its mate

Answer on page 325

ACROSS

1. Egg dish with its own station, often
2. Egg preparation served with hollandaise sauce
6. Trendy topping for 4-Down
8. They may be shoestring or waffle
10. Drink from fresh-squeezed fruit
12. Sweet dish served with maple syrup
17. Dish with oats and berries
18. 'Brunch' is a portmanteau of 'breakfast' and this
19. Southern brunch staple

DOWN

1. Fruit used in 7-Down
3. Menu items that can be served scrambled, fried, or sunny-side-up
4. Recooked bread
5. Caffeinated breakfast drink
7. Traditional brunch booze
9. Melon and berries
11. Popular breakfast meat
13. Healthy veggie dish
14. Egg dishes that may be single-serve
15. Fried pork strips
16. Type of 13-Down with chicken and tomato

Answer on page 326

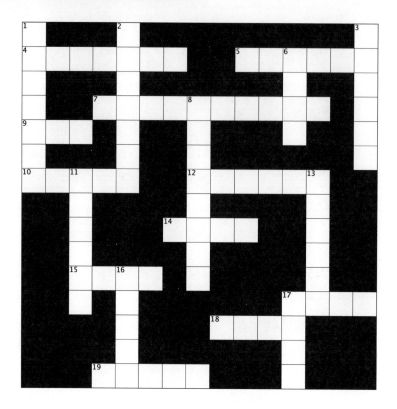

ACROSS
4. Steamed soybeans
5. Spicy green garnish
7. Utensils traditionally used for eating sushi
9. Long, slender fish
10. Basic Japanese soup and cooking stock
12. Pink-fleshed fish found in a Philadelphia roll
14. _____ tataki
15. Japanese word for 17-Down
17. Staple of Japanese cuisine
18. Type of soup often served with sushi
19. Traditional Japanese 'lunch box'

DOWN
1. 'Nori' is the Japanese word for this
2. Raw fish eaten on its own
3. Pickled condiment that can be used as a palate cleanser
6. Japanese wine… or the Japanese word for 12-Across
8. Sushi dip
11. Seeds that are add to sushi rice
13. Raw fish atop rice
16. Sushi chef's need
17. Piece of sushi

Answer on page 326

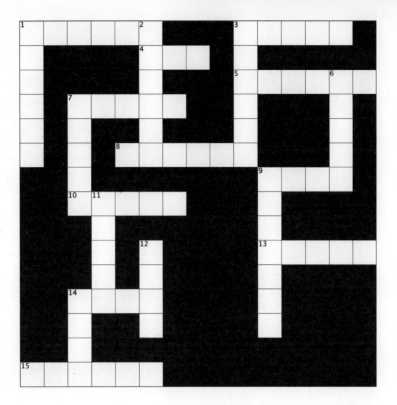

ACROSS

1. Newbies might use these to avoid 1-Downs
3. Locale where bowling occurs
4. Number of 9-Across
5. ____pin bowling
7. Bowler's trouble
8. Organized bowling group with teams
9. Bowler's targets
10. Term for knocking down all pins in two tries
13. Each one consists of two chances
14. It can weight between 6–16 lbs
15. Impressive bowling feat

DOWN

1. Boundary bowlers try to avoid
2. Score marked by an 'X'
3. Videogame venue sometimes located in a bowling alley
6. Places to bowl
7. Rented equipment
9. Like a score of 300
11. Meal eaten while bowling, maybe
12. One of three on a ball, usually
14. Bowling beverage, perhaps

Answer on page 326

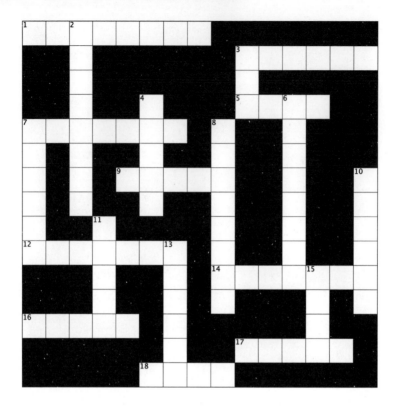

ACROSS
1. Long-legged, pink bird
3. Loggerhead or green ____
5. Org. with a location in Cape Canaveral
7. Gentle sea creature related to the dugong
9. City northwest of 12-Across
12. Tourist paradise
14. Key ____, state dessert
16. Florida has 1,350 miles of it
17. Southern city with a large Cuban expat population
18. Collection of islands off the tip of Florida

DOWN
2. Body of water bordering Florida to the east
3. Lay in the sun
4. West Palm, Cocoa, or Daytona
6. The ____ State
7. Gulf of ____, body of water to Florida's west
8. Marine amusement park
10. Walt ____ World
11. Florida predator
13. State fruit of Florida
15. Shake one of these trees for a coconut

Answer on page 326

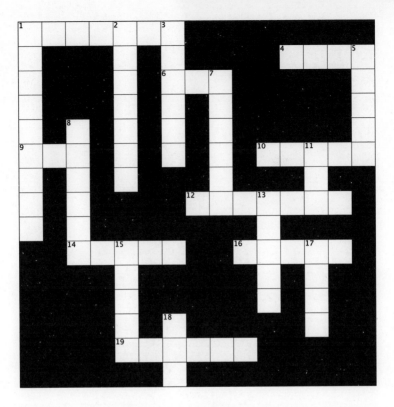

ACROSS

1. Establishment selling beer made on the premises

4. Bitter flowers used in brewing

6. On ____

9. Particularly bitter beer (abbr.)

10. Beer served directly from casks

12. ½ gallon container used to sell beer to-go

14. Beer associated with crisp, clean flavors

16. Fungus key to fermentation

19. ____ Artois

DOWN

1. Its mascots have included frogs and Clydesdales

2. Type of pale 14-Across

3. Breakable green or amber container

5. It may be imperial, milk, or oatmeal

7. Dark, malted beer

8. Wooden vessel used to age beer

11. The "A" of 9-Across

13. Grain used in brewing

15. Material for a 12-Across or 3-Down

17. Beer with an intentionally acidic or tart flavor

18. Large storage container for beer

Answer on page 326

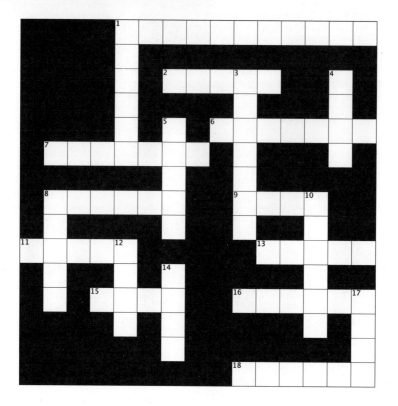

ACROSS

1. Most prestigious title in chess
2. Word of warning
6. Initial moves of a game
7. Casual chess player
8. Play involving 9-Across and 4-Down
9. Piece that can only move laterally
11. Surface on which the game is played
13. Color that moves first
15. Word that ends the game
16. Piece that can only move diagonally
18. Withdraw when there's no way to win

DOWN

1. Risky play in which a piece is sacrificed on purpose
3. When one piece takes another
4. Piece to protect at all costs
5. Most powerful piece
8. How chess players keep time
10. Piece represented by a horse and rider
12. Game ending in a tie
14. _____ Blue, computer that beat Garry Kasparov in 1996
17. Least valuable piece

Answer on page 326

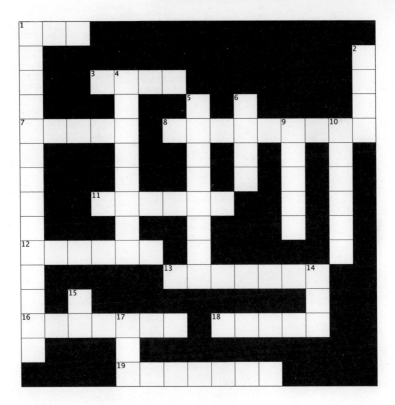

ACROSS

1. There's no consensus on the model of this token
3. Fee paid upon landing on an owned property
7. Rich _____ Pennybags
8. Most valuable property on the board
11. Color of St. James, Tennessee, and New York
12. One of two mystery spots
13. Yellow property
16. Dog breed that's a token
18. Ownership papers
19. See 6-Down

DOWN

1. The other mystery spot
2. With 'Place,' second-most valuable spot on the board
4. _____ Company
5. You can do this to unimproved properties
6. With 19-Across, spot that's often the subject of house rules
9. _____ Works
10. $75 tax
14. Reading and B&O (abbr.)
15. Collect $200 when you pass it
17. Type of hat that's a token

Answer on page 327

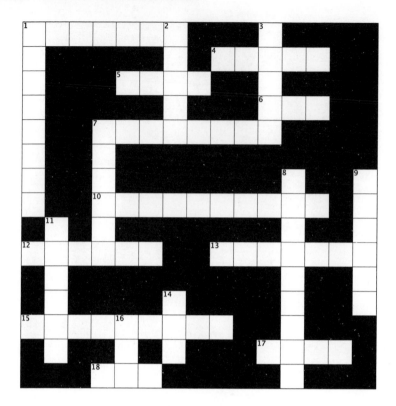

ACROSS

1. Ocean sought by Lewis and Clark
4. St. _____, departure point for the expedition
5. Enslaved man who was the only Black person on the expedition
6. 7-Down's species
7. Sacagawea's tribe
10. Lewis's first name
12. Country with whom the US negotiated 15-Across
13. Herd animal also called bison
15. With 1-Down, transaction in which the US acquired 828,000 square miles of land
17. _____ Clatsop, encampment built near the Columbia River
18. Number of people who died on the expedition

DOWN

1. See 15-Across
2. _____ of Discovery, official name of the expedition
3. One of many of Sacagawea's roles on the journey
7. Newfoundland explorer
8. President who commissioned the expedition
9. Tribe of Indigenous people often encountered by the explorers
11. State in which the expedition ended
14. Month in which the expedition began
16. Family member brought along by Sacagawea

Answer on page 327

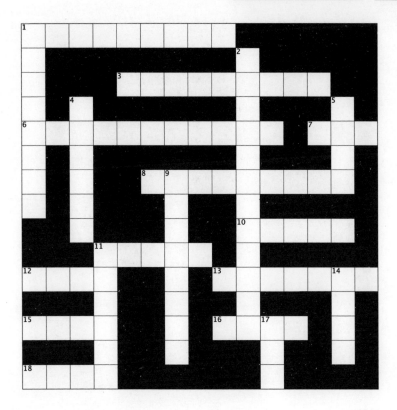

ACROSS

1. '_____ Mountain' (2005)

3. Best Picture winner, 2016

6. 'But I'm A _____' (1999)

7. 'To Wong _____, Thanks for Everything! Julie Newmar' (1995)

8. With 'The,' period drama with Rachel Weisz and Olivia Colman

10. 'Hedwig and the _____ [16-Down]' (2001)

11. 2015 drama set in the 1950s

12. 'Y Tu _____ Tambien' (2001)

13. '_____ Jessica Stein' (2001)

15. 'The Danish _____' (2015)

16. See 10-Across

18. '_____ is the Warmest Colour' (2013)

DOWN

1. With 'The,' film based on 'La Cage aux Folles' (1996)

2. 'The _____ of Cameron Post' (2018)

4. 'Priscilla, Queen of the _____' (1994)

5. '_____, Simon' (2018)

9. 2020 film with Kate Winslet and Saoirse Ronan

11. '_____ By Your [14-Down]' (2017)

14. See 11-Down

17. 'Boys Don't _____' (1999)

Answer on page 327

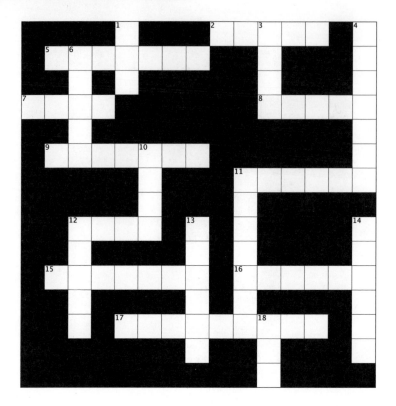

ACROSS

2. Grassroots political group working to end AIDS

5. Mattachine _____, early gay rights organization

7. See 11-D

8. Celeb who came out on a magazine cover

9. Wyoming town where Matthew Shepard was killed

11. Civil rights activist Bayard

12. Color of the triangle used to identify LGBTQ+ people in WWII

15. Activist Edie whose Supreme Court case advanced marriage equality

16. '_____ marriage,' early 20th-century term for two women living together

17. New York gay bar where a rebellion began in 1969

DOWN

1. Virus discovered in 1983

3. Magazine in which 8-Across came out

4. Marsha P. who threw the first brick at 17-Across

6. First president to declare support for gay marriage

10. Politician and activist Harvey

11. With 7-Across, flying symbol

12. Self-affirmation and celebration within the LGBTQ+ community

13. British mathematician Alan

14. Sexologist Alfred

18. Game-changing AIDS drug

Answer on page 327

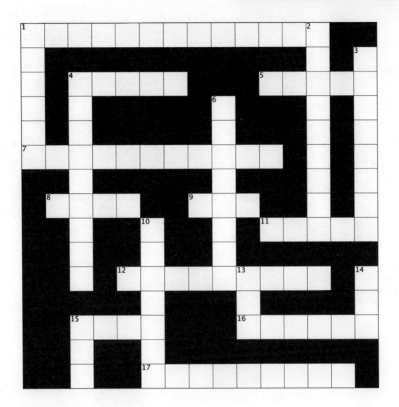

ACROSS
1. Sign-off line
4. See 15-Down
5. Coyote whose nemesis is the Road Runner
7. Red-mustached character
8. Hunter Elmer
9. He's a real devil
11. Pig with a stutter
12. Bird who says 'You're dethpicable!'
15. Where Marvin is from
16. Preferred food for 4-Down
17. Lover who stinks

DOWN
1. Frequent prey for 2-Down
2. Tuxedo cat
3. Creator and animator
4. Main 'Looney Tunes' protagonist
6. Wabbit descriptor, for 8-Across
10. Part 1 of a catchphrase of 4-Ddown
13. Part 2 of the phrase
14. Weapon for 5-across
15. With 4-Across, 'Looney Tunes' voice actor

Answer on page 327

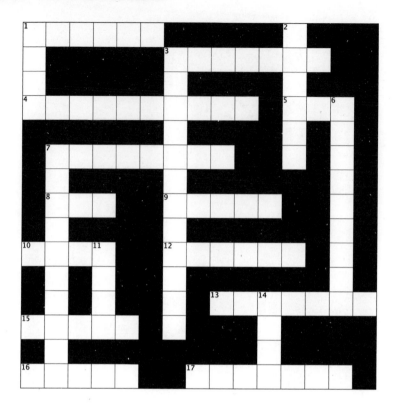

ACROSS

1. It may be loose or compressed
3. Makeup chain
4. Base layer
5. Canadian makeup brand
7. Color for the kissers
8. UV protecting initials
9. Shiny stuff
10. What you might use 6-Down to cover up
12. Cosmetic applicator
13. Users may hold their mouths open when applying this
15. Puts a little color in those cheeks
16. Makeup tool with bristles
17. Makeup often advertised with the word 'sun-kissed'

DOWN

1. Tool used to apply 1-Across
2. Product used before applying 4-Across
3. Liquid mist to help makeup stay in place
6. Makeup to hide unwanted blemishes
7. Tool used before applying 13-Across
11. Parts of the face that shadow and liner accentuate
14. Makeup canvas

Answer on page 327

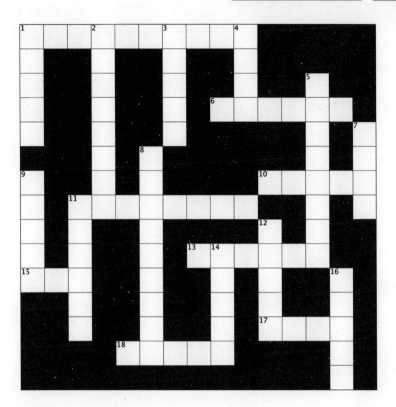

ACROSS

1. Sandwich bread associated with healthy eating
6. Traditional Ethiopian bread
10. Falafel holders
11. Long, thin, French bread
13. Breakfast bread that originated in Scotland
15. Grain used to make bread...or whiskey
17. Thin South Indian bread
18. Basic sandwich bread type

DOWN

1. Unleavened bread in Jewish cuisine
2. Mesoamerican flatbread
3. Basketful on a dinner table
4. Versatile Asian bread
5. Bread cubed, rebaked, and used in salads
7. Effect of 16-Down on dough
8. Bread made from starter
9. Basic ingredient of most breads
11. Dozen you can get at a deli
12. What bakers do to develop the gluten in dough
14. Thin breakfast pancake
16. The fungus among us

Answer on page 328

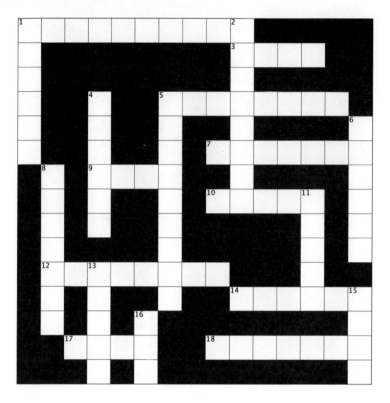

ACROSS

1. Common type of dolphin
3. See 16-Down
5. Dolphin relative
7. Endangered everglades animal
9. Apex predator of the ocean
10. Mammal that keeps its favorite rock in a pocket under its armpit
12. Type of whale often sought on a sightseeing trip
14. Flippered mammal with tusks
17. Blow _____
18. Rarest marine mammal

DOWN

1. Subject of a Raffi song
2. Type of 15-Down with a prominent proboscis
4. Relative of 7-Across found in the Indian Ocean
5. Arctic animal
6. Steller's _____ (now extinct)
8. Unicorn of the sea
11. Type of dolphin found in the Amazon
13. _____-headed whale, who shares part of its name with a fruit
15. Harp or harbor
16. With 3-Across, mammal that may be trained to do tricks

Answer on page 328

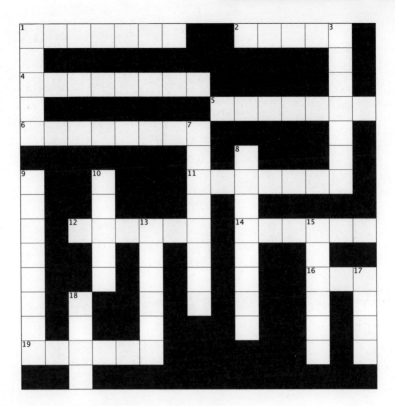

ACROSS

1. Nation that's home to Shuri and M'Baku
2. Treelike creature voiced by Vin Diesel
4. Samuel L. Jackson character
5. Alter ego of Tony Stark
6. Superhero team
11. Captain played by Chris Evans
12. Captain played by Brie Larson
14. '____ Strange' (2016)
16. '____-Man and the Wasp' (2018)
19. He's played by Anthony Mackie

DOWN

1. The Scarlet Witch
3. King of 1-Across
7. Peter Quill's superhero alter ego
8. Merc with a mouth
9. 1-Down's surname
10. ____ Widow, character played by Scarlett Johansson
13. Android played by Paul Bettany
15. Supervillain who sought the Infinity Gauntlet
17. Viking god played by Chris Hemsworth
18. Big green hero played by Ed Norton and Mark Ruffalo

Answer on page 328

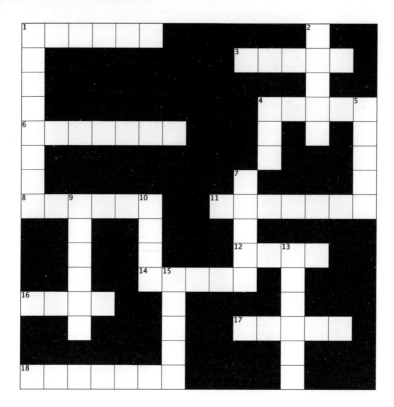

ACROSS

1. Theroux, Trudeau, or Bieber
3. Boitano, Eno, or May
4. Leto, Polis, or Harris
6. Hutton, Dalton, or Leary
8. Lane, Hale, or Fillion
11. Gere, Kind, or Nixon
12. Rickman, Alda, or Arkin
14. Bacon, Durant, or Smith
16. Pitt, Garrett, or Paisley
17. Rock, Pine, or Evans
18. Colbert, Hawking, or King

DOWN

1. Demme, Groff, or Swift
2. Houdini, Nilsson, or Styles
4. Pesci, DiMaggio, or Alwyn
5. Spade, Duchovny, or Bowie
7. Quinn, Gillen, or Turner
9. Edison, Jefferson, or Aquinas
10. Cannon, Hornby, or Nolte
13. Garfield, Johnson, or W.K.
15. Allen, Embry, or Hawke

Answer on page 328

ACROSS

1. Christmas visitor
5. 1-Across makes one of these – and checks it twice
7. Along with green, traditional Christmas color
8. Goods from the North Pole
9. One of 1-Across's helpers
11. You might sing one
12. Rudolph or Comet
16. Something to unwrap
17. Sweet treat for 1-Across
19. Belly laugh from 1-Across

DOWN

1. Notorious Christmas cynic
2. Edible decorations
3. 'Tis the _____
4. 'Hark, hear the _____'
6. Plant brought inside for the holiday
10. Evergreen
13. Naughty or _____
14. Christmas drink
15. Christmas decor
18. Unwanted stocking stuffer

Answer on page 328

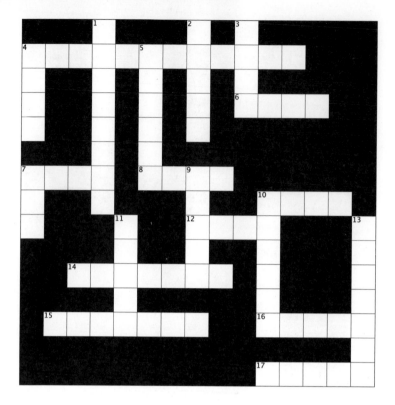

ACROSS

4. The value of one country's currency in relation to another's
6. Ten-cent piece
7. Chinese currency
8. Current currency of Turkey and former currency of Italy
10. Vietnamese currency
12. Currency that translates literally to 'weight'
14. It's worth twenty-five cents
15. Currency that doesn't exist in a physical form
16. Currency used by Olga and Vladimir
17. Currency in Warsaw and Krakow

DOWN

1. British coin no longer minted
2. Coin worth one cent
3. Currency in South Africa
4. Currency used in 19 countries
5. Coin on which a buffalo once appeared
7. Japanese currency
9. Currency in India
10. Basic American unit of currency
11. Swiss currency
13. President who appears on the US fifty-cent piece

Answer on page 328

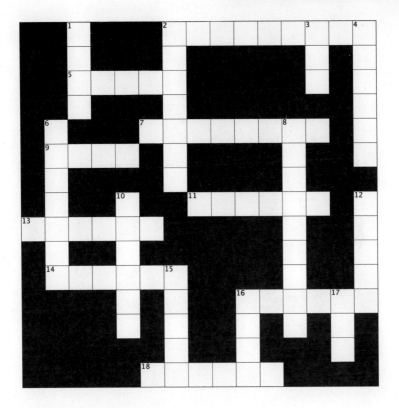

ACROSS

2. Asian mountain range

5. One of two countries home to the mountain

7. Spot from which an expedition may set off

9. Creature you might meet on the mountain, in legend

11. Tenzing ____, one of two first known climbers to reach the top

13. Element that's more scarce the higher you climb

14. Climb

16. Document needed to climb the mountain

18. Elite local mountaineer and guide

DOWN

1. Where a climber might bed down

2. Edmund ____, the other first known climber

3. Shaggy mountain creature

4. Climber's goal

6. Condition in which the brain is deprived of 13-Across

8. Rongbuk ____, religious pilgrimage site near the mountain

10. ____ Spur, geological feature that shares its name with a set of international accords

12. The other country that lays partial claim to the mountain

15. Discarded cans, bottles, et cetera

16. More than 14 tons of this is left on the mountain each year

17. What crampons might help a climber deal with

Answer on page 329

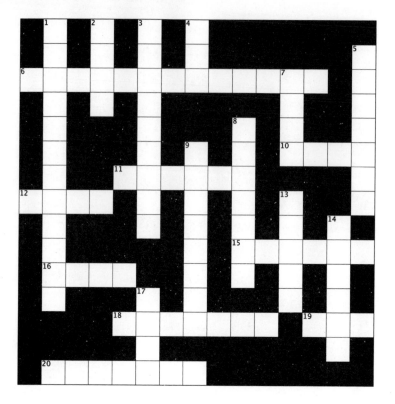

ACROSS

6. 1960s musical based on 'Romeo and Juliet'

10. 'A _____ is Born'

11. Musical featuring 'Sandy' and 'Summer Nights'

12. He played both P.T. and Valjean

15. First movie musical to win Best Picture

16. Musical that gets its source material from 'La Boheme'

18. Life was a _____ for Liza Minnelli

19. With 'The,' 1978 film based on one from 1939

20. Next movie musical to win Best Picture

DOWN

1. Lane and Broderick played these title characters

2. Musical with characters Grizabella, Rumpleteazer, and Mr. Mistoffelees

3. Musical with the opening number 'Good Morning Baltimore'

4. When doubled, what Ann-Margret said to Birdie in 1963

5. James Corden, Meryl Streep, and Nicole Kidman all went here in a 2020 Netflix film

7. Cult favorite featuring Frank-N-Furter, in short

8. 'Fiddler on _____'

9. Jukebox musical featuring ABBA songs

13. Titular Madonna role

14. French Revolution musical, familiarly

17. '_____ Land'

Answer on page 329

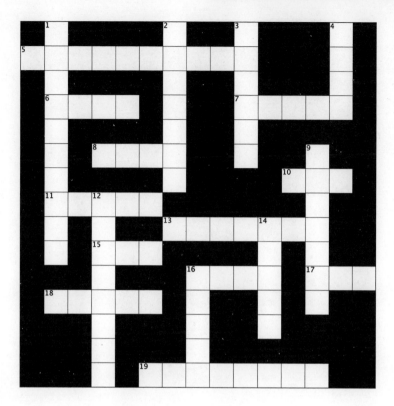

ACROSS

5. Luke's father
6. Simba's uncle
7. Cruella _____
8. Keyser _____
10. Murderous computer system
11. Norman _____
13. See 3-Down
15. Kylo _____

16. With 12-Down, Danny's father in 'The Shining'
17. Rose's fiancé in 'Titanic'
18. Menace in 'Jaws'
19. Sherlock Holmes' foil

DOWN

1. He takes a tumble off the Nakatomi Tower
2. Nurse _____ ('One Flew Over the Cuckoo's Nest')
3. With 13-Across, 'A Nightmare on Elm Street' villain

4. Buffalo _____ ('The Silence of the Lambs')
9. _____ Bateman ('American Psycho')
12. See 16-Across
14. Gordon _____ ('Wall Street')
16. Aladdin's nemesis

Answer on page 329

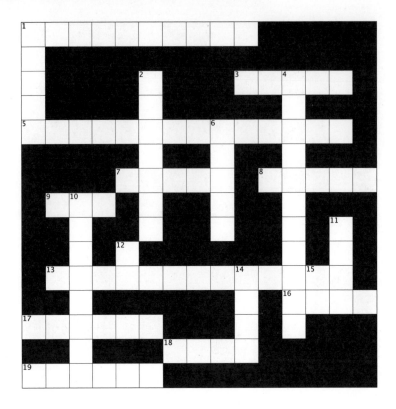

ACROSS

1. 2007 film based on a graphic novel about growing up in Iran

3. 'The Silence of the _____' (1991)

5. 2000 slasher film with Christian Bale

7. 'The _____ Purple' (1985)

8. '_____ Club' (1999)

9. 'No Country for Old _____' (2007)

13. Gritty 1996 British film with Ewan McGregor

16. 2015 film with Brie Larson and Jacob Tremblay

17. 'Crazy Rich _____' (2018)

18. 'Harry Potter and the Goblet of _____' (2005)

19. '_____ Women' (1994, 2019)

DOWN

1. 'The Devil Wears _____' (2006)

2. 'One Flew Over the _____ Nest' (1975)

4. 'To Kill A _____' (1962)

6. 'The _____ of Being a Wallflower' (2012)

10. With 'The,' movie with 'The power of Christ compels you!' (1973)

11. 2011 fantasy film set in 1930s Paris

12. 'Life of _____' (2012)

14. 'The Handmaid's _____' (1990)

15. 'Dr. _____' (1963)

Answer on page 329

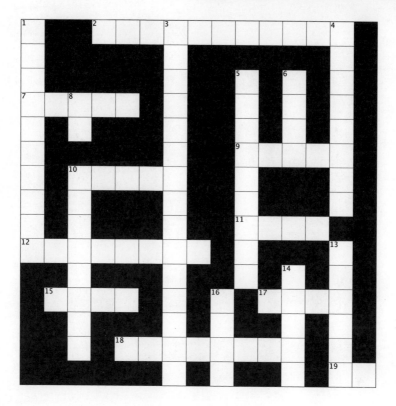

ACROSS

2. 'They're heeeeere.'

7. 'This is Ripley, last survivor of the Nostromo, signing off.'

9. 'I guess that was your acquaintance in the wood chipper.'

10. 'It's like War of the Worlds out there.'

11. 'You is kind. You is smart. You is important.' (with 'The')

12. 'I am serious. And don't call me Shirley.'

15. 'You're gonna need a bigger boat.'

17. 'That'll do, pig. That'll do.'

18. 'Mrs. Robinson, you're trying to seduce me.'

19. 'Phone home.'

DOWN

1. 'Here's looking at you, kid.'

3. 'These go to eleven.'

4. 'To infinity and beyond!'

5. 'I'm gonna make him an offer he can't refuse.' (with 'The')

6. 'I find your lack of faith disturbing.' (with 'Wars')

8. 'We all float down here.'

10. 'Say hello to my little friend!'

13. 'Tell me about it, stud.'

14. 'I will look for you, I will find you, 'and I will kill you.'

16. 'I'm going to live every minute of it.'

Answer on page 329

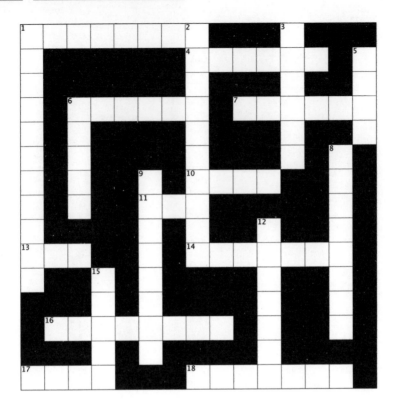

ACROSS

1. Its features include Half Dome and El Capitan
4. Death or Cuyahoga
6. Hot spring that erupts intermittently
7. Only national park in Maine
10. Gateway _____
11. _____ Faithful
13. Org. responsible for park stewardship
14. General Sherman is the largest tree in this park
16. Mostly underwater park that shares its name with a bay
17. Park with sandstone features
18. Carlsbad _____

DOWN

1. First national park
2. Floridian wetlands
3. Park formerly known as Mt. McKinley
5. State that's home to Bryce Canyon
6. President when the first national park was created
8. One of two parks in South Dakota
9. With 'Dry,' islands at the western end of the Florida Keys
12. Natural phenomenon that's a sight to behold at the Grand Canyon
15. You might spot one of these animals in 1-Down

Answer on page 329

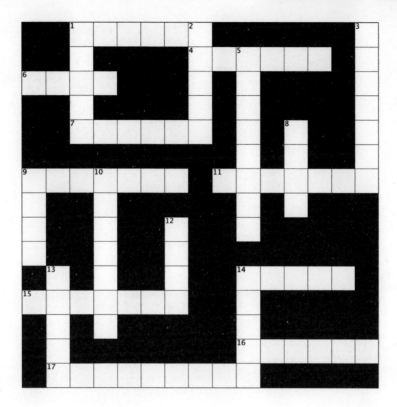

ACROSS
1. New York
4. Indiana
6. Phoenix
7. Philadelphia, familiarly
9. Charlotte
11. Boston
14. Milwaukee
15. Toronto
16. Los Angeles
17. Cleveland

DOWN
1. Sacramento
2. San Antonio
3. Washington, D.C.
5. Los Angeles
8. Brooklyn
9. Miami
10. Denver
12. Dallas, familiarly
13. Orlando
14. Chicago

Answer on page 330

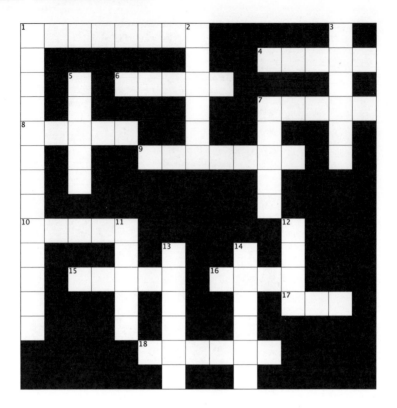

ACROSS

1. Breakfast fritters with powdered sugar
4. Marshy outlet of a lake or river
6. _____ Armstrong, trumpeter
7. Cafe du _____, where you can get 1-Across
8. They might be tossed from floats
9. Bivalves eaten raw
10. Fortune telling cards
15. Soup with celery, bell peppers, onions, meat or shellfish, and spices
16. See 7-Down
17. 'Where _____?' (greeting)
18. Traditional Creole music

DOWN

1. In New Orleans, it's Party Central
2. Local NFL team
3. _____ doll
5. Types of instruments you might see at a New Orleans funeral
7. With 16-Across, annual New Orleans celebration
11. _____-Picayune, New Orleans newspaper
12. 'The Big _____'
13. Local sandwich often made with fried seafood
14. _____ Quarter, neighborhood in which 1-Down is located

Answer on page 330

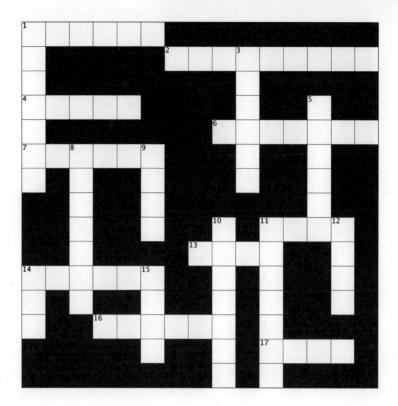

ACROSS

1. Writer and philosopher Susan
2. Transportation Secretary Pete
4. Poet and playwright Oscar
6. Singer going down the old town road
7. Creator of a famous drag race
11. Politician Harvey
13. Actor Elliot
14. Journalist Anderson
16. Journalist Rachel
17. 'Velvet Underground' frontman Lou

DOWN

1. Actress Kristen
3. Mathematician Alan
5. Artist Andy
8. Actress Sarah
9. 'Schitt's Creek' showrunner Dan
10. Writer James
11. Musician Freddie
12. Tennis player Billie Jean
14. Actress Laverne
15. Astronaut Sally

Answer on page 330

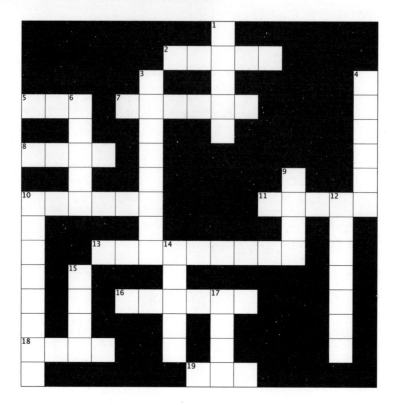

ACROSS

2. Cook using direct heat at a high temperature
5. Fuel for cooking
7. Cook by transferring from boiling to freezing water
8. Cook in liquid
10. Cook in hot liquid over a period of time
11. Cook in a pan using minimal oil
13. Cook using electromagnetic radiation
16. Cook using wet and dry heat, as in meat
18. Kitchen appliance used to 9-Down
19. Cook in oil

DOWN

1. Cook by submerging in a liquid, as in pears or eggs
3. Modern type of 18-Across
4. Cooking style using broth or melted cheese
6. Cook using water vapor
9. Cook with dry heat, as in bread
10. Kitchen appliance used to 11-Across
12. 18-Across made of clay and used in Asia
14. Cook with dry heat, often over an open flame
15. Primitive heat source
17. Cook at high heat until a crust is formed

Answer on page 330

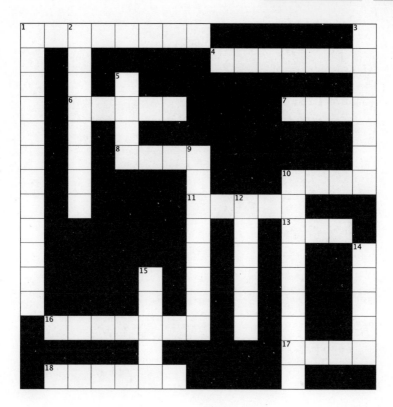

ACROSS

1. Surgery performed by an OB/GYN
4. One may help with a home birth
6. Person providing labor support
7. Uterus
8. Part of the baby that usually emerges first
10. One may be identical or fraternal
11. It has latent and active phases
13. What a laboring person may eat
16. Where the baby might be taken afterwards
17. Ova
18. Sign of the onset of labor

DOWN

1. Braxton-Hicks, for example
2. Birth anesthetic
3. Infant
5. Instruction heard during a birth
9. The end of a pregnancy
10. First, second, or third
12. Term for when baby's feet come out first
14. A laboring person might feel these in their abdomen and back
15. Important but hard to come by activity for a new mom and baby

Answer on page 330

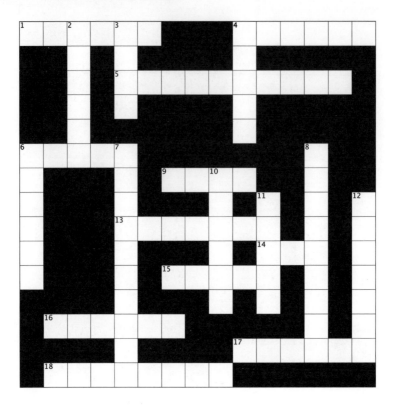

ACROSS
1. 1908, 1948, 2012 (United Kingdom)
4. 1980 (USSR)
5. 1932 (USA)
6. 1988 (South Korea)
9. 1960 (Italy)
13. 1996 (USA)
14. 2016 (Brazil)
15. 2014 (Russia)
16. 1936 (Germany)
17. 1896, 2004 (Greece)
18. 1952 (Finland)

DOWN
2. 1998 (Japan)
3. 1952 (Norway)
4. 2026 (Italy)
6. 2000 (Australia)
7. 1932, 1984, 2028 (USA)
8. 1956 (Australia)
10. 1972 (West Germany)
11. 1924, 2024 (France)
12. 1904 (USA)

Answer on page 330

ACROSS
1. Straw man
6. Storage space
8. Young members of a flock
10. The smartest animals on the farm
12. Autumn activity
15. Woolly mamas
17. Where most farm animals live
19. 13-Down and 14-Down, for example

DOWN
2. Dairy animals
3. Animals on the farm to catch mice
4. Earth
5. The farm's alarm clock
7. Animal that'll eat anything
9. Chore you could do with 2-Down or 7-Down
11. Wool producers
12. Coop dwellers
13. It can be made into whiskey or bread
14. Grass cultivated for flour and cereal
16. They're produced by 12-Down
18. Young 7-Downs

Answer on page 331

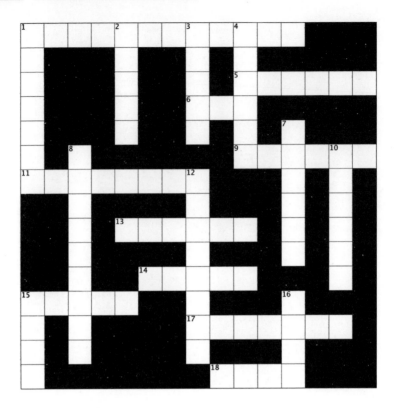

ACROSS
1. Washington, D.C.
5. New York
6. Administrative org. for pro football
9. New Orleans
11. Seattle
13. Baltimore
14. Indianapolis
15. Chicago
17. Las Vegas
18. Los Angeles

DOWN
1. Atlanta
2. Buffalo
3. Detroit
4. Philadelphia
7. Tennessee
8. Arizona
10. Houston
12. Pittsburgh
15. Tampa Bay, familiarly
16. New York

Answer on page 331

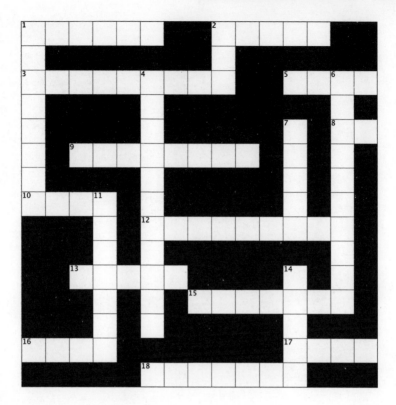

ACROSS

1. 1997 Hanson hit
2. '_____ No. 5' (1999)
3. Where Lipps, Inc. was going to take you in 1979
5. 'What Is _____' (1993)
8. With 16-Across, song that begins 'All I can say is that my life is pretty plain'
9. They had a 1981 hit with 'Tainted Love'
10. She sang about luftballons in 1983
12. 1979 The Knack hit
13. 'Rockin' _____' (1958)
15. With 'the,' what Musical Youth asked you to pass in 1982
16. See 8-Across
17. Singer Basil with 'Mickey' (1982)
18. 'Teenage Dirtbag' band

DOWN

1. Bobby with 'Don't Worry, Be Happy'
2. Baha _____
4. 1997 song about getting knocked down but getting up again
6. Their one hit included the line 'A1A, Detroit Avenue!'
7. 'Rock Me Amadeus' band
11. 'Because I Got High' singer
14. '_____ Up?' (1997)

Answer on page 331

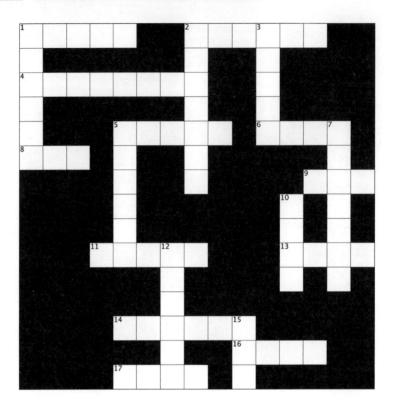

ACROSS

1. Fledgling bird
2. Urban birds
4. Red bird that mates for life
5. Subject of much of Darwin's research
6. They're laid by mama birds
8. Bird that can rotate its head as much as 270 degrees
9. Noisy blue bird
11. Bird that brings babies, supposedly
13. Intelligent member of the corvid family
14. Orange and black bird that's also a baseball mascot
16. Lose one's feathers
17. Where a baby bird spends most of its time

DOWN

1. Species that engages in brood parasitism
2. Bird with a large throat pouch for catching aquatic prey
3. America's mascot
5. How most birds get around
7. Common brown bird
10. Mallard
12. Harbingers of spring
15. Australian bird

Answer on page 331

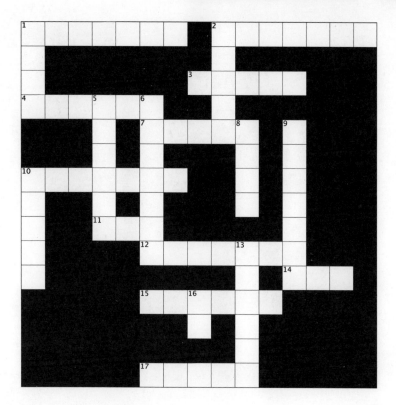

ACROSS

1. It has an 88-day year
2. Invisible force that pulls objects toward each other
3. Life-giving substance
4. Orb with a distinctive belt
7. You're on it right now
10. Several answers in this puzzle
11. Star that gives us light and heat
12. Astronomical event that may be lunar or solar
14. Color of 9-Downs's great spot
15. Moon that shares its name with a character from 'The Little Mermaid'
17. Features of 4-Across

DOWN

1. Missions there have included Perseverance and Curiosity
2. Type of planet
5. Planet that has a cheeky name
6. Blue planet named after the god of the ocean
8. What 7-Across is to all of us
9. Planet named for the king of the Roman gods
10. Orb demoted in 2006
13. One of two moons of 1-Down
16. Most volcanically active moon in the solar system

Answer on page 331

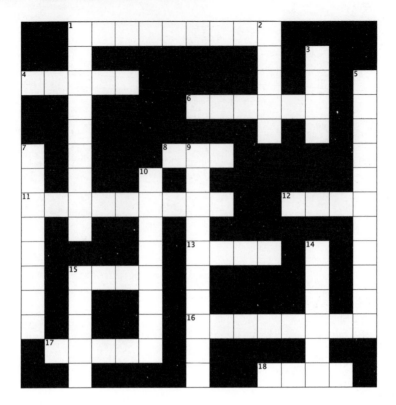

ACROSS

1. French breakfast pastry
4. With 3-Down, 'our lady'
6. Louvre or d'Orsay
8. French friend
11. A little bit of bubbly
12. Material 2-Down is made out of
13. With 18-Across, famous Louvre resident
15. Fromage, par example
16. Arc de _____
17. River running through Paris
18. See 13-Across

DOWN

1. Religious building at the heart of Paris
2. Eiffel _____
3. See 4-Across
5. Nightclub of renown (and of a 2001 film)
7. French sandwich cookies
9. Arts district in Paris
10. Long, thin French bread
14. French street food
15. Stereotypical French hat

Answer on page 331

ACROSS

1. Fictional 'Parks and Rec' setting
6. Apathetic intern-turned-assistant
9. Leslie's love interest
10. Office manager played by Retta
11. Entrepreneur with businesses Rent-A-Swag and Entertainment 720
12. Councilman Jeremy _____
14. Ron's girlfriend and eventual wife
16. Andy's off-and-on band
17. Chris Traeger's catchphrase... and I don't mean figuratively

DOWN

1. Newscaster Hapley
2. Preferred breakfast food of Leslie Knope
3. Rival town of 1-Across
4. With 'Li'l,' beloved celebrity horse
5. Daddy's girl with an artful name
7. State that's home to 1-Across
8. Leslie's best friend
12. ...or is it Garry? Or Larry?
13. Showrunner Schur
14. Ron's saxophonist alter ego
15. Unhinged librarian

Answer on page 332

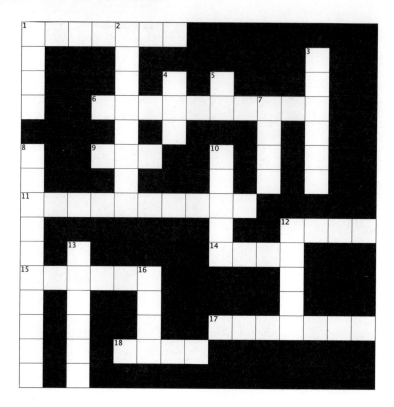

ACROSS

1. Charizard or Pikachu
6. Toy that needed to be taken care of like a pet
9. With 12-Down, fad toys packaged with straw in a cardboard box
11. 2000s video game franchise
12. Jewelry that purported to tell your mood
14. Toy used it to 'walk the dog' or 'rock the baby'
15. With 13-Down, toys that included Princess, Garcia, and Squealer
17. Plastic disc enjoyed by dogs
18. Hula _____

DOWN

1. '90s fad based on a game called 'milk caps'
2. '90s dance craze
3. '50s apparel with poodles
4. With 5-Down, '90s fitness craze
5. See 4-Down
7. Type of 'pet' that grows 'hair'
8. Finnish smartphone game involving pigs and eggs
10. Robotic toy that speaks its own language
12. See 9-Across
13. See 15-Across
16. Ticklish Sesame Street character

Answer on page 332

ACROSS

1. Xylophone relative

3. Instrument that gets its name from its shape

4. Japanese drum

5. Drummer for The Who

7. Collection of percussion instruments

8. Type of 16-Across that produces a staccato sound

11. Two 12-Downs, stacked

12. Subject of a 2000 SNL sketch

15. Flat, suspended disc

16. Any instrument with a taut membrane

17. Bluegrass band staple

DOWN

1. Instrument used to strike a 1-Across

2. Rumba shakers

3. Kettle drums

6. Type of drum associated with reggae

9. Type of bell used in Christmas music

10. Beatles drummer

12. Thin brass plates

13. Afro-Cuban 16-Across that comes in pairs

14. Percussion stick named after an Indigenous tribe

Answer on page 332

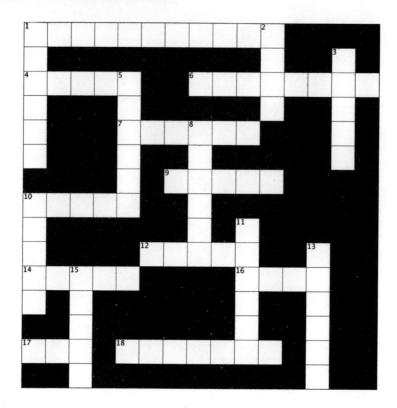

ACROSS
1. 'Where the Sidewalk Ends'
4. 'Lady Lazarus'
6. 'Howl'
7. 'The Hill We Climb'
9. 'The Love Song of J. Alfred Prufrock'
10. 'Auld Lang Syne'
12. 'Inferno'
14. 'Ode on a Grecian Urn'
16. 'Diving into the Wreck'
17. 'Annabel Lee'
18. 'I Sing the Body Electric'

DOWN
1. 'Ode to Aphrodite'
2. 'The Cow'
3. 'The Road Not Taken'
5. 'The Weary Blues'
8. 'Paradise Lost'
10. 'The Tyger'
11. 'Soneto XVII'
13. 'Do Not Go Gentle into that Good Night'
15. 'September 1, 1939'

Answer on page 332

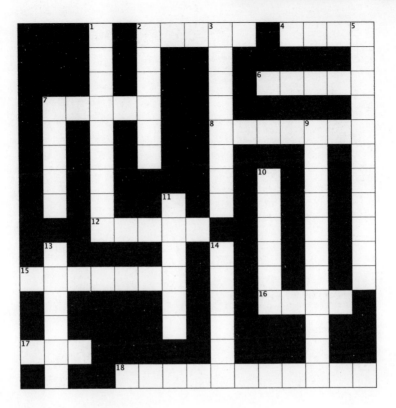

ACROSS
2. Male 'My Little Pony' fan
4. Online journal
6. Hybrid offspring of two big cats
7. Wrinkle treatment
8. Art form seen at Comic-Con
12. Miley Cyrus dance move, notably
15. C, K, or B$_{12}$
16. Urban air pollution
17. Basic unit of digital information
18. Celebrity tabloid name for Natalie and Jacques?

DOWN
1. Two-week period
2. 2020 breakup that made headlines
3. TV or radio show about current events
5. Manipulate political boundaries
7. Teen's woe, perhaps
9. Hypoallergenic hybrid dog
10. Not quite as fancy as hotels
11. Sunday meal with the gals, maybe
13. Film that dramatizes a person's life
14. '30 Rock' or 'Cheers'

Answer on page 332

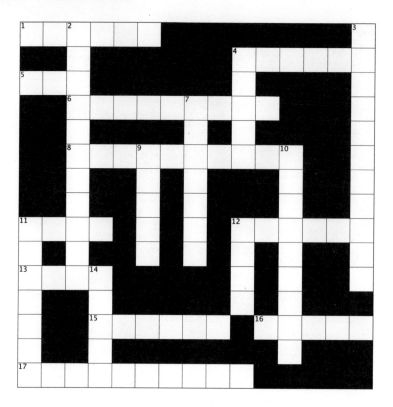

ACROSS

1. Author of 'The Handmaid's Tale'
4. Havarti or Brie
5. Trident-shaped letter
6. Swiss chocolate bar with a distinctive shape
8. 1995 TLC song
11. Wobegon or Titicaca
12. Locust relative
13. Filmmaker Ephron
15. Famous snowman
16. It has five stages, per Elisabeth Kubler-Ross
17. Pop punk band from the 2000s

DOWN

2. 'Game of Thrones' monster
3. Farm fixture
4. Panama or Suez
7. Person in charge of the rules, in sports
9. Poet Dickinson
10. Detail-oriented folks
11. Actress Lohan of 'Mean Girls'
12. 11-Down's character in 'Mean Girls'
14. Just terrible

Answer on page 332

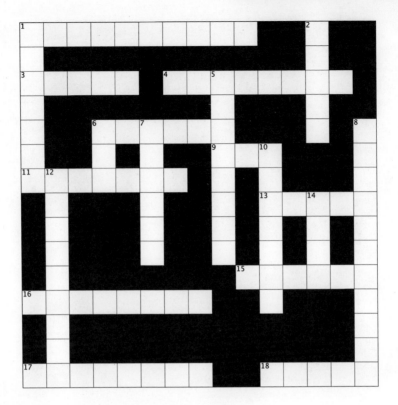

ACROSS

1. Host of 'Last Week Tonight'
3. Some Iraqis
4. Syrian city
6. Hole to be filled by a dentist
9. Lagasse's catchphrase
11. Dancer Fred
13. He had a hit with 'Yeah!' in 2004
15. Place for a tasting
16. 'The Remains of the Day' author
17. Skills honed by 6-Down officers
18. 'It's all _____ to me'

DOWN

1. Indonesian capital
2. Pinken
5. Hometown of Opie and Aunt Bee
6. Agency that began as the OSS
7. Certainly, quaintly
8. Borrowed reading material
10. Overly sentimental
12. Position played by Jeter and Ripken
14. Courtney Love's band

ACROSS

2. Iowa college town
5. Witty remark
6. Entertainment form with queens
9. Musical with 'Day by Day' and 'Bless the Lord'
10. Great avidity
11. Short knife used as a weapon
13. Country that calls itself Magyarorszag
14. Ambient music pioneer Brian
15. Folk singer Dar
18. Flower that's poisonous to cats

DOWN

1. Whelk, conch, or junonia
3. Kid lit whiz kid
4. 'Morning Edition' org.
5. Paper craft with spirals
7. Quiz show that was hosted by Trebek
8. Top banana, so to speak
9. Outgoing
12. Actress Katharine
16. Python alum Eric
17. Unit of measurement in chemistry

Answer on page 333

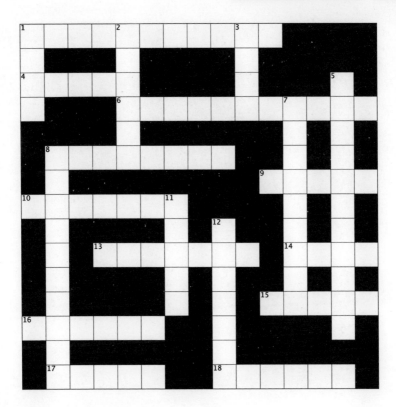

ACROSS

1. With 6-Across, Tim Curry film with a cult following
4. Goodyear or Hindenburg
6. See 1-Across
8. iOS app for video calls
9. $100, in slang
10. Knowles fandom
13. 'Pod Save ____,' political podcast
14. Creator Alan of 'Six Feet Under' and 'True Blood'
15. Embarrass or disconcert
16. 'My ____ Vinny'
17. Bookish, maybe
18. Sitcom set in a Boston bar

DOWN

1. Bones held together by intercostal muscles
2. Demographic term now used pejoratively
3. Unpleasant aroma
5. Art technique used by Seurat
7. Bikini Bottom's most notable resident
8. Brass instrument with a reputation for being difficult to learn
11. Spooky
12. Biting

Answer on page 333

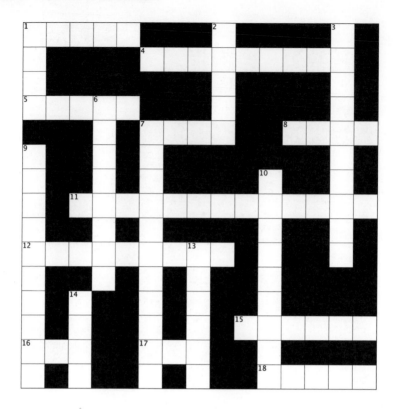

ACROSS

1. Nye and Nighy
4. 2008 song that begins 'I wanna hold 'em like they do in Texas, please'
5. Wash oneself
7. Earl _____ tea
8. Actor Wilson of 'Meet the Parents'
11. Phenomenon when robots seem *almost* human
12. Band with hits 'The Sign' and 'Cruel Summer'
15. With 18-Across, 'Paper Rings' and 'Betty' singer
16. Long-term birth control
17. Night class for an immigrant, maybe
18. See 15-Across

DOWN

1. News channel in the UK, affectionately
2. Her number is 867-5309
3. Physicist with an uncertainty principle
6. Time of day when the sun's directly overhead
7. Canadian folk rock band
9. Electropop music duo
10. They protect workers
13. They go to the victors
14. Sans clothing

Answer on page 333

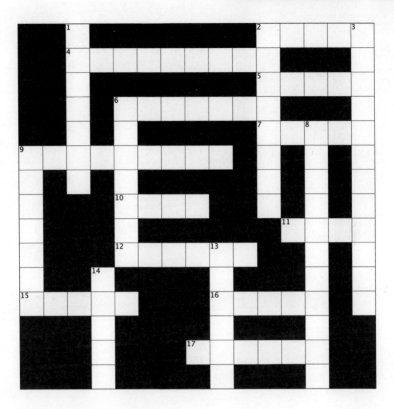

ACROSS

2. Philosopher with a razor
4. TV show created by Trey Parker and Matt Stone
5. Arms and legs
6. State with Weeki Wachee and Pensacola
7. Prefix meaning 'sun'
9. It gets the worm, proverbially
10. Disgusting
11. Character voiced by Isaac Hayes in 4-Across
12. Catholic prayer beads
15. Etiquette expert Post
16. Person with no fixed home
17. Bell, serrano, or poblano

DOWN

1. Transition zone between river and ocean
2. Musical with 'Oh, What a Beautiful Morning'
3. 1993 title role for Robin Williams
6. Low flight by an aircraft
8. Southpaws
9. Superstitious curse that's cast by looking at someone
13. Texas MLBer
14. Feature of '90s Nickelodeon

Answer on page 333

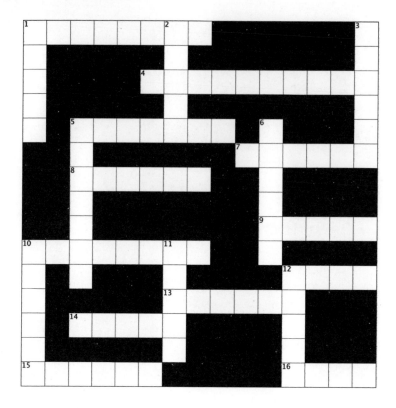

ACROSS

1. 1857–1861
(15th, James)

4. 1789–1797
(1st, George)

5. 1829–1837
(7th, Andrew)

7. 1853–1857
(14th, Franklin)

8. 1929–1933
(31st, Herbert)

9. 2009–2017
(44th, Barack)

10. 1923–1929
(30th, Calvin)

12. 1909–1913
(27th, William)

13. 1881–1885
(21st, Chester)

14. 1969–1974
(37th, Richard)

15. 1981–1989
(40th, Ronald)

16. 1845–1849
(11th, James)

DOWN

1. 2021–(46th, Joe)

2. 1797–1801
(2nd, John)

3. 1817–1825
(5th, James)

5. 1865–1869
(17th, Andrew)

6. 1913–1921
(28th, Woodrow)

10. 1977–1981
(39th, Jimmy)

11. 1869–1877
(18th, Ulysses)

12. 2017–2021
(45th, Donald)

Answer on page 333

ACROSS

1. Gorilla who climbed the Empire State Building
3. Reddish ape found in Borneo
8. When doubled, the largest nocturnal primate
9. Also known as the 'lesser ape'
10. First primate to be launched into space
12. All primate are this type of animal
14. You, me, and everyone we know
16. She was discovered in 1974
17. Primates may use sticks or rocks to make these
18. '_____ of the Apes'

DOWN

1. Gorilla trained in American Sign Language
2. Wise mandrill in 'The Lion King'
4. Their lack of tails differentiates them from monkeys
5. Largest living primates
6. First non-human primate to achieve Earth orbit
7. 10-Across and 6-Down were these, familiarly
11. How primates communicate
13. Primates native to Madagascar
14. Humans belong to this genus
15. Primates tend to be not solitary but _____

Answer on page 334

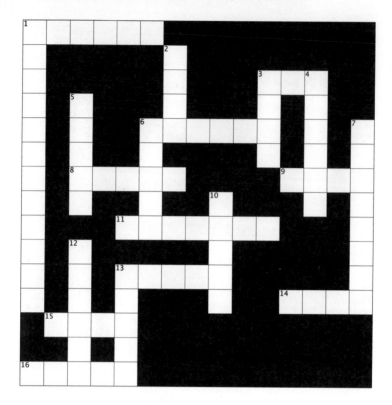

ACROSS

1. French dance popular in music halls
3. Dance style with moves that include the shuffle, the brush, and the buffalo
6. Type of dance with five positions
8. Miley made news with this dance move
9. Many of these make up 1-Down
11. Skintight rehearsal wear
13. Dance style popular in the Big Band Era
14. Celebratory dance in Jewish culture
15. Lively Irish dance
16. Group dance involving a line

DOWN

1. Sequence of dance movements
2. Hawaiian dance
3. Performance garb for a ballerina
4. Dance style on the very tips of the toes
5. Triple time dance
6. Fixture in a dance studio
7. Brazilian dance that's also a martial art
10. Argentinian dance that's also a letter of the NATO alphabet
12. Free, expressive style of dance
13. Partnered Latin dance popularized in New York City

Answer on page 334

ACROSS

1. Drink with rum and mint

5. Rum and coke

6. Brunch beverage

7. Drink garnished with an olive

10. Fruit-infused wine

12. Christmas quaff

16. Drink associated with 'Sex and the City'

17. Long Island iced ____

18. Old-fashioned base liquor

DOWN

1. Drink traditionally served in a copper mug

2. Italian cocktail

3. Tequila and grapefruit juice

4. Alcohol in 1-Down

6. Drink with a rhyming name

8. Seven and Seven or Scotch and soda

9. Drink named after a Scottish folk hero

11. Alcohol that's juniper-flavored

13. Cocktail with 11-Down and 15-Down

14. Drink with an egg white, sometimes

15. Green citrus fruit

Answer on page 334

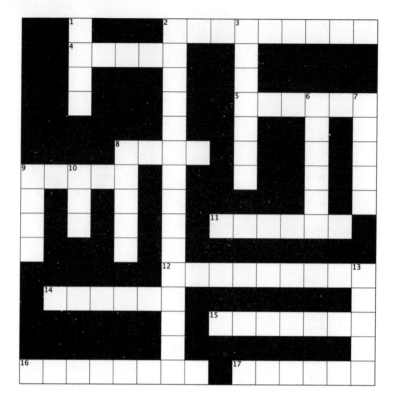

ACROSS

2. Reptile that changes its appearance to match its surroundings
4. Small reptile often kept as a pet
5. Protective skin covering
8. With 3-Down, venomous Southwestern reptile
9. Hooded, legless reptile
11. With 14-Across, reptile large enough to eat water buffalo
12. Extinct class of reptile
14. See 11-Across
15. Reptile unusual for its 'third eye'
16. Subject for Aesop, perhaps
17. Shelled reptile

DOWN

1. Most reptiles begin life inside these
2. Quality of having a body temperature that varies with the environment
3. See 8-Across
6. It might be an anole, a monitor, or an iguana
7. Type of 6-Down that might have a blue tail
8. 'Later, _____'
9. Predatory river dweller, for short
10. Reptile with a main squeeze
13. Legless reptile

Answer on page 334

ACROSS

1. Riding style that requires both hands
4. It may be braided for competitions
5. Gait that's faster than the trot and slower than the gallop
7. Tool used for grooming
9. Slow, easy gait
11. Rider's place
12. Metal tool worn on riding boots, sometimes
14. Activity disparagingly referred to as 'horse dancing'
17. Equipment used by the rider to control the horse
18. Hair that covers a horse's neck

DOWN

2. Where the rider's feet are placed
3. Metal in the horse's mouth
5. Rider's aid
6. Parts of the horse made of keratin
8. Rider's head protection
9. Riding style used by cowboys
10. Equipment that includes a 17-Across and 3-Down
13. A horse might wear one to keep flies off their face
15. A horse that's shod is wearing these
16. Together, all accessories and equipment worn by a horse

Answer on page 334

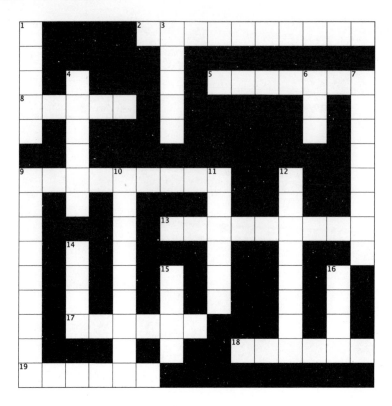

ACROSS

2. Rodent often raised for fur

5. Ground dwellers which typically live in the mountains

8. These parts of a rodent's body never stop growing

9. Rodent with a namesake February holiday

13. Rodent with protective quills

17. Close relative of 9-Down

18. You might associate this rodent with its prominent tail

19. Garden burrower and, at times, destroyer

DOWN

1. Percentage of the world's mammals that are rodents

3. They're rodents, but rabbits aren't

4. Desert rodent with enormous ears

6. Flighted predator of rodents

7. Common backyard rodent

9. Domestic rodent also known as a cavy

10. Type of objectively ugly 'rat' also known as the sand puppy

11. Domestic rodent akin to a hamster

12. South American animal, largest of the rodents

14. South American rodent with dotted and striped fur

15. Urban dwellers that were the subject of a 2007 Pixar film

16. Lemming relative similar in appearance to a mouse

Answer on page 334

ACROSS

1. Michael Cera played him in 2010
5. '27 ____' (2008)
6. 'Bringing Up ____' (1938)
7. '____ Got Mail' (1998)
8. Spike Jonze film with Scarlett Johansson's voice (2013)
9. 'The Big ____' (2017)
10. Sweet way to connect, in rom-com tropes
12. Director Nora
14. 'She's All ____' (1999)
15. 'The ____ Singer' (1998)
16. Renee played her in 2001, then again in 2004 and 2016

DOWN

1. '____ in Seattle' (1993)
2. 1990 film starring Julia Roberts and Richard Gere
3. 'Always Be My ____' (2019)
4. 'There's Something About ____' (1998)
5. 'How to Lose a Guy in 10 ____' (2003)
8. '10 Things I ____ About You' (1999)
11. '____ Amy' (1997)
12. 2010 film that's a loose interpretation of 'The Scarlet Letter'
13. He met Sally in 1989

Answer on page 335

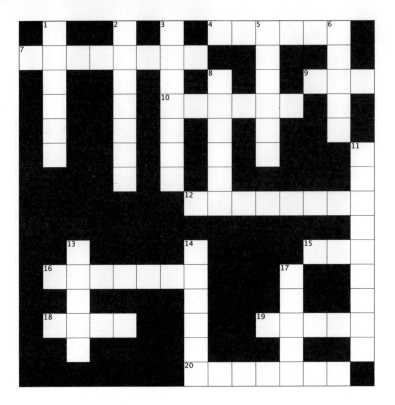

ACROSS

4. 'A pair of star-crossed _____ take their life'
7. Romeo's surname
9. The fairy queen
10. 'Parting is such sweet _____'
12. '_____ Story,' 1957 musical
15. 'Thus with a kiss, I _____'
16. Site of a famous love scene
18. What one might do to one's thumb as an insult
19. Romeo's confidante
20. Dramatic genre

DOWN

1. Method of Romeo's suicide
2. Juliet's surname
3. '_____! What light through yonder window breaks?'
5. Italian town
6. 'Then I defy you, _____'
8. _____ Escalus, who tries to stop the feud
11. Word meaning why (not where)
13. Juliet's intended
14. John Leguizamo played him in the 1996 film
17. Juliet's confidante

Answer on page 335

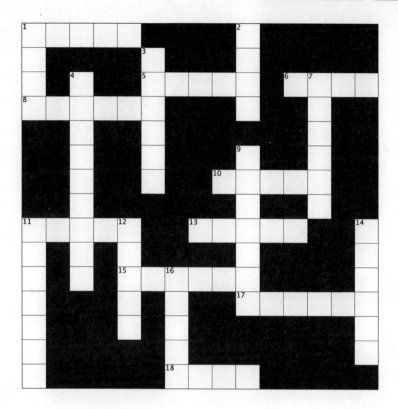

ACROSS
- **1.** Meretricious
- **5.** Noisome
- **6.** Vexation
- **8.** Deleterious
- **10.** Idiosyncratic
- **11.** Tranquil
- **13.** Incise
- **15.** Ambulatory
- **17.** Precarity
- **18.** Buss

DOWN
- **1.** Hyperborean
- **2.** Monotonous
- **3.** Pandemonium
- **4.** Loquacious
- **7.** Intimate
- **9.** Perspicacious
- **11.** Accelerate
- **12.** Diffident
- **14.** Clandestine
- **16.** Fracture

Answer on page 335

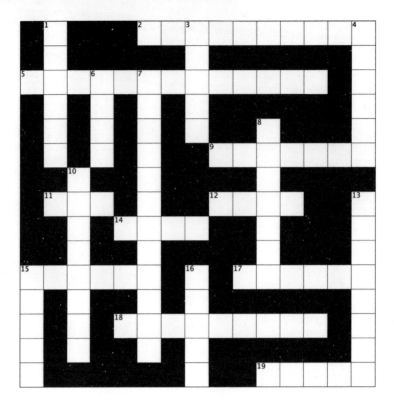

ACROSS

2. Where Matt Foley's van is parked
5. Recurring news segment
9. She played Clinton
11. And she played Palin
12. And she played Kamala
14. The person in this role changes every week
15. Rachel who played Debbie Downer
17. Form of comedy on SNL
18. One of the earliest SNL bits
19. Farley, Kattan, or Parnell

DOWN

1. He always knows New York's hottest club
3. Baldwin played him
4. Gilda who played Roseanne Roseannadanna
6. _____ McKinnon
7. 'Mr. Robinson's _____'
8. 'Live from _____, it's Saturday Night!'
10. 'Celebrity _____'
13. Showrunner Lorne
15. _____ S. Pumpkins, viral character played by Tom Hanks
16. Cast member with rhyming first and last names

Answer on page 335

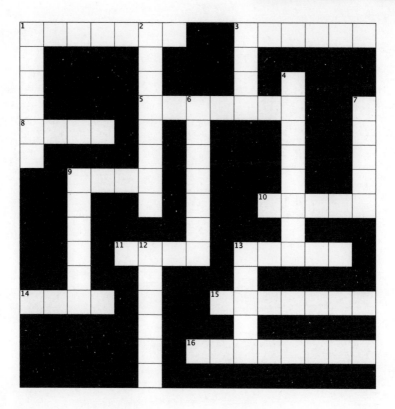

ACROSS

1. Sharp cheese popular all over the world
3. How Parmesan cheese is often sold
5. Soft, sweet cheese used in Italian desserts
8. Pepper ____, cheese flavored with chilis and herbs
9. Crumbly Greek cheese
10. Key ingredient in poutine
11. Cheese made with Penicillium mold
13. Do this to a cheese sandwich for a treat
14. Byproduct of cheese manufacturing
15. Italian cheese made from mozzarella and served in balls
16. Crunchy cheese plate items

DOWN

1. Salty Mexican cheese
2. Processed cheese sold in slices
3. Earthy cheese often sold in logs
4. Mediterranean cheese often fried
6. Type of cheese curd sold in tubs
7. Cheese identifiable by its trademark holes
9. Melted cheese dish
12. Middle Eastern cheese made from yogurt that's been salted and strained
13. Dutch cheese

Answer on page 335

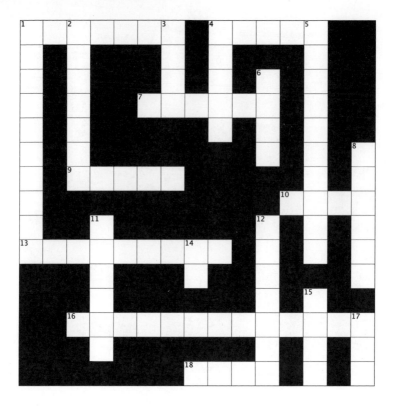

ACROSS

1. Roland's wife
4. She's played by Catherine
7. You just…fold it in
9. 10-Across proprietor
10. _____ Tropical
13. Local vintner specializing in fruit wines
16. Tina Turner love song
18. Adult son of 1-Across

DOWN

1. Former video rental chain CEO
2. Musical performed in the season 5 finale
3. Actor Reid who plays Patrick
4. Living quarters for the Roses
5. Business opened by David
6. Eugene or Daniel
8. David's deadpan friend
11. 'A Little Bit _____'
12. 'Best wishes!' ' _____ regards!'
14. '_____, David'
15. Infant, per Moira
17. Vet who ends up moving to the Galapagos

Answer on page 335

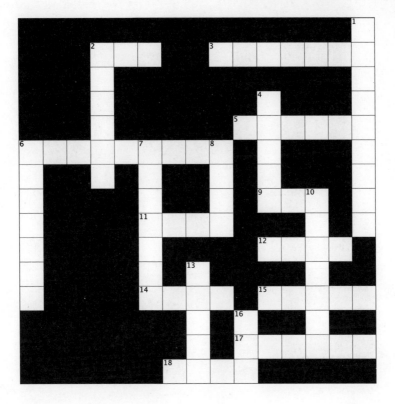

ACROSS

2. With 'ed,' where students learn about the birds and the bees

3. Classroom leader

5. Quaintly, class where students learned to cook and keep house

6. Where a naughty student might be sent

9. Vehicle for getting to and from school

11. Where a student sits

12. Mini-18-Across

14. It might come in a bottle or a stick

15. Midday meal

17. Time to play tag

18. Exam

DOWN

1. School administrator

2. _____ studies, class akin to geography

4. List of new words to learn, for short

6. They're made of wax

7. Skill built with books

8. It comes in cartons

10. Biology or chemistry

13. Medic who deals with skinned knees and tummy aches

16. Class in which students express themselves

Answer on page 336

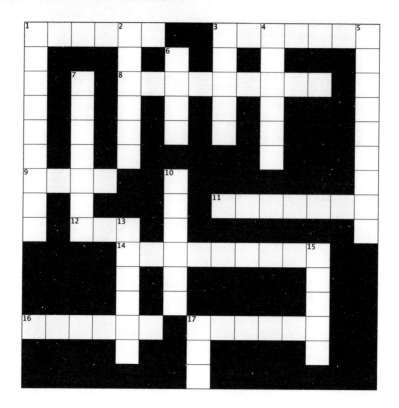

ACROSS

1. Band with Roger Daltrey and Pete Townshend
3. With 'the,' band who sang 'I Wanna Be Sedated' and 'Blitzkrieg Bop'
8. Boston band with 'Walk This Way'
9. Frontman of U2
11. Grunge band from Seattle
12. English prog rock band with 'Owner of a Lonely Heart'
14. 'Another Brick in the Wall' band
16. Nicks who provided vocals on 'Dreams' and 'Gold Dust Woman'
17. Singer Mick

DOWN

1. What the Clash rocked in 1982
2. 'Stairway to ____' (1971)
3. Guns n' ____
4. See 6-Down
5. What Def Leppard wanted you to pour on them in 1987
6. With 4-Down, band named after a torture device
7. 'Don't Stop Believin'' Band
10. The Rolling ____
13. 'Smells Like Teen ____' (1991)
15. With 'the,' band that took its name from a Huxley title
17. Morrison of 15-Down

Answer on page 336

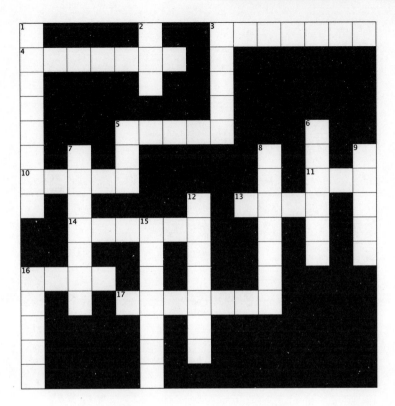

ACROSS

3. Appetizer in which seafood is 'cooked' with citric acid
4. Seafood that requires butter and a bib
5. In the Mid-Atlantic, they're eaten with Old Bay
10. Seafood used in calamari
11. Fish eggs
13. Doubled, its name means 'very strong'
14. Migratory fish rich in omega-3s
16. Dover _____
17. This cephalopod is too smart to eat, some say

DOWN

1. Japanese chefs train for at least three years to qualify to serve this seafood
2. Long, thin fish
3. They're served 'casino'-style with breadcrumbs and bacon
5. The 'fish' in 'fish and chips'
6. Crustacean whose name is a synonym for 'small'
7. Black-shelled bivalve
8. Patagonian toothfish
9. Citrus often served with seafood
12. Tiny fish that can go on your pizza or into your Caesar salad
15. Fish high on the food chain may contain high levels of this element
16. Japanese dish with rice and raw fish

Answer on page 336

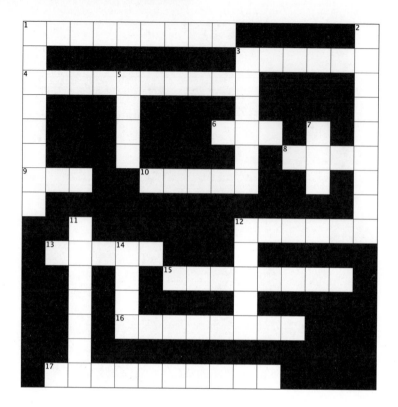

ACROSS
1. First meal of the day
3. Drink with 1-Across, often
4. Crest or Oral-B
6. Earl Grey or oolong
8. Gentle stretching
9. School vehicle
10. Inbox contents
12. Bath alternative
13. Houseplants need
15. B₁₂, K, and C
16. Morning footwear
17. Mindfulness activity

DOWN
1. Terry cloth garment
2. The Globe or The Times
3. Kix or Special K
5. Locks
7. Pet that may need to be let out
11. With 'bed,' a morning chore
12. Use a razor
14. They might be sunny-side-up or scrambled

Answer on page 336

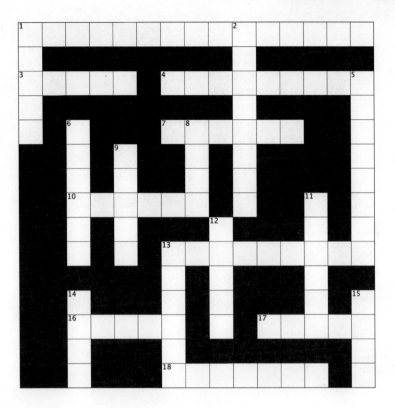

ACROSS

1. Location to buy fresh fish or produce
3. Seattleite Bill
4. Coffee company founded in Seattle
7. Music genre that got its start in Seattle
10. Company headquartered in Seattle
13. What Tom Hanks and Meg Ryan were in Seattle, in 1993
16. With 17-Across, Seattle amusement ride
17. See 16-Across
18. Seattle glass artist Dale

DOWN

1. Sound on which Seattle is located
2. Seattle AL MLB team
5. Seattle NFL team
6. Bainbridge or Vashon
8. Weather associated with Seattle
9. With 11-Down, Seattle's most notorious landmark
11. See 9-Down
12. How one might get around in Seattle
13. Airport serving Seattle and Tacoma, familiarly
14. Demographic representing 12.9% of Seattle's population
15. Seattle _____, Triple Crown winner

Answer on page 336

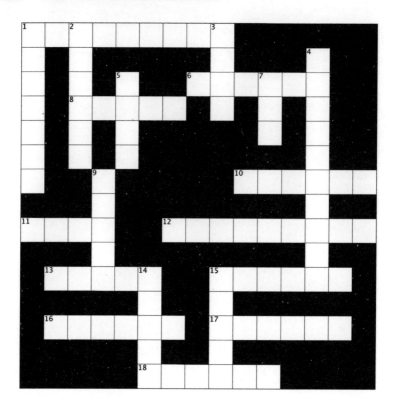

ACROSS

1. In a formal setting, you'll have one for red and one for white
6. It might come in pats
8. Utensil with a serrated edge
10. Spice that might be ground fresh
11. It comes in a shaker
12. Seating assignment indicator
13. Utensils with tines
15. Small dish
16. Mood lighting, maybe
17. Shellfish served with lemon and crackers
18. Evening meal

DOWN

1. Formal event with a meal and a reception, usually
2. Cloth used to protect the lap
3. Gazpacho or bouillabaisse
4. Dish in the upper left of a place setting
5. Family members whose chore it might be to set the table
7. After-dinner drink, maybe
9. Drink served from a pitcher
14. Pre-meal greens
15. Tiny bowl on a handle, essentially

Answer on page 336

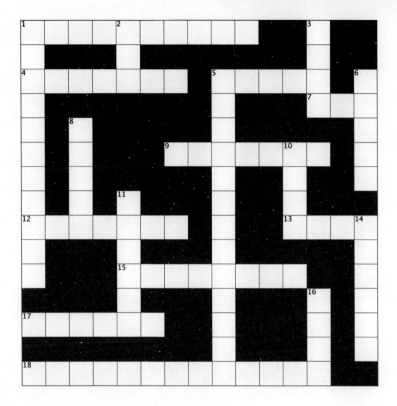

ACROSS

1. Rich, crumbly cookie
4. Spherical chocolate cookie
5. Annual cookie recipient
7. Whoopie _____, dessert in a sandwich cookie format
9. Delicate French cookie
12. Type of cookie at a Chinese restaurant
13. You might find them in a cookie with raisins
15. Cookie that means 'twice baked' in Italian
17. Tool for making shapes out of cookie dough
18. Classic cookie recipe on the back of a Nestle's bag

DOWN

1. Dutch cookie with caramel
2. Drink with cookies, maybe
3. It can be brandy or ginger
5. Classic cookie with cinnamon
6. Nut featured in Mexican wedding cookies
8. Sweet cookie ingredient
10. Black-and-white sandwich cookie
11. Type of cookie also called 'kitchen sink'
14. Christmas cookie made with a press
16. Style of cookie made using a spoon

Answer on page 337

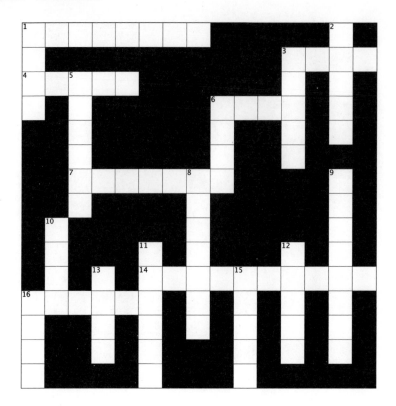

ACROSS

1. What most countries call the game of soccer

3. Brazilian soccer legend

4. An attempt to fake out another player

6. An attempt to score

7. Megan in the 2012 Olympics

14. Protective equipment

16. Soccer shoes

DOWN

1. Body which governs international soccer

2. Along with white, traditional soccer ball color

3. Field

5. It's customary to take a knee when this happens

6. Goalie's feat

8. Rule technically called 'Law 11'

9. Quadrennial event that will next be held in Qatar

10. It's shouted upon scoring

11. Pass that leads directly to a goal

12. Body parts with which most players aren't allowed to touch the ball

13. Mia in the 1996 Olympics

15. Surface on which soccer is played

16. It can be red or yellow

Answer on page 337

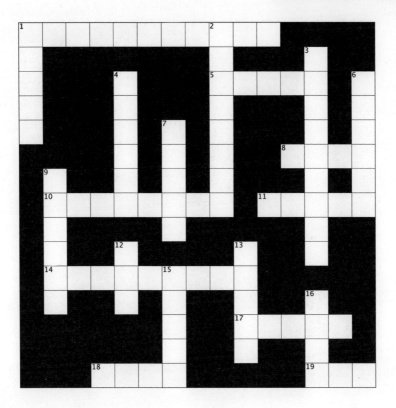

ACROSS

1. Its varieties include Code Red and Live Wire
5. Drink that had a 'Crystal' version in the 1990s
8. On 'M*A*S*H,' Radar's favorite drink
10. Soda made from sassafrass bark
11. Soda flavor often dyed purple
14. Soft drink generally flavored with vanilla
17. Fizzy drink with quinine
18. Soda that once contained cocaine
19. Soda brand with a cult following

DOWN

1. The official soft drink of Maine
2. Its slogan was once 'Drink it slow. Doctor's orders.'
3. Tummy soother
4. Grapefruit soda
6. Soda flavored with lemon and lime
7. Indie soda brand known for odd flavors
9. Calorie-free citrus soda
12. It's usually made of aluminum
13. Fruit-flavored soda brand
15. 1-Across competitor with a high caffeine content
16. Adjective for sugar-free soda

Answer on page 337

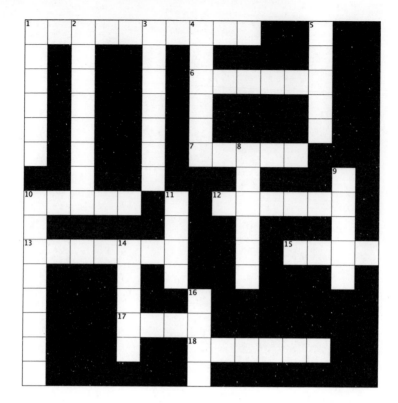

ACROSS

1. The Beach Boys, 1965
6. Elvis Costello, 1977
7. The Rolling Stones, 1973
10. Barry Manilow, 1974
12. Dolly Parton, 1974
13. Simon & Garfunkel, 1970
15. The Beatles, 1967 (with 'Lovely')
17. The Kinks, 1970
18. The Beach Boys, 1965 (with 'Help Me')

DOWN

1. Looking Glass, 1972
2. Fleetwood Mac, 1975
3. The Police, 1978
4. Boston, 1986
5. Tommy Tutone, 1981
8. Van Morrison, 1964
9. Taylor Swift, 2020
10. The Beatles, 1965
11. Michael Jackson, 1982 (with 'Billie')
14. Eric Clapton, 1970
16. Fleetwood Mac, 1979

Answer on page 337

ACROSS

1. Edwin who gave his name to a telescope
2. Soviet satellite
4. First Black woman in space
6. First space station
8. 11-Down that can take selfies
9. Water was discovered in this form on the Moon in 2008
12. Program that sent US astronauts to the Moon
14. 'The Blue _____,' famous photo of Earth from space
15. Space exploration firm owned by Elon Musk
16. First person in space
18. It carried two golden records into space in 1977

DOWN

1. '_____, we have a problem'
3. Scott and Mark, American astronaut twins
5. The 'red planet'
7. First dog in space
8. 1986 disaster
10. First American in space
11. Motor vehicle sent to explore Mars
13. Trajectory around a planet or star
17. First name of 4-Across

Answer on page 337

ACROSS

1. With 13-Across, 2020 George Clooney film
4. 'High ____' (2018)
6. 2009 film that largely takes place on Pandora
9. '____ 13' (1995)
11. '____ Astra' (2019)
13. See 1-Across
14. Film series with Skywalker, Vader, and Ren
16. '____ Man' (2018)
17. 'Close Encounters of the Third ____' (1977)
18. Stranded, lovable alien (1982)
19. Trash-collecting robot (2008)

DOWN

1. With 'The,' 2015 Matt Damon film
2. Film with Paul Atreides and flowing spice (1984, 2021)
3. Affectionate 'Star Trek' send-up (1999)
5. 2013 Cuaron film with Sandra Bullock
7. It can precede 'Attacks!' (1996) or follow 'Mission to' (2000)
8. '____ of the Galaxy' (2014)
10. '2001: A Space ____' (1968)
12. 2016 film that takes place entirely on Earth
15. 1979 film set on the Nostromo

Answer on page 337

ACROSS

1. Meat in ropa vieja
4. Cheese from La Mancha
6. City home to the San Fermin festival
9. Midday rest
10. Architect from Catalonia
13. Main ingredient in gazpacho
15. Fried dough rolled in cinnamon sugar
16. Animals you might encounter in 6-Across
17. Palace in Granada
18. Quixote's creator

DOWN

2. Cuisine involving small plates
3. Chef Jose of World Central Kitchen
4. Spain's capital
5. In Spanish, it's jamon
6. Rice dish flavored with saffron
7. Dance with castanets
8. Creme caramel
11. Peninsula on which Spain is located
12. Language spoken in Valencia
14. Spanish crop that can be black or green

Answer on page 338

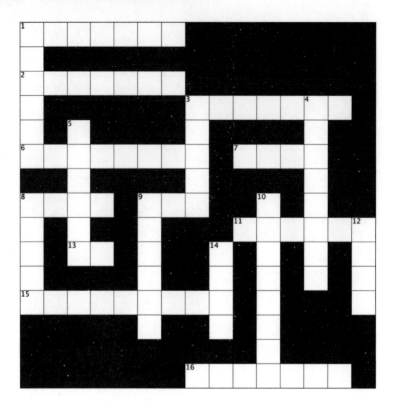

ACROSS

1. '_____ of the Lost Ark' (1981)

2. 'Saving _____ [7-Across]'

3. Do this…if you can

6. With 'The,' 2004 film in which Tom Hanks is stuck in an airport

7. See 2-Across

8. 'West _____ Story,' 2021 remake of a 1961 classic

9. '_____ of the [9-Down],' 2005 science fiction thriller

11. 2005 thriller that shares its name with a German city

13. Alien who was a long way from home

15. He had a list in a 1993 film

16. Day-Lewis played him in 2012

DOWN

1. See 4-Down

3. 'The _____ Purple' (1985)

4. With 1-Down, 2002 film with 'pre-cogs'

5. '_____ of [8-Down],' 2015 Cold War thriller

8. See 5-Down

9. See 9-Across

10. With 14-Down, research facility on Isla Nublar

12. Captain played by Hoffman (1991)

14. See 10-Down

Answer on page 338

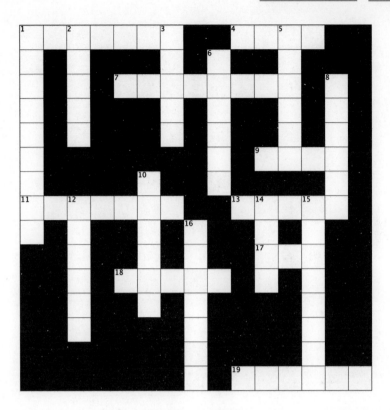

ACROSS
1. Seattle and Skokie
4. Lahore and Karachi
7. Beijing and Shanghai
9. Bangkok and Phuket
11. Manila and Makati
13. Prague and Pilsen
17. Vientiane and Pakse
18. Kuala Lumpur and Jakarta
19. Paris and Quebec

DOWN
1. International language constructed in the 1800s
2. Crete and Santorini
3. Agra and Bhopal
5. Aarhus and Copenhagen
6. Kabul and Khost
8. Warsaw and Krakow
10. Seoul and Busan
12. Bonn and Berlin
14. Cape Town and Soweto
15. Dubrovnik and Split
16. Madrid and Managua

Answer on page 338

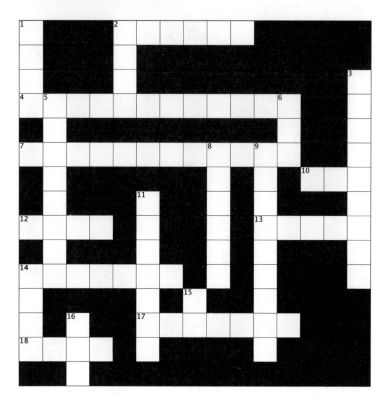

ACROSS

2. Author of 'The Exorcist'

4. Part 1 of a title of a short story collection for children

7. Mary Shelley's masterpiece

10. Author of 'The Raven' and 'The Tell-Tale Heart'

12. Lestat's creator

13. 'The Haunting of Hill ____'

14. Novel that opens 'Last night I dreamed I went to Manderley again.'

17. With 'The,' classic short story by Shirley Jackson

18. '____ After Dark,' first book in the Southern Vampire Mystery series

DOWN

1. Book by Benchley

2. 'Rosemary's ____'

3. Post-apocalyptic horror novel adapted for film in 2007

5. Dark fantasy novel by Neil Gaiman

6. '____ of Rosemary'

8. Part 2 of the title

9. Part 3 of the title

11. Classic vampire novel

14. With 'The,' post-apocalyptic McCarthy novel

15. Book with Pennywise

16. 'The Running ____,' 1982 Bachman novel

Answer on page 338

ACROSS

1. 2004 US Olympic hockey film
6. Margot played her in a 2018 film
8. See 9-Across
9. With 8-Across, 1988 baseball romcom
10. Best Picture winner in 1976
11. 'A ____ of Their Own' (1992)
14. '____ the Titans' (2000)
17. 2001 biopic starring Will Smith
18. '____ Runnings' (1993)
19. 'Any Given ____' (1999)

DOWN

1. 2011 film in which Brad Pitt plays Billy Beane
2. 1993 film about an aspiring Notre Dame football player
3. Film released on the 40th anniversary of the release of 10-Across
4. 2014 wrestling film with Channing Tatum and Steve Carell
5. With 'The,' movie featuring Smalls, Yeah-Yeah, and the Beast
7. 'Million Dollar ____' (2004)
12. 2009 roller derby film
13. With 'The,' 1984 film with Robert Redford
15. '____ League' (1989)
16. Youth baseball team in a 1976 Matthau flick

Answer on page 338

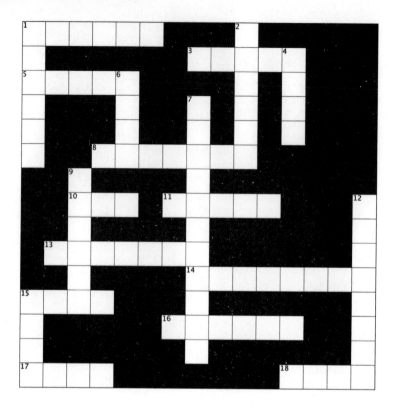

ACROSS

1. Thanksgiving bird (AL, MA, OK, SC)
3. Ground-nesting bird (CA, GA, MO, TN)
5. Red-breasted bird (CT, MI, WI)
8. Bird with a built-in scoop (LA)
10. Chicken breed (RI)
11. Purple _____ (NH)
13. Lark _____, type of sparrow (CO)
14. Bird with azure feathers (ID, MO, NV, NY)
15. Small songbird (AZ, SC)
16. Baseball team mascot (MD)
17. Bird symbolizing peace (WI)
18. Common seabird (UT)

DOWN

1. Bird with a spotted breast (DC, VT)
2. Peregrine _____, fastest bird (ID)
4. Bird with a crazy-sounding name (MN)
6. Tropical goose (HI)
7. Bird that's a master imitator (AR, FL, MS, TN, TX)
9. One might hunt for them (PA)
12. Species in which the male is red and the female is brown (IL, IN, KY, NC, OH, VA, WV)
15. _____ duck (MS)

Answer on page 338

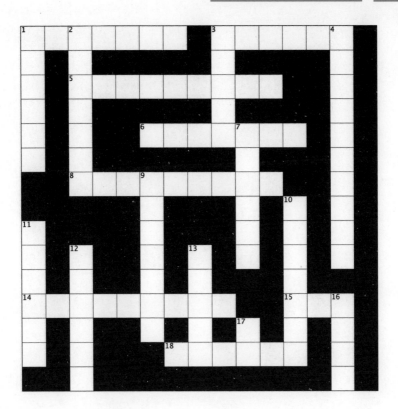

ACROSS
1. Mississippi
3. Minnesota
5. Tennessee
6. Washington
8. Iowa
14. Maryland
15. Utah (abbr.)
18. Montana

DOWN
1. Alaska
2. New Hampshire
3. Oregon
4. Arkansas
7. South Dakota
9. Wisconsin
10. Maine
11. New York
12. Colorado
13. Idaho
16. Carson _____, Nevada
17. Santa _____, New Mexico

Answer on page 339

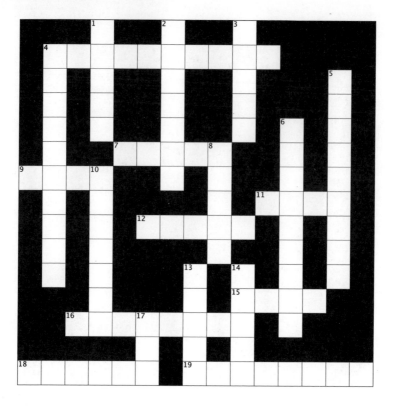

ACROSS

4. Flower resembling a pioneer woman's headwear (TX)

7. Flower with large, showy blossoms (IN)

9. Flower that shares its name with part of the eye (LA, MI, TN)

11. _____ lily (UT)

12. _____-eyed [1-Down] (MD)

15. Classic flower (GA, IA, NY, ND, OK)

16. It may be steel, in a film title (LA, MS)

18. Flower that shares its name with its color (IL, NJ, RI, WI)

19. _____ rose (GA)

DOWN

1. See 12-Across

2. Tree with fragrant blossoms (NC, VA)

3. _____ blossom (DE-oddly not GA)

4. Culturally significant plant for some Indigenous peoples (MT)

5. Spring-blooming wildflower particularly apropos for this state (MA)

6. Woody shrub (NV)

8. Flowering succulent (NM)

10. Also known as mock-orange (ID)

13. Another flower that shares its name with its color (NH, NY)

14. Oregon _____, plant with dark blue berries (OR)

17. Forget-me-_____ (AK)

Answer on page 339

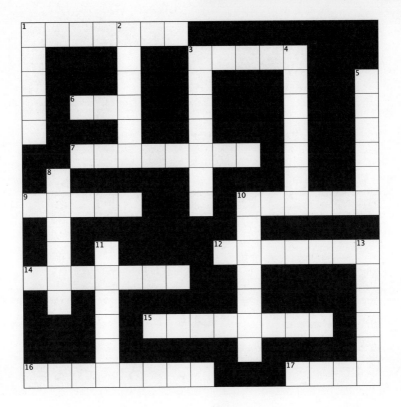

ACROSS
1. Louisiana
3. Rhode Island
6. Massachusetts
7. Florida
9. Delaware
10. California
12. Iowa
14. Utah
15. Pennsylvania
16. Texas
17. Maine (with 'tree')

DOWN
1. Georgia
2. Arizona (with 'grand')
3. Maryland
4. Arkansas
5. New Jersey
8. Nevada
10. New Hampshire
11. Missouri
13. New York

Note to the solver: Each answer in this puzzle fits into the "The _____ State" format.

Answer on page 339

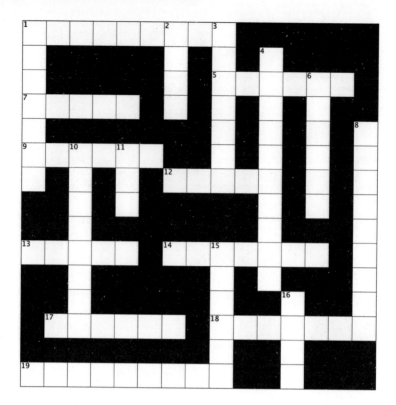

ACROSS
1. 'L'Etoile du Nord'
5. 'North to the Future'
7. 'Friendship'
9. 'All for Our Country'
12. 'Esto Perpetua'
13. 'Dirigo'
14. 'In God We Trust'
17. 'Ua Mau Ke Ea O Ka 'Aina i Ka Pono'
18. 'Wisdom, Justice, Moderation'
19. 'Forward'

DOWN
1. 'Oro y Plata'
2. 'With God, All Things Are Possible'
3. 'We Dare Defend Our Rights'
4. 'Eureka'
6. 'Ad Astra Per Aspera'
8. 'Union, Justice, and Confidence'
10. 'Sic Semper Tyrannis'
11. 'Liberty and Independence' (abbr.)
15. 'She Flies with Her Own Wings'
16. 'God Enriches' (abbr.)

Answer on page 339

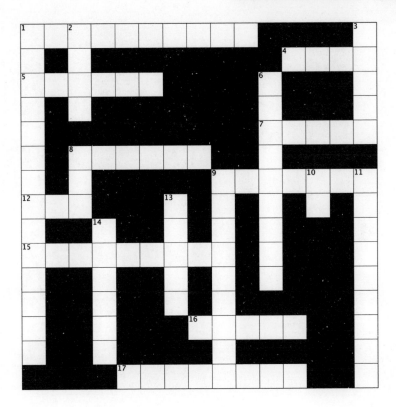

ACROSS

1. 'Rita Hayworth and Shawshank _____' (1982)
4. 1981 novel with rabies
5. King's first novel
7. With 'The,' 1978 post-apocalyptic novel
8. '_____ Sleep,' 2013 sequel to 9-Across

9. With 'The,' 1977 book about a Colorado winter
12. '_____ of Bones' (1998)
15. 1983 novel about a possessed car
16. Spooky creature at the heart of 10-Down
17. 'Pet _____' (1983)

DOWN

1. King nom de plume
2. 'The _____ Tower,' series with eight books and one short story
3. 'The Girl Who _____ Tom Gordon' (1999)
6. With 'The,' 2019 thriller about kids with special powers
8. 4-Across species

9. King's second published novel
10. Tim Curry and Bill Skarsgard have both played this title role
11. With 'The,' 1996 novel set in a prison
13. State where much of King's work is set
14. 1987 novel made into an Oscar-winning film in 1990

Answer on page 339

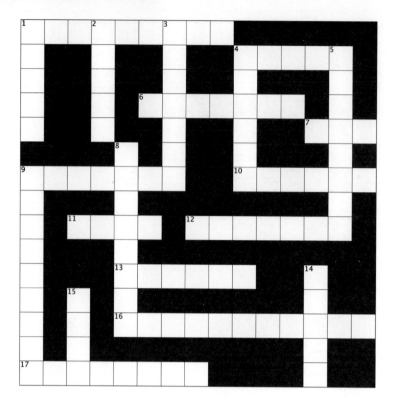

ACROSS

1. Shoes often seen at the beach
4. Shoes associated with Holland
6. Slip-on shoes
7. Dance shoes for when you want to be heard
9. Shoes that leave your toes exposed
10. Roller _____
11. Type of shoe that's also British English for a part of a car
12. Low-heeled shoes with decorative perforations
13. Trademarked name for shoes with wheels
16. Black-and-white footwear
17. A dog might fetch them

DOWN

1. Shoes with no heel
2. Some heels
3. Shoes that share their name with a British university
4. Athletic shoes with studs
5. Trainers or tennis shoes
8. Shoes worn in the rain
9. Very high heels named after a weapon
14. Comfortable shoes often worn by nurses
15. Japanese shoes traditionally worn with kimono

Answer on page 339

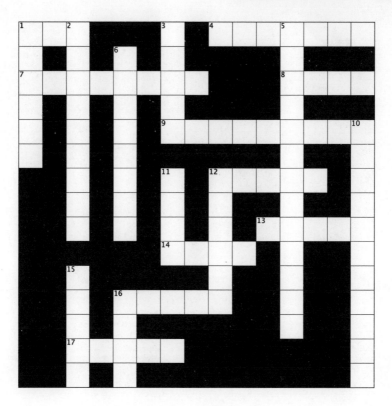

ACROSS

1. Kit ____
4. Jolly ____
7. Candy bar with chocolate, peanuts, nougat, and caramel
8. Chocolates with caramel centers
9. They're square, chewy, and fruit-flavored
12. Maligned Easter candy
13. Sweet ____, a contradiction in terms
14. Slang for clothes...or what follows 'milk' in a candy name
16. Word that can follow saltwater or laffy
17. ____-o-stick, vintage candy with coconut and peanut butter

DOWN

1. Chocolate drops made by Hershey's
2. Strawberry-flavored licorice
3. Sugar crystals sold in small boxes
5. Marshmallow candy dating to the 19th century
6. Varieties include sour, tropical, or Xtreme
10. Chocolate candy named after the inventor's daughter
11. ____ 'n Plenty
12. Candy bar with peanuts and caramel
15. Maker of Wafers and Sweethearts
16. Chocolate bar with caramel and shortbread

Answer on page 340

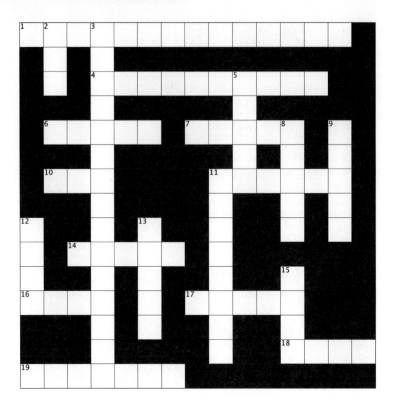

ACROSS
1. Game with 'New Leaf' and 'New Horizons' editions
4. With 11-Down, crossover fighting game
6. Pink character who can float
7. 'Mario ____,' franchise with a board game and minigames
10. Nintendo ghost
11. Primary antagonist
14. Teleporting devices
16. Donkey or Diddy
17. 'The Legend of ____'
18. Character with a mushroom-shaped head
19. Luigi's occupation

DOWN
2. Vid. game console
3. Nintendo universe
5. Protagonist who wears red
8. Dinosaur sidekick of 5-Down
9. 5-Down's rival
11. See 4-Across
12. 17-Across protagonist
13. Princess in a pink dress
15. 'Mario ____,' racing franchise

Answer on page 340

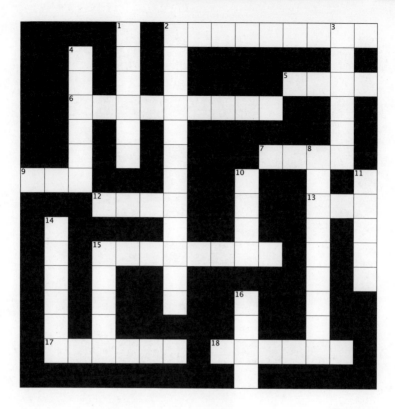

ACROSS

2. Stroke that shares its name with an insect
5. Position in which a diver's body forms a ball
6. Very basic swimming style
7. Diving position with the knees to the face
9. Like an unused towel
12. Swimming competition also called a gala
13. Swimmer's headwear
15. Pool chemical
17. What a diver doesn't want
18. Swimwear brand

DOWN

1. In an Olympic pool, it's 50 meters
2. Most popular recreational style of swimming
3. Ryan who competed in Rio
4. Race in which four different strokes are combined
8. Swimmer's aid
10. Dive style named after a bird
11. Mark who medaled in Munich
14. Most decorated American swimmer of all time
15. Freestyle
16. Swimmer's reps

Answer on page 340

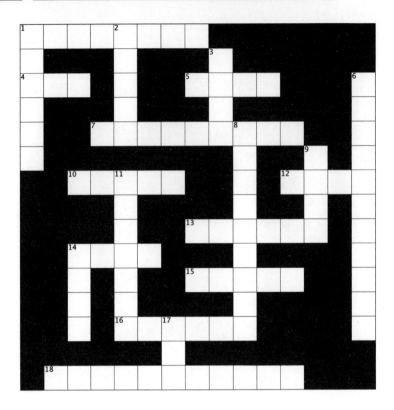

ACROSS

1. Lefthanded pitcher
4. A team's best starting pitcher
5. A ball hit deliberately gently
7. Hit that results in four runs
10. Defensive realignment used against lefthanded batters
12. When a pitcher starts to pitch… and then doesn't
13. Next to bat
14. 14-Down's opposite
15. A base runner in a rush can do this
16. When a batter swings and misses
18. Alliterative phrase for a 9-Down

DOWN

1. How a batter stands
2. Slang term for hitting a ball out of the park
3. Reaching three of them ends a half-inning
6. Erratic type of pitch
8. A hard-hit ball with a low arc
9. Occurs when a batter is allowed to proceed to first base
11. Game divisions
14. Out of play
17. In baseball, a point is called this

Answer on page 340

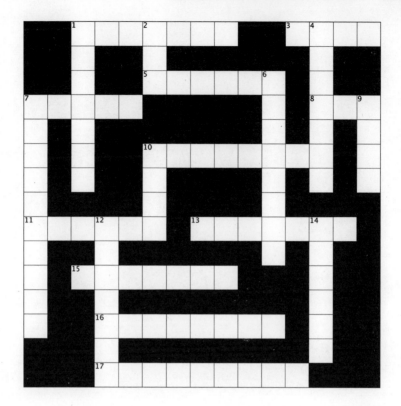

ACROSS
1. Pain reliever
3. Antidepressant abbr.
5. Syrup that induces vomiting
7. Tummy soother, familiarly
8. Anti-HIV drug
10. The mother of all acne medication
11. Element that's also an antiseptic
13. Malaria preventive
15. It may reduce the risk of heart attack
16. Take this to go
17. Antibiotic ointment for cuts and scrapes

DOWN
1. Family-planning medication
2. _____-Pen
4. Brand whose name sounds similar to 'pseudoephedrine'
6. Lotion that soothes poison ivy rashes
7. Antibiotic originally obtained from mold
9. Chewable heartburn relievers
10. Gel for a sunburn
12. Hormone that helps metabolize sugar
14. Brand name medicine for drug overdoses

Answer on page 340

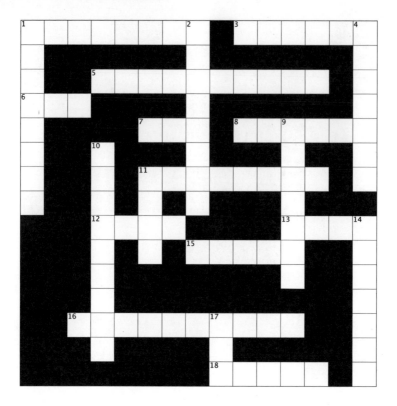

ACROSS

1. First surprise album of 2020

3. 'Invisible _____' (2020)

5. Self-references in Swift's music videos

6. 2012 album with 'We Are Never Ever Getting Back Together'

7. With 8-Across, Swift's first hit, named after a fellow country artist

8. See 7-Across

11. Lead single of 1-Across

12. What the haters gonna do, per a 2014 song

13. Lead single from 'Speak Now'

15. 'Love _____' (2008, 2021)

16. Where she'll write your name, in a 2014 song

18. Along with guitar, instrument Swift is known for playing

DOWN

1. 2008 album with 'You Belong With Me' and 'White Horse'

2. Second surprise album of 2020

4. '_____ Car' (2017)

9. Swift has eleven of these awards

10. Swift's hometown

11. Film in which Swift appeared…or, her preferred pets

14. In a 2019 song, what Swift forgot you did

17. Genre to which Swift pivoted

Answer on page 340

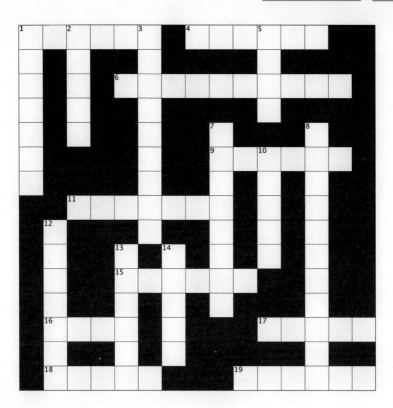

ACROSS

1. Dog breed that adorned many skirts
4. Crooner Bing
6. It opened in Anaheim in 1955
9. TV show with a collie namesake
11. First artificial Earth satellite
15. Along with 13-Down, one of two to achieve statehood in 1959
16. ____ hoop
17. Defendant in a landmark 1954 case, informally
18. March of Dimes concern
19. Cowboy Roy

DOWN

1. Children's toy sold in cans
2. 'The Adventures of ____ and Harriet'
3. Across the pond, she was crowned Queen in 1953
5. Vaccine pioneer
7. 1952 presidential campaign slogan
8. They taught millions of schoolkids how to read
10. Popular putty
12. Dance event for teens
13. See 15-Across
14. Activist Rosa

Answer on page 341

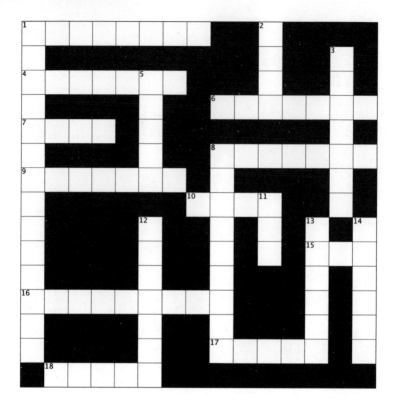

ACROSS

1. He welcomed us into his 'Neighborhood' in 1963
4. He was assassinated in 1963
6. Demographic associated with the '60s
7. Faddish type of lamp
8. First man in space
9. Controversial 1960s conflict
10. McDonald's founder Ray
15. With 'The,' band with the hit 'My Generation'
16. 1969 music festival
17. Timothy who advocated for psychedelic drugs
18. Vehicle in which 6-Across were sometimes spotted

DOWN

1. Peaceful slogan
2. 'That's one small _____ for man...'
3. Innovation in birth control
5. Motown singer Ross
8. One-half of a folk duo
11. Argentinian revolutionary
12. They landed in America in 1964
13. British cultural icon and model
14. Singer-songwriter Janis

Answer on page 341

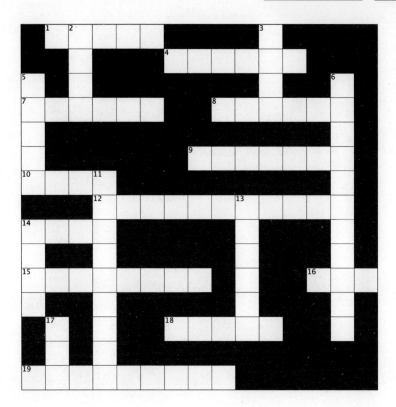

ACROSS

1. Ill-fated Ford
4. With 10-Across, TV program with Fozzie and Robin
7. With 17-Down, one of a pair of prominent artists and anti-war activists
8. He became the US President in 1977
9. Place where you might have encountered a line
10. See 4-Across
12. College comedy with John Belushi
14. With 18-Across, university at which the National Guard killed four students in 1970
15. 1977 blockbuster
16. Plaintiff in a landmark 1973 Supreme Court case
18. See 14-Across
19. Settlement established by the Peoples Temple

DOWN

2. A hostage crisis began here in 1979
3. Israeli Prime Minister who resigned in 1974
5. He died at Graceland in 1977
6. Achievement by Secretariat in 1973
11. Hotel with a namesake scandal
13. Notable member of the Symbionese Liberation Army
14. Rock band with makeup and pyrotechnics
17. See 7-Across

Answer on page 341

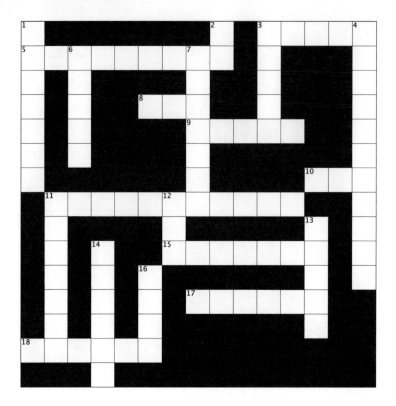

ACROSS

3. Hungarian architect with a namesake cube

5. Memorial project created by Cleve Jones

8. Channel launched with the words 'Ladies and gentlemen, rock and roll'

9. _____ Valdez

10. Line of Chrysler automobiles, with 'K'

11. New Coke spokesman portrayed by Matt Frewer

15. Democratic VP nominee in 1984

17. TV character with a playhouse and red bowtie

18. Arcade game with ghosts and dots

DOWN

1. Mobile music device

2. He needed to phone home

3. Film franchise with Sylvester Stallone

4. TV series with David Hasselhoff

6. When doubled, 'Hungry Like the Wolf' band

7. Benefit concert held in 1985

11. Anti-apartheid activist

12. Cat-eater from Melmac

13. Halley's _____

14. Hip hop group from Queens, NY

16. Beatle that was assassinated in 1980

Answer on page 341

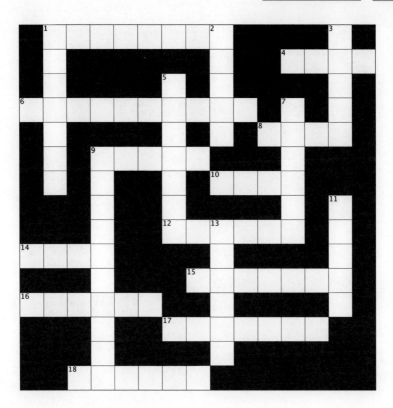

ACROSS

1. A show about nothing
4. Apple desktop introduced in 1998
6. Group with Baby, Scary, Ginger, Sporty, and Posh
8. Site of a 1993 siege
9. Rapper with the middle name Amaru
10. Game with a 'slammer'
12. Grunge pioneer
14. His beating at the hands of the LAPD sparked a riot
15. 1990s president
16. British teen wizard
17. Sitcom with Ross and Rachel
18. Oriole who broke an MLB record in 1995

DOWN

1. Passenger in a white Bronco
2. First cloned mammal
3. Where is he?
5. 1997 film with Kate and Leo
7. They had a hit with 'MMMBop'
9. Handheld digital 'pet'
11. She was killed in a Paris car crash in 1997
13. 'The Fresh Prince of _____'

Answer on page 341

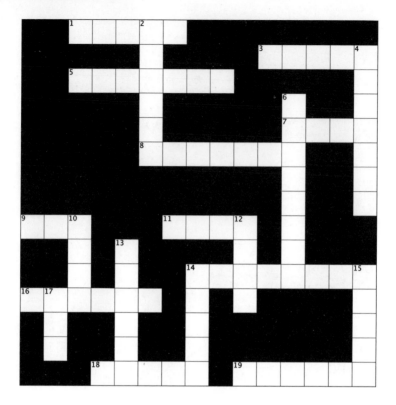

ACROSS

1. He was elected president in 2008
3. He was killed by a stingray in 2006
5. Hurricane that ravaged New Orleans in 2005
7. Fuzzy boots, informally
8. Social media site for 'microblogging'
9. Nintendo gaming system
11. Noted 2000 loser
14. It malfunctioned at the 2004 Super Bowl
16. Where the 2000 Olympics were held
18. Foam shoes
19. AMC series starring Jon Hamm

DOWN

2. It crashed in 2008
4. Shady music download site
6. Early reality show hosted by Jeff Probst
10. Portable music device
12. Currency that had coins and banknotes introduced in 2002
13. Justin with hits 'Baby' and 'One Time'
14. Pro golfer Tiger
15. Company that went under in 2001
17. Computer bug dreaded in the run-up to 2000

Answer on page 341

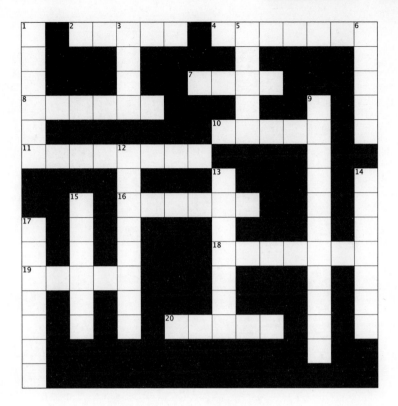

ACROSS

2. Virus discovered in 2019
4. Gorilla killed at the Cincinnati Zoo in 2016
7. Ride-sharing app
8. Social movement against economic inequality, in brief
10. Social movement drawing attention to sexual harassment
11. Climate activist Greta
16. Consequential 2016 referendum
18. ____ Go, augmented reality app
19. Singer with hits 'Juice' and 'Good as Hell'
20. Electric car company owned by Elon Musk

DOWN

1. Jordan Peele's directorial debut
3. HBO show featuring Julia Louis-Dreyfus
5. Singer with albums '21' and '25'
6. Juul or Blu, casually
9. International event on January 21, 2017
12. Adorable character on 'The Mandalorian' whose real name is Grogu
13. Easily losable iPhone accessories
14. Fidget ____
15. Disney movie with Anna and Elsa
17. Solar phenomenon in 2017

Answer on page 342

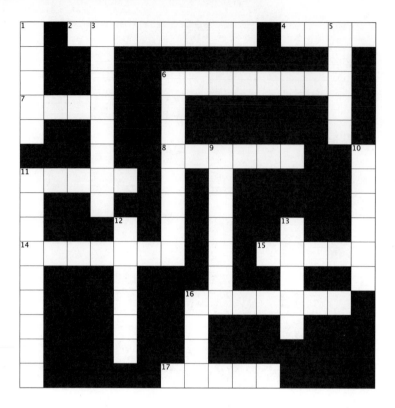

ACROSS

2. Cape of _____
4. Ethnic group in Nigeria
6. One of three of South Africa's capital cities
7. Where the Pyramids and Sphinx are
8. African desert
11. Ghanaian capital
14. Plant whose name means 'red bush'
15. Largest city in Egypt
16. Capital city of 17-Across
17. Its oldest city is Mombasa

DOWN

1. Neighbor of Gabon
3. Where you might go to see African wildlife
5. Language group including Swahili, Zulu, and Tiv
6. Grain staple in North Africa
9. Tunisian chili pepper paste
10. Rice dish popular in sub-Saharan Africa
11. Caste system against which Nelson Mandela fought
12. Nguni Bantu term meaning 'humanity'; also a Linux OS
13. Most populous city in Nigeria
16. Famed Egyptian river

Answer on page 342

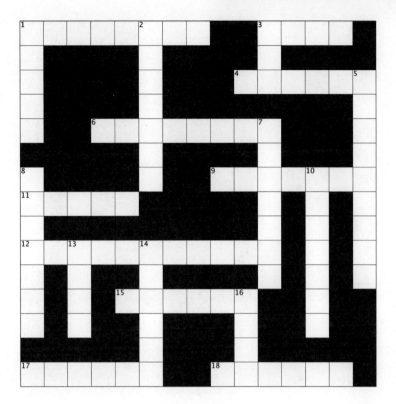

ACROSS

1. Where the Dodgers used to play
3. Crosstown rivals of 7-Down
4. Historically Black neighborhood in Manhattan
6. Give my regards to this place
9. He popularized 'New York, New York'
11. _____ Island, historic immigrant entry point
12. On New Year's Eve, watch the ball drop here
15. They're boiled, baked, and schmeared
17. One of three New York City rivers
18. Neighborhood grocery spot

DOWN

1. With 'the,' one of five New York boroughs
2. Center or Tunnel
3. NYC subway org.
5. Borough with a cocktail named after it
7. Crosstown rivals of 3-Across
8. _____ Park, dedicated green space in the middle of the city
10. Neighborhood name short for 'Triangle Below Canal'
13. Where you might see a Klee or Dali
14. _____ Island, the smallest borough
16. Upscale neighborhood whose name stands for 'South of Houston'

Answer on page 342

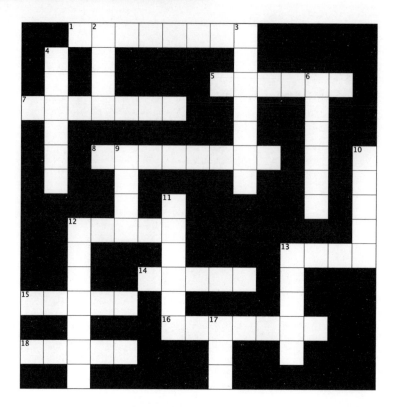

ACROSS

1. Ocean between the Americas and Africa
5. Coldest ocean
7. Sea cow
8. Intelligent marine mammals
12. Seashore
13. Prey for 9-Down
14. They create the regular rise and fall of the sea surface
15. Marylanders have a particular affinity for them
16. Ocean surrounding Australia
18. Surfer's needs

DOWN

2. Albacore or bluefin
3. Movement of seawater, e.g. the Gulf Stream
4. Giant sea mammals
6. Ocean south of Asia
9. Black-and-white apex predator
10. Primary food for 4-Down
11. Small crustaceans sometimes eaten in scampi or cocktail
12. Sea creature with two shells
13. Animal that can squirt ink
17. The most common fish found in 'fish and chips'

Answer on page 342

ACROSS
1. Vernon and Petunia _____
4. How wizard mail is delivered
5. The Fat _____, guardian of Gryffindor Tower
8. Wizard equivalent of a "nastygram"
9. The Marauder's _____.
10. Harry's nemesis at school
11. See 14-Down
13. Magical sport
16. _____ Bagman, Head of the Department of Magical Games and Sports
17. Tom Marvolo _____
19. Non-wizard

DOWN
2. House represented by a snake
3. He Who Must Not Be Named
6. House for the Weasleys
7. Hogwarts gamekeeper and, later, professor
12. Behemoth spider living in the Forbidden Forest
14. With 11-Across, Harry's crush
15. Viktor _____ of Durmstrang Institute
16. _____ Jordan, Harry's housemate and pal
18. Fluffy, the Grim, and Sirius Black's Animagus form are all this type of animal

Answer on page 342

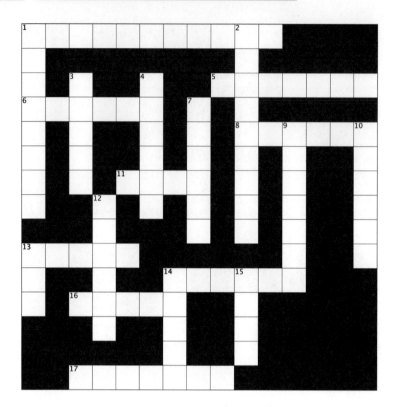

ACROSS

1. Surname adopted by Prince Philip
5. First name for the Duke of Cambridge
6. Prince born on July 22, 2013
8. Son of 13-Across and 4-Down
11. She married 5-Across in 2011
13. Prince whose real name is Henry
14. Notorious divorcee Simpson
16. The 'People's Princess'
17. _____ Castle

DOWN

1. The Queen's late sister
2. Current monarch
3. One of many canine members of the family
4. Family member who had an acting career
7. The Queen's late father
9. Elizabeth's current heir
10. Youngest son of the Queen
12. Former wife of Prince Andrew, familiarly
13. Royal honorific (abbr.)
14. Princess of _____
15. _____ of succession

Answer on page 342

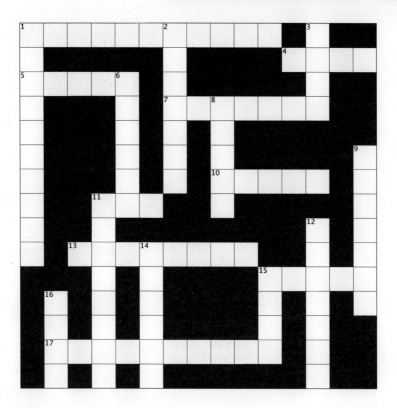

ACROSS

1. '77 ____'
4. Photographers seen about town, for short
5. With 'The,' LGBT drama set in LA
7. Brooklyn transplants
10. Venice, Huntington, or Redondo
11. Airport code
13. Event held in LA in 1932 and 1984
15. Avenue of the ____
17. LA nickname

DOWN

1. East LA neighborhood with painted staircases
2. Paramount, Columbia, and Universal
3. LA NFL team
6. 'Black ____'
8. Academy Awards ceremony venue
9. Grauman's ____ Theatre
11. 2016 film with Emma Stone and Ryan Gosling
12. Persistent LA complaint
14. They're often shot in LA
15. Hollywood ____, prominent LA landmark
16. LA industry

Answer on page 343

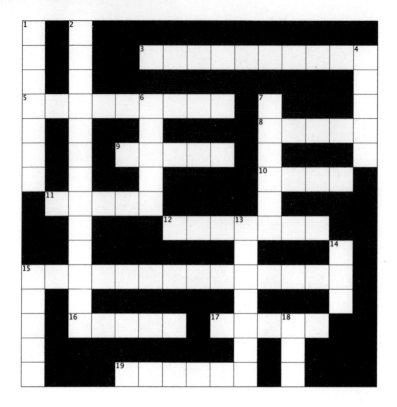

ACROSS

3. Deadliest battle of the Civil War

5. Mississippi town with a key Civil War battle and siege

8. Another name for the North

9. He led a raid on Harpers Ferry

10. Maritime military force

11. _____ and Bars, nickname for the flag of the CSA

12. Site of the first major battle of the Civil War

15. Demarcation indicating the boundary between free and slave states

16. Month in which the war ended in 1865

17. The side that lost the war

19. Harriet who guided approximately 70 enslaved people to freedom

DOWN

1. Cause of the war

2. Sherman led it in 1864

4. Northern general

6. Civil War documentarian

7. Enslaved man who led a rebellion in 1831

13. President during the Civil War

14. Southern general

15. Winning general at 3-Across

18. Owner of a cabin in an influential 1852 novel

Answer on page 343

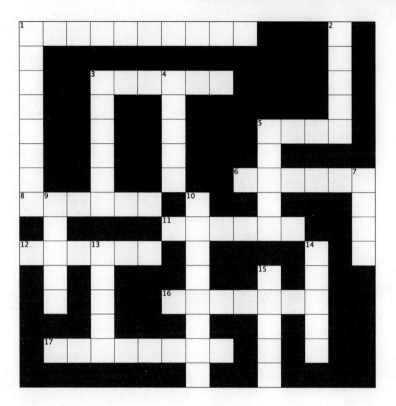

ACROSS
1. It's sought by farmers entering animals in fair contests
3. Arts and _____
5. Swine
6. Raffle purchase
8. Ride also known as a yo-yo
11. Type of cake served with powdered sugar
12. Area of the fairgrounds with amusements
16. Frankfurters
17. Pet won at a fair

DOWN
1. They're filled with helium
2. Bumper cars and carousel
3. _____ candy
4. How much fair food is prepared
5. 1-Across, for example
7. _____-a-[9-Down], dizzying ride
9. See 7-Down
10. Building with trick mirrors and shifting floors
13. Ferris _____
14. Entertainment provided by a band
15. Rodeo animal

Answer on page 343

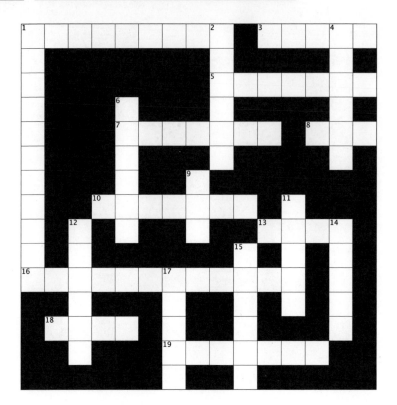

ACROSS

1. Perpetual political issue in DC
3. DC public transit system
5. DC river
7. War memorialized by Maya Lin
8. DC MLBer, familiarly
10. _____ and Poets, noted bar and bookstore
13. Historically Black DC neighborhood
16. Landscaped park with monuments
18. Music subgenre associated with funk
19. Hirshhorn and Renwick

DOWN

1. Administrator of 20 DC museums and galleries
2. _____ Circle
4. DC airport
6. Pennsylvania or Constitution
9. Its residents include Tian Tian
11. Ben's _____ Bowl
12. Foggy _____, neighborhood that's home to the State Department
14. The _____ House, president's home
15. Rose _____, photo op spot for POTUS
17. _____ Morgan

Answer on page 343

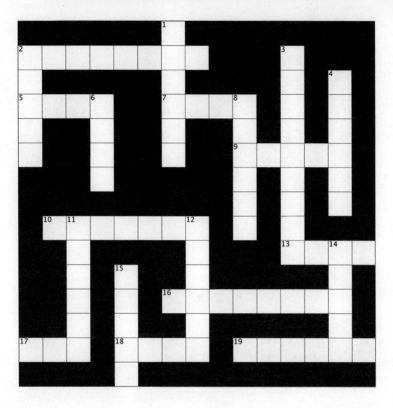

ACROSS

2. Cheery flower symbolizing hope
5. Flower that shares its name with a part of the eye
7. _____ of the valley
9. Pale shade of purple
10. Gather flowers to make one of these
13. Traditional Valentine's Day gift
16. Tropical bloom
17. Flower stage after 6-Down
18. Autumn flowers, familiarly
19. Flower lacking pigmentation

DOWN

1. Purple ground-cover flower
2. Duke or Duck
3. Baseball players may eat the seeds of this flower
4. First sign of spring, it's said
6. All flowers start as this
8. 2-Across color
11. Flower notoriously difficult to grow
12. Flower that's a homophone with a part of the face
14. Black-eyed _____
15. Pleasant smell

Answer on page 343

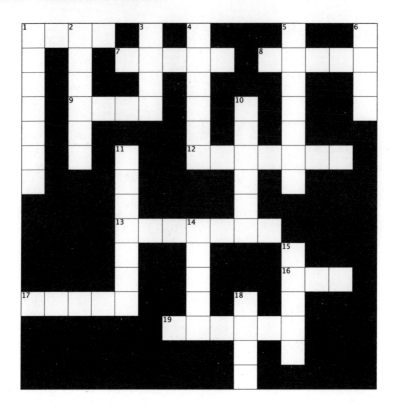

ACROSS

1. Element used in Las Vegas, maybe?

7. Element deriving its name from the Latin for 'strange'

8. Substance made of hydrogen and 2-Down

9. Element found in some jewelry

12. Element that is liquid at room temperature

13. Positive particles

16. Alloys of it include pewter and bronze

17. Buy a test kit to see if this radioactive gas is present in your home

19. Element lighter than air

DOWN

1. The heart of an atom

2. Fire and humans need it to live

3. Element represented by the symbol Pb

4. Combine this element with chloride to get table salt

5. In your body, much of it is stored in your bones

6. A deficiency of this causes anemia

10. Word with 'copy' or 'dioxide'

11. Superman's least favorite element

14. The periodic ____

15. They're made of neutrons, electrons, and 13-Across

18. Rub an oxide of this on your nose to prevent sunburn

Answer on page 343

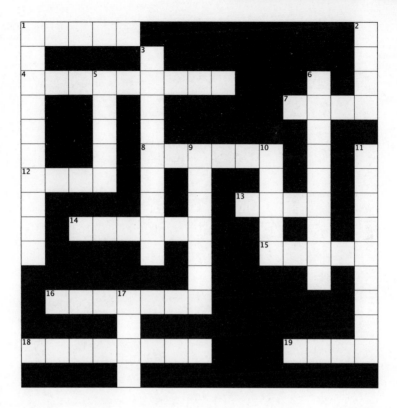

ACROSS

1. '_____ Raccoon' (1968)
4. Song that includes the lyric 'Take these sunken eyes and learn to see'
7. _____ Best, the 'fifth Beatle'
8. The color of the Beatles' submarine
12. '_____ Sadie' (1968)
13. '_____ Prudence' (1968)
14. Half of a Beatles mantra meaning 'life goes on'
15. Ringo _____
16. Song with a seemingly interminable coda of 'na'
18. What the Beatles wanted to hold in 1963
19. An urban legend in the late '60s held that he was actually dead

DOWN

1. Album with 'Drive My Car' and 'Girl'
2. 'Penny _____' (1967)
3. Album with an iconic cover
5. What you need to do with 'that weight'
6. When the Beatles' troubles seemed so far away
9. Song that reassures the listener that 'there will be an answer'
10. 'While My Guitar Gently _____' (1968)
11. Beatles' British hometown
17. He married Yoko

Answer on page 344

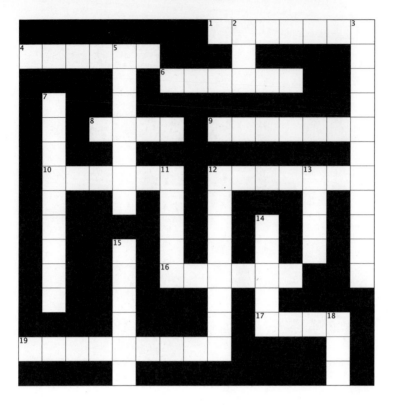

ACROSS

1. 'Dr. Strangelove or: How I Learned to Stop Worrying and Love _____' (1964)
4. He starred in Kubrick's final film
6. 16-Across antagonist
8. Character played by Malcolm McDowell in 1971
9. She played Wendy in 'The Shining'
10. Ominous word appearing in a mirror in 'The Shining'
12. '2001: A Space _____' (1968)
16. Kubrick film based on a Nabokov novel
17. Sue _____, actress who played the title role in 16-Across
19. 'A _____ Orange' (1971)

DOWN

2. He wouldn't open the pod bay doors
3. 1975 period piece with Ryan O'Neal
5. Actor who starred in 'Dr. Strangelove'
7. 1960 film starring Kirk Douglas in the title role
11. 'Full _____ Jacket' (1987)
12. With 14-Down, setting for 'The Shining'
13. 'Eyes Wide _____,' 1999 film released after Kubrick's death
14. See 12-Down
15. Author of the novella on which '2001' is based
18. Conflict in which 11-Down is partially set, informally

Answer on page 344

ACROSS

1. Matter entering Earth's atmosphere
4. The path of an object around another object
5. Super____
6. Group of stars that forms a shape
7. 6-Across that looks like a lion
8. Term for forgotten satellites, old rocket parts, etc
9. Fine particles in space
10. Feature of 12-Down
11. Small, rocky object sometimes called a 'minor planet'
14. Little green men, for short
15. The dog star
16. Nearest star to Earth

DOWN

1. Natural satellite
2. You can make wishes on these
3. ____ sequence, series of star types to which most stars belong
6. Halley's or Hale-Bopp
7. How distance in space is measured
9. Big or Little 6-Across
12. Archer in the sky
13. This type of star may be red, orange, or yellow

Answer on page 344

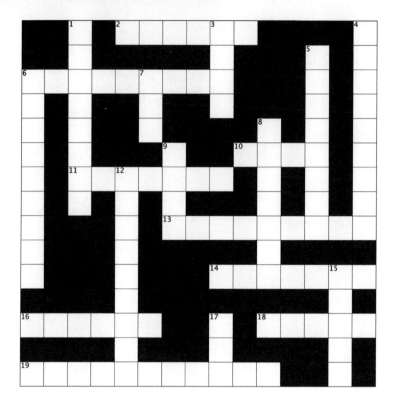

ACROSS

2. Daytime procession
6. 4th of July finale
10. One of three patriotic colors
11. Country celebrated on the 4th of July
13. Hand-held wires that can be set on fire
14. Food served between two buns
16. Outdoor meal
18. Live entertainment
19. Despite its name, it's not from Italy

DOWN

1. This might take place in a city park
3. When 6-Across usually begin
4. Bloodsucking bug
5. As American as _____
6. A kid might get one of these of a butterfly or a flag
7. Reaction to 6-Across, maybe
8. Spread one of these on the grass
9. Messy barbecued food
12. Blast
15. Place to cook burgers
17. One of three patriotic colors

Answer on page 344

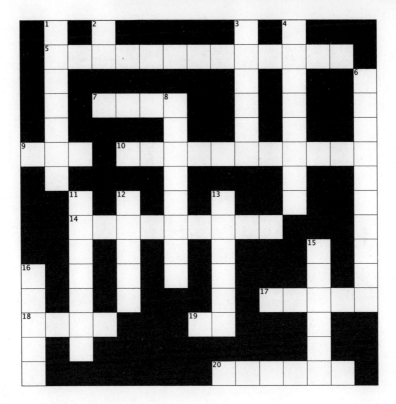

ACROSS

5. A woman suffers a devilish pregnancy (1968)

7. The first summer blockbuster, arguably (1975)

9. 'A Nightmare on _____ Street' (1984)

10. First horror film to be nominated for Best Picture (1973)

14. In which Jamie Lee Curtis plays the 'final girl' (1976)

17. 'The _____,' low-budget film in which all crime is legal for one night a year (2013)

18. 'The _____,' a film about a haunted videotape (2002)

19. Pennywise emerges from the sewer (1990)

20. 'The _____ Man,' 1973 film subjected to a 2006 remake with Nicolas Cage

DOWN

1. Bela Lugosi plays the title character (1931)

2. Film featuring 'tethered' souls (2019)

3. The blood in the shower scene is actually chocolate syrup (1960)

4. 'Texas Chainsaw _____' (1974)

6. 'The _____ Horror' (1979)

8. Town where the women are almost too good to be true (1975)

11. 'The _____,' in which all work and no play makes Jack a dull boy (1980)

12. 'A Quiet _____' (2018)

13. Jordan Peele's directorial debut (2017)

15. She has a bloody awful time at the prom (1976)

16. 'The _____,' Hitchcock film based on a du Maurier story (1963)

Answer on page 344

ACROSS

1. Fluid that carries oxygen
3. First stop along the digestive tract
5. Arm joint
7. Space in the head that's Latin for 'curve'
8. It detects odors
10. Backbone
13. Their three types are skeletal, smooth, and cardiac
15. Opening
17. Arteries and _____

DOWN

1. The 'nerve center'
2. Throat glands often removed
3. Filters blood and combats infections
4. Organ with four chambers
6. There are 206 of them in the body
7. The largest organ
9. The iris, the pupil, and the retina are part of it
11. These organs perceive sound
12. Organs damaged by smoking
14. Organ that processes alcohol and toxins
16. Ten fingers, ten _____

Answer on page 344

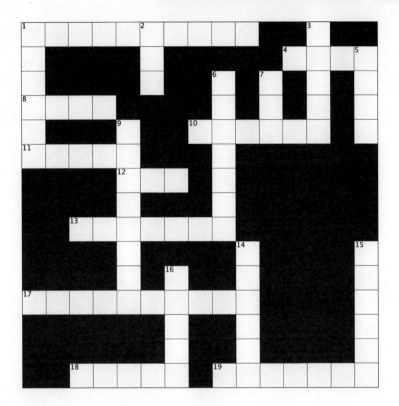

ACROSS

1. State flower
4. 'Don't _____ with Texas'
8. With 'black,' slang term for 2-Down
10. It should be kept weird, according to its unofficial motto
11. Competitive equestrian event
12. _____ Braunfels, Texas
13. US president from Texas
17. Texas's state motto
18. Remember it
19. Texas NFL team

DOWN

1. 'Everything's _____ in Texas'
2. Petroleum
3. Official tree of Texas
5. Film, media, and music festival, for short
6. Most-populous Texas city
7. Head topper
9. Type of cattle that shares its name with a university mascot
14. It's Spanish for 'the pass'
15. Home to 19-Across
16. Houston athlete involved in a 2019 scandal

Answer on page 345

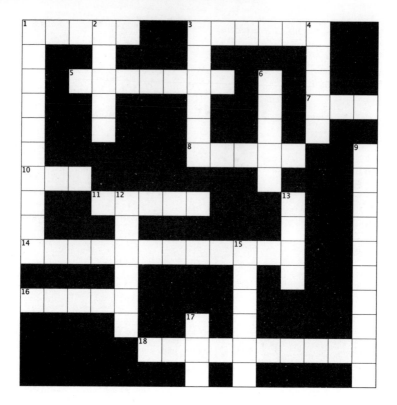

ACROSS

1. Bearer of the One Ring
3. 10-Across's surname
5. Ian McKellen plays him in the films (both the Grey and the White)
7. Tree creature
8. With Pippin, one of two hobbit pals of 1-Across
10. Best friend of 1-Across
11. Dragon and antagonist
14. Director of 'Lord of the Rings' films
16. 1-Across's cousin
18. Creator of Middle-earth

DOWN

1. 'The ____ of the Ring' (2001 film)
2. Gimli is one of these creatures
3. Character who refers to the ring as 'my precious'
4. Legolas and Galadriel, for example
6. With 'the,' idyllic land where hobbits dwell
9. Country where all filming was completed
12. Land where 15-Down rules
13. 'The Return of the ____' (2003 film)
15. Evil character depicted as a flaming eye
17. Goblin-like monster

Answer on page 345

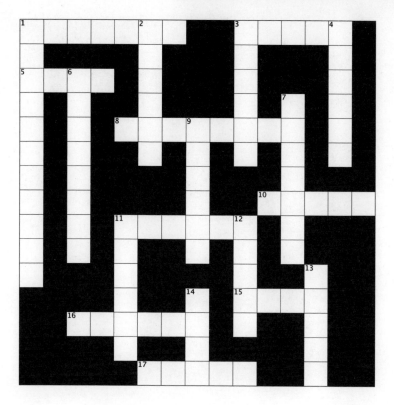

ACROSS

1. French island with Italian culture
3. Croatian city that shares its name with a gymnastics move
5. French city that lives up to its name
8. Mediterranean summers provide plenty
10. Along with blue, traditional Greek color
11. ____, Italian tourist spot
15. Italian dough, once
16. Principality and microstate
17. Largest island in Greece

DOWN

1. In Italian, 'five lands'
2. Mediterranean country that sounds like a tree
3. ____ of Gibraltar
4. Country with the capital city Ankara
6. Ride one of these up a Dubrovnik hillside
7. Vacation spots
9. Italian island
11. Home to the Acropolis and the Parthenon
12. Country shaped like a boot
13. Archipelago with Valletta as its capital
14. 12-Down's capital

Answer on page 345

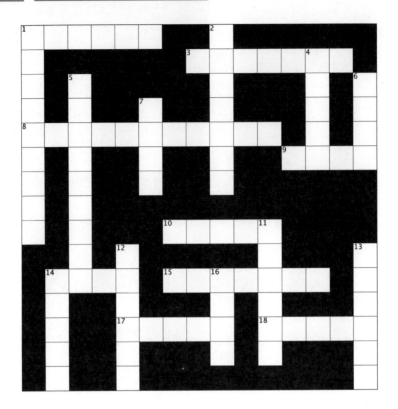

ACROSS

1. Greek god for whom the mission was named
3. Where Mission Control is located
8. Sea of _____
9. 'That's one small _____ for man...'
10. 'The _____ has landed'
14. Mission commander's first name
15. President who proposed the moon landing mission in 1961
17. Types found on the moon included basalt and breccia
18. 12-Down's real first name

DOWN

1. Surname of the mission commander
2. 'Forgotten' astronaut who remained in the spacecraft
4. The path of an object around a star or planet
5. International competition to be the first country to make it to the moon
6. '...one giant _____ for mankind.'
7. 12-Down's nickname
11. Moon landing mission number
12. He took Communion on the moon
13. Astronauts' feet left these behind
14. President during the moon landing
16. Org. responsible for the moon landing

Answer on page 345

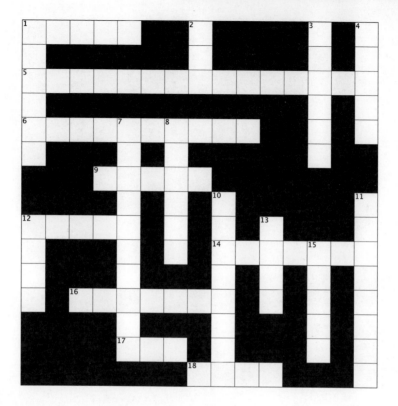

ACROSS

1. With 2-Down, ABBA musical that takes its name from one of their songs

5. Song that begins 'If you change your mind...'

6. Contest won by ABBA in 1974

9. With 16-Across, rhyming song title

12. What ABBA demands you do with a man after midnight

14. 'When I Kissed the ____'

16. See 9-Across

17. Distress signal

18. Number of ABBA members

DOWN

1. 'Does Your ____ Know'

2. See 1-Across

3. This person takes it all

4. 'Dancing ____'

7. In French, 'do you want?'

8. ABBA's home country

10. Song with which ABBA won 6-Across

11. War ballad with a man's name

12. Greatest hits album

13. 'Our ____ Summer'

15. Doubled, song that contains the line 'I feel like I wanna sing when you do your thing'

Answer on page 345

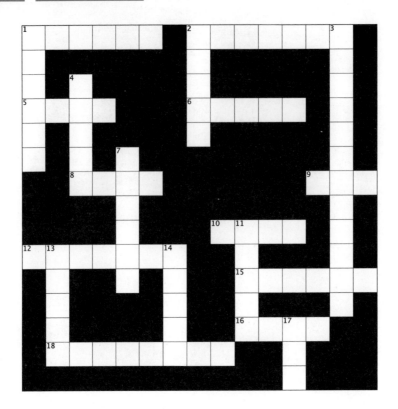

ACROSS

1. With 2-Across, company at the center of 'The Office'
2. See 1-Across
5. _____ Daniels, showrunner
6. _____ Wallace, Michael's long-suffering boss
8. Number of seasons of 'The Office'
9. Receptionist played by Jenna
10. _____ Krasinski
12. Wife of Bob Vance (Vance Refrigeration)
15. Steve _____
16. Self-described wunderkind played by BJ
18. Pennsylvania town where 'The Office' takes place

DOWN

1. Office weirdo played by Rainn
2. _____ Kaling, actress and writer
3. Where a pivotal wedding scene occurs in season 6
4. Bumbling accountant
7. Her cats included Bandit, Sprinkles, and Princess Lady
11. Accountant who is often the voice of reason
13. Funnyman Ed who played Andy
14. Michael _____, Branch Manager
17. She played HR rep Holly

Answer on page 345

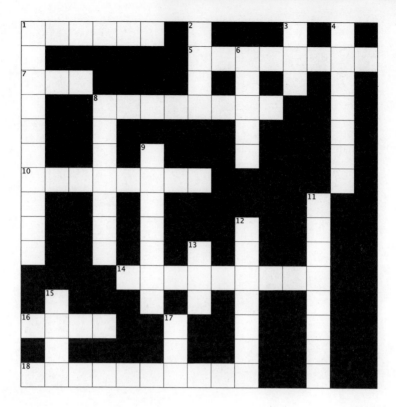

ACROSS

1. It went coed in 1969
5. DC university noted for international affairs
7. Its two locations are in Manhattan and Brooklyn (abbr.)
8. Liberal arts college in Northfield, Minnesota
10. Women's college whose name means 'large hill' in Welsh
14. Where Sonia Sotomayor went to law school
16. Empire State educ. system
18. Their mascot is the hoya

DOWN

1. Nashville university
2. College in New Haven
3. This univ. is represented by the saluki
4. Women's college associated with Columbia
6. Research university in Atlanta
8. Andy Bernard's alma mater
9. Oldest institute of higher ed in the United States
11. Alma mater of 17 astronauts
12. Ohio school famed for its music conservatory
13. With NC State and 15-Down, it makes up the Research Triangle
15. See 13-Down
17. Scientific univ. in Cambridge

Answer on page 346

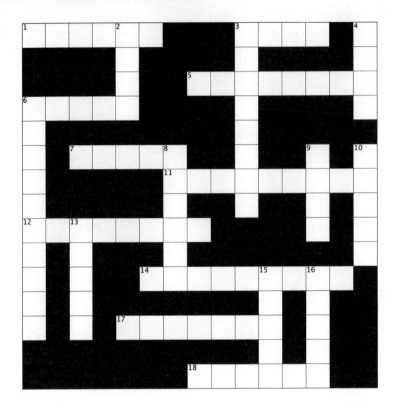

ACROSS

1. _____ Road, toll path towards the end of the trail
3. Laramie, Bridger, or Knox
5. Westward migrants
6. Vehicle for traveling the train
7. Shoshone, Kettle, or Twin
11. Heavy type of 6-Across
12. State in which the trail began
14. 'You have died of _____'
17. Disease resulting from poor sanitation
18. Party that ended early?

DOWN

2. Pack animals
3. Boundary between settled land and wilderness
4. South _____
6. Valley in which the trail ends
8. Eating berries and currants helped prevent this disease
9. Chimney or Independence
10. Doubled, a Washington town
13. A bite from this creature could be fatal
15. Caravan
16. Ford it, or caulk the wagon and float

Answer on page 346

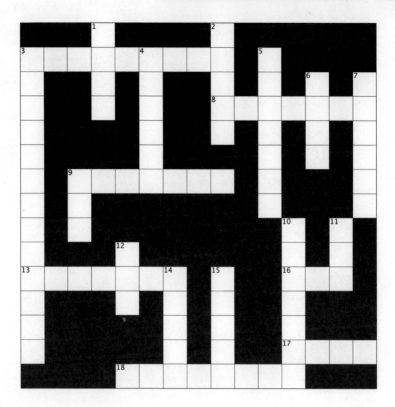

ACROSS

3. In the world of the film, it means 'I love you'

8. With 2-Down, he played Vizzini

9. Patinkin played him

13. Fictional poison

16. Number of fingers on the Count's left hand

17. Water creatures that shriek

18. Cliffs of _____

DOWN

1. Fearsome beast (abbr.)

2. See 8-Across

3. Pro wrestler who played Fezzik

4. Robin who played Buttercup

5. 11-Down's wife

6. Peter who played Grandpa

7. Film's director

9. The only thing better than true love, per 11-Down

10. Dread Pirate Roberts / Man in Black / Farm Boy

11. Miracle _____, healer played by Billy Crystal

12. 'You killed my father. Prepare to _____.'

14. Actor who portrayed 10-Down

15. The man sought by 9-Across

Answer on page 346

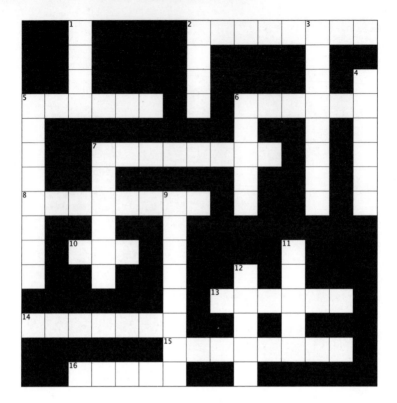

ACROSS

2. Burr's competitor in a duel
5. Location of 3-Down
6. 'We the _____'
7. The first US ambassador to 7-Down
8. River famously crossed by Washington
10. Stamp or Townshend
13. British king
14. Creator of a 2015 musical about 2-Across
15. Number of original colonies
16. Financial charges imposed by Britain

DOWN

1. Flagmaker Betsy
2. Patriot spy Nathan
3. Protest held in a harbor
4. Subject of an 1860 Longfellow poem
5. First name of a noted traitor
6. Author of 'Common Sense'
7. Ally of the Continental Army
9. British soldiers
11. Valley _____, winter military camp
12. Patrick who said 'Give me liberty, or give me death!'

Answer on page 346

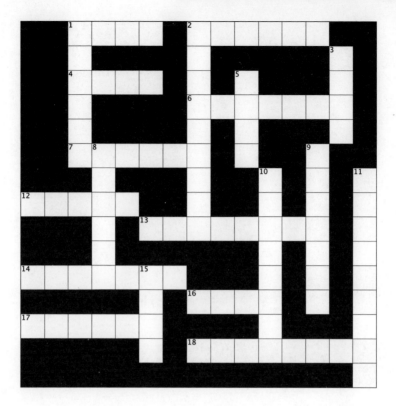

ACROSS

1. Only person to have been both President and Chief Justice

2. Body responsible for confirming justices

4. Word used to call the Court to order

6. First woman on the Supreme Court

7. Justice who died in 2016

12. Roger who was the fifth Chief Justice

13. First Black justice

14. Term for the minority opinion

16. How long a justice's term lasts

17. He wrote the majority opinions in Brown v. Board and Loving v. Virginia

18. She was 'notorious'

DOWN

1. Anita Hill testified against him at his hearing

2. First Latina on the court

3. Defendant in a 2000 Supreme Court case

5. Traditional court garb

8. Legal aides

9. Merrick who missed out

10. First Jewish justice

11. Justice at whose confirmation hearing Christine Blasey Ford testified

15. Number of justices on the court

Answer on page 346

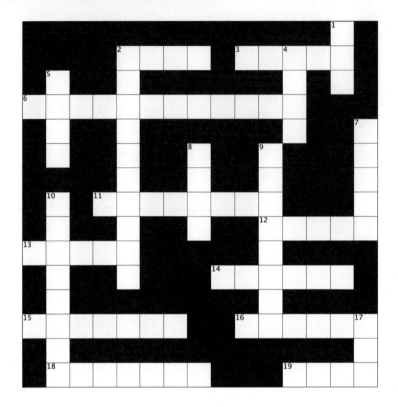

ACROSS

2. The West ____
3. President elected in 2020
6. City that's home to the President
11. Month in which presidential elections take place
12. It can precede lady, dog, or family
13. Acronym used to refer to the President
14. ____ Corps, military branch that oversees presidential helicopters
15. Month in which a president is inaugurated
16. ____ Service
18. Museum/archive traditionally established by former presidents
19. The President has the power to do this to bills

DOWN

1. It follows 14-Across and 9-Down
2. It was previously known as the Executive Mansion
4. See 5-Down
5. With 4-Down, term for a president in the final days of office
7. With 'the,' nickname for the President's armored limo
8. ____ David
9. Branch of the military that oversees fixed-wing aircraft used by the President
10. Nickname for the briefcase containing nuclear codes
17. Maximum number of terms for a president

Answer on page 346

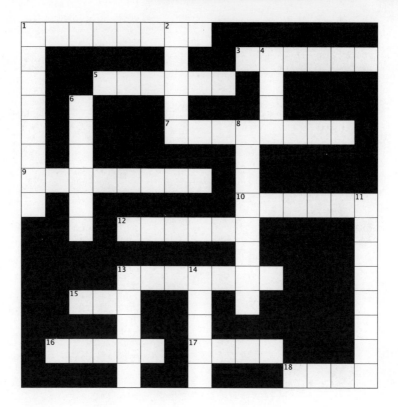

ACROSS

1. Military branch dealing with aviation
3. They're said to be 'up' when the plane takes off
5. 737 manufacturer
7. Onboard recording device
9. Close-range aerial battle
10. Force creating forward motion
12. Engineless aircraft
13. It's also called the flight deck
15. Aviation org.
16. Their parts include flaps, slats, and ailerons
17. Structure at the rear of the aircraft that provides stability
18. The plane's steering wheel, essentially

DOWN

1. Measure of an airplane's distance from the ground
2. Ascent
4. Kitty _____, North Carolina
6. Orville or Wilbur
8. Sign in the sky that an airplane's been there
11. Device that controls engine power
13. Goods carried on an aircraft
14. Units of air speed measurement

Answer on page 347

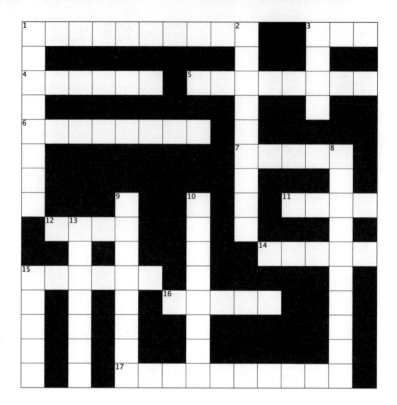

ACROSS

1. She sings 'Colors of the Wind' and 'Just Around the Riverbend'

3. 'The ____ and the [7-Across]' (1981)

4. Film with the song 'You'll Be in My Heart'

5. With 'The,' 1994 film loosely based on 'Hamlet'

6. They went 'down under' in a 1990 sequel

7. See 3-Across

11. She adopted Stitch in 2002

12. Female protagonist in 5-Across

14. 1998 animated film remade with live actors in 2020

15. '____ and the Beast' (1991)

16. 1941 film with the songs 'Baby Mine' and 'Pink Elephants on Parade'

17. With 'The,' 1970 film about French felines

DOWN

1. 1953 film with Smee, Nana, and Wendy Darling

2. She ate a poisoned apple in 1938

3. Hummingbird friend of 1-Across

8. Dogs sought by Cruella de Vil

9. 1940 film set to classical music

10. 1997 film based on a Greek myth

13. Film in which Robin Williams voiced the Genie

15. Deer whose friends include Thumper and Flower

Answer on page 347

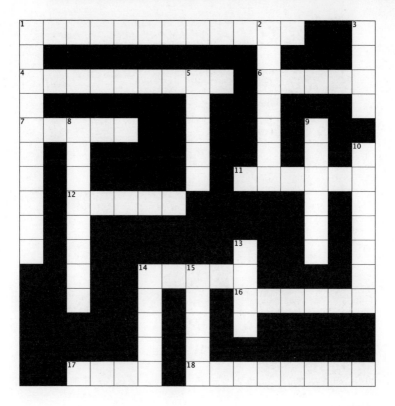

ACROSS

1. He starred in several Hitchcock films
4. 'North by ____'
6. Norman or Norma
7. She played Melanie in 'The Birds'
11. 1964 film with Hedren and Connery
12. 'Blackmail' was his first film to feature this
14. Hitchcock trademark
16. 1960 classic beloved by audiences, but panned by critics at the time
17. 'The Man Who Knew Too ____'
18. Hitchcock film that shares its name with a seagoing vessel

DOWN

1. She was promoted as the star of 16-Across, despite only appearing in the first act of the film
2. 1940 film that was Hitchcock's first American project
3. '____ Virtue'
5. 'The 39 ____'
8. TV series 'Alfred Hitchcock ____'
9. 'Rear ____'
10. Film in which Kim Novak plays Madeleine
13. Film shot to look like it was made with one continuous take
14. 'To ____ a Thief'
15. Setting for 16-Across

Answer on page 347

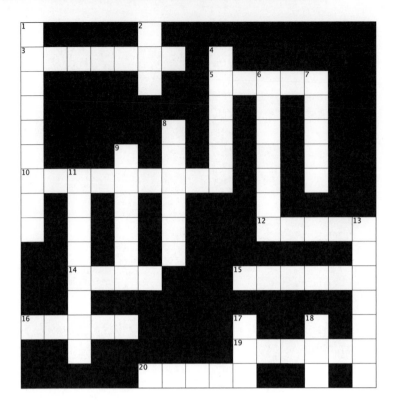

ACROSS

3. 'Dear Mr. _____'
(1983)
5. Motorcycling
mouse
10. Beverly Cleary's
day job
12. 1973 novel in
which a cat has to
get used to a new
baby
14. 'Drop everything
and _____'
15. Relationship
of 9-Down to
11-Down
16. Doubled, the
name of the family
pet
19. 'Muggie _____'
(1990)
20. 7-Down's dog

DOWN

1. Car/doll name
2. 16-Across is this
type of household
pet
4. State in which
most Cleary
novels are set
6. How the two
protagonists
communicate in
3-Across
7. _____ Huggins
8. Surname of
9-Down and
11-Down
9. 'The pest'
11. Beezus's real
name
13. Dog adopted
in the sequel to
3-Across
17. 'Mitch and _____'
(1967)
18. Food item
cracked over
9-Down's head

Answer on page 347

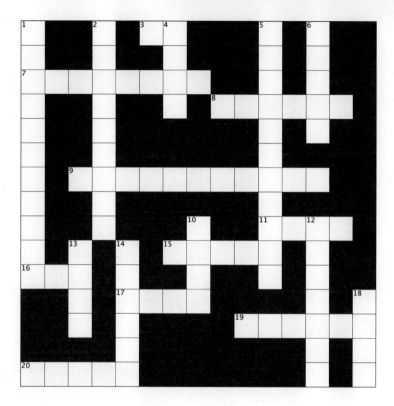

ACROSS

3. 2009 film with a notoriously tearjerking opening sequence

7. Pixar's first feature-length film

8. Red-headed protagonist of 20-Across

9. 2001 film featuring Mike Wazowski

11. 'A Bug's ____'

15. Garbage-collecting robot

16. 15-Across's love interest

17. 2021 Best Animated Feature Oscar winner

19. Primary setting of 18-Down, along with the Land of the Dead

20. Pixar's first film with a female protagonist

DOWN

1. 2007 film in which a rodent becomes a chef

2. 2015 depicting anthropomorphized emotions

4. Surname in 5-Down

5. With 'The,' 2004 film about a family of superheroes

6. Cowboy hero of 7-Across

10. Cranky 3-Across protagonist

12. '____ Nemo' (or Dory)

13. 1-Down character voiced by Patton Oswalt

14. 6-Down's cowgirl sidekick

18. 2017 film inspired by Dia de los Muertos

Answer on page 347

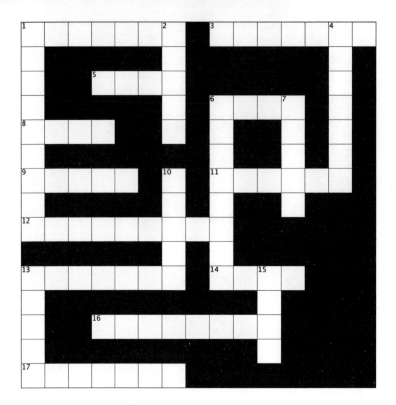

ACROSS
1. Shakespeare wrote 154 of them
3. It's unlucky to say this in a theater
5. 'Exit, pursued by a ____'
6. With 'the,' term used to refer to Othello
8. Part 1 of a famous Shakespeare quote
9. Part 2 of the quote
11. 'As You Like It' or 'The Winter's Tale'
12. Othello's wife
13. Fairy queen
14. Part 3 of the quote
16. Titular character with three daughters
17. 6-Down antagonist

DOWN
1. ____-upon-Avon
2. Unkind name for Katarina
4. 'Hamlet' or 'Cymbeline'
6. 'The ____ of Venice'
7. Star-crossed lover
10. 'Twelfth Night' protagonist
13. '____ Andronicus'
15. Shakespeare's nickname, with 'the'

Answer on page 347

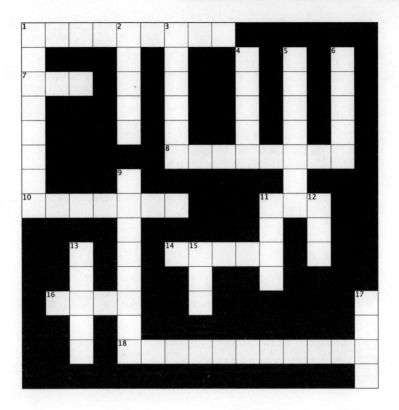

ACROSS

1. Sparking wine
7. Oft-derided wine packaging method
8. 2004 film starring Paul Giamatti as a wine aficionado
10. Event where many wines are sampled
11. Color of wine made from dark grapes
14. Traditional method of sealing a wine bottle
16. California region famous for wine
18. Port, Madeira, or sherry

DOWN

1. _____ Sauvignon
2. Noir or Grigio
3. Fruit traditionally associated with winemaking
4. Color of wine that's actually more like yellow
5. The year in which a wine was bottled
6. Vessel for drinking wine
9. Where fruit is grown for wine
11. Type of wine known as 'rosato' in Spanish
12. In wine terms, non-sweet
13. Fungus key to fermentation
15. Wood used for wine barrels
17. Part of plant or a 6-Down

Answer on page 348

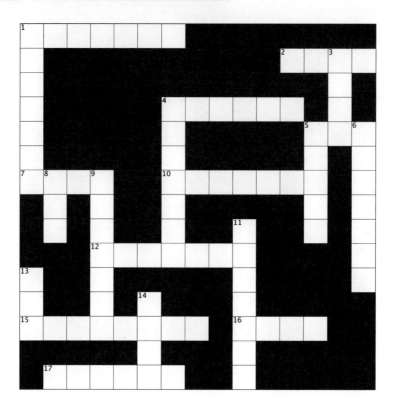

ACROSS
1. Defunct social media site
2. Protocol used to transfer data over the web
4. Irritating ads
5. Comcast or Verizon (abbr.)
7. Site for crafty folks
10. They record your web activity
12. Site started by Jack Dorsey
15. Social media site that's often a source of misinformation
16. To hang ten…or to visit websites
17. 11-Down made by Google

DOWN
1. It includes worms and Trojan horses
3. Things open in windows
4. Digital audio series
5. Photo-sharing app, for short
6. Internet music player
8. Software for using the dark web
9. Where you might find a vlog
11. It's used to access the web
13. Animated image
14. Video-chatting platform that experienced a boom in 2020

Answer on page 348

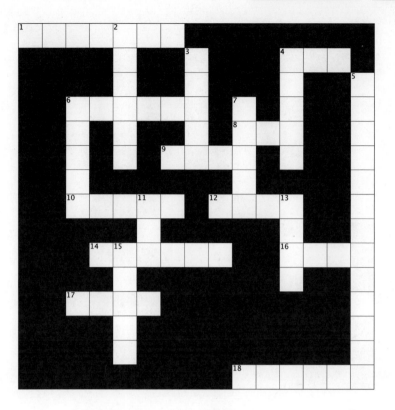

ACROSS

1. Only sign represented by an insect

4. Midsummer sign

6. Symbol of Sagittarius

8. Gemini, Libra, and Aquarius are all this type of sign

9. Capricorn's symbol

10. Written in the ____

12. Animal that represents Cancer

14. Late spring sign

16. Symbol of 4-Across

17. Element that represents Aries, Leo, and Sagittarius

18. Inanimate object representing 4-Down

DOWN

2. Fishy sign

3. Sign represented by a maiden

4. Autumn sign

5. The zodiac gets its name from the ancient Greek phrase 'cycle of ____'

6. Sign ruled by Mars

7. Element that represents Scorpio, Pisces, and Cancer

11. Symbol of 6-Down

13. Animal that represents Taurus

15. Element representing Taurus, Virgo, and Capricorn

Answer on page 348

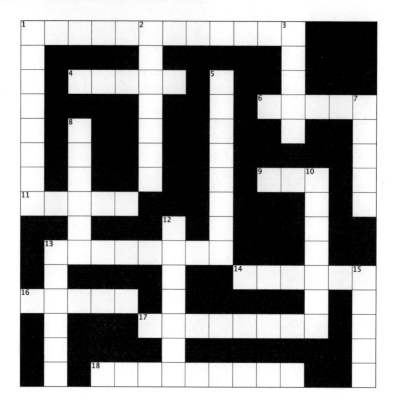

ACROSS

1. 1993 film for which Hanks won an Oscar
4. With 10-Down, romcom involving AOL
6. 'Saving Mr. _____,' 2013 film starring Hanks as Walt Disney
9. 1988 film in which David Moscow plays Young Josh
11. 2016 drama/disaster film
13. Film franchise in which Hanks voices Sheriff Woody
14. 1984 romcom with Daryl Hannah
16. 'The _____ Mile' (1999)
17. With 'The,' 2004 film set in an airport
18. '_____ You Do!', 1996 film which Hanks also directed

DOWN

1. 'Captain _____' (2013)
2. 'The _____ Code,' 2006 film in which Hanks plays Robert Langdon
3. 'Cloud _____,' 2012 scifi film
5. 2000 film in which Hanks's most wrenching line is 'Wilson!'
7. 'Bridge of _____,' 2015 Cold War thriller
8. 1995 space docudrama
10. See 4-Across
12. Role for which Tom won his 1994 Oscar
13. '_____ and [15-Down],' buddy cop film
15. See 13-Down

Answer on page 348

ACROSS

1. Main stem of a tree
5. It may be weeping
7. Sleeping spot in a tree
8. Its wood makes baseball bats
10. '...under his own vine and _____ tree'
11. They are smaller than boughs, bigger than twigs
13. Dutch _____ disease
14. How a tree stays anchored
17. Tree you might find on the beach
18. Coniferous tree
19. Wood used in boatbuilding

DOWN

1. Secret hideaway
2. Tree that sounds like a pronoun
3. It might be made from a tire
4. A grove of fruit trees
6. Foliage
9. Its fruit is a main ingredient in Nutella
12. Home in a tree
15. Its branches are a sign of peace
16. A leafy tree creates this

Answer on page 348

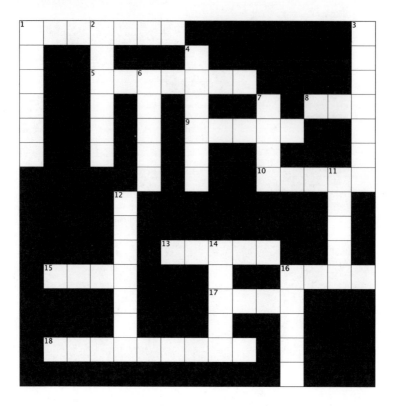

ACROSS
1. This fruit has milk inside
5. Alligator pear
8. Fruit used in pudding in a Christmas song
9. Coat it in caramel at Halloween
10. Its cultivars include Alphonse and Tommy Atkins
13. Yellow citrus fruit
15. Fruit with fuzz
16. Bosc or Bartlett
17. Green citrus fruit
18. Fuzzless variety of 16-Down

DOWN
1. The stem of this fruit is often involved in a party trick
2. Fruit whose name and color are the same
3. Citrus hybrid
4. Yellow fruit that's easily bruised
6. It can be green, black, or Kalamata
7. Jack Horner found one in the nursery rhyme
11. Small tropical fruit with pink flesh
12. Stone fruit often eaten dried
14. Anagram of 13-Across
16. Fruit with fuzz

Answer on page 348

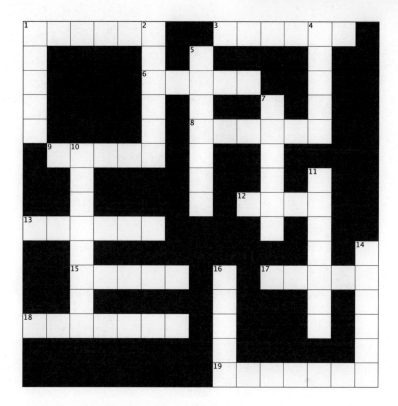

ACROSS
1. Archie or Edith
3. Danny, Stephanie, or Michelle
6. Phil, Vivian, or Carlton
8. Morticia, Wednesday, or Pugsley
9. Walter, Skyler, or Holly
12. Sonny or Cher
13. George, Jane, or Elroy
15. Marcia, Jan, or Cindy
17. Frasier, Niles, or≈Daphne
18. Ward, June, or Wally
19. Peter, Lois, or Meg

DOWN
1. Lucille, George Michael, or Gob
2. Barney, Betty, or Bam-Bam
4. Florida, James, or Michael
5. Mary, Laura, or Charles
7. John-Boy, Olivia, or Jim-Bob
10. Cliff, Clair, or Rudy
11. Tony, Carmela, or Meadow
14. Elyse, Steven, or Alex P.
16. J.R., Bobby, or Jock

Answer on page 349

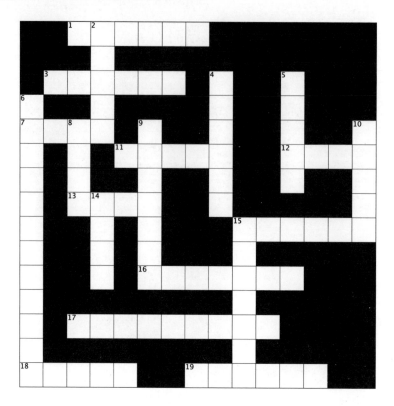

ACROSS
1. Endocrinologist
3. Oncologist
7. Ophthalmologist
11. Hepatologist
12. ENT
13. Dermatologist
15. Neurologist
16. Gastroenterologist
17. General practitioner
18. Cardiologist
19. ENT

DOWN
2. Pulmonologist
4. Gynecologist
5. Phlebologist
6. Psychiatrist
8. ENT
9. Nephrologist
10. Obstetrician
14. Pediatrician
15. Urologist

Note to the solver: *All answers in this puzzle are the body part treated by the type of doctor specified in the clue.*

Answer on page 349

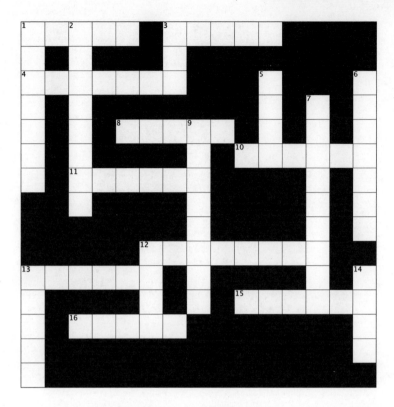

ACROSS

1. Weapon of choice for vampire slayers
3. See 12-Down
4. When vampires come out
8. Where a vampire needs an invitation
10. This allium repels vampires
11. Surname in 12-Across
12. Stephenie Meyer series revolving around Bella and Edward
13. See 14-Down
15. What a vampire can't see himself in
16. A vampire family or group

DOWN

1. 'What We Do in the ____' (TV series with Nadja, Laszlo, and Nandor)
2. Lestat creator
3. A vampire can turn into this creature
5. ____ Lugosi
6. Most notorious vampire
7. This fluid wards off vampires
9. It will burn a vampire's skin
12. With 3-Across, HBO TV series about vampires in Louisiana
13. Inner essences that vampires lack, it's said
14. With 13-Across, author of the most famous vampire novel

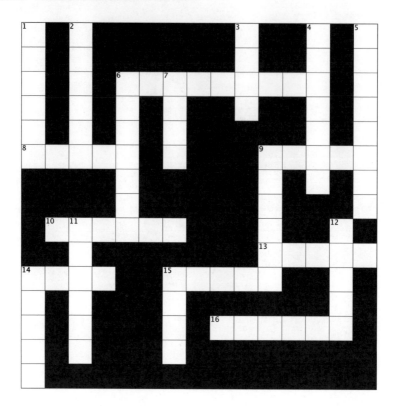

ACROSS

6. 1791–1801, under Adams

8. 1953–1961, under Eisenhower

9. 1841, under Harrison I

10. 2001–2009, under Bush II

13. 1969–1973, under Nixon

14. 1993–2001, under Clinton

15. 2009–2017, under Obama

16. 1989–1993, under Bush I

DOWN

1. 1861–1865, under Lincoln

2. 1869–1873, under Grant

3. 1801–1805, under Jefferson

4. 1977–1981, under Carter

5. 1965–1969, under Johnson II

6. 1865, under Lincoln

7. 1973–1974, under Nixon

9. 1945, under Roosevelt

11. 2021–, under Biden

12. 2017–2021, under Trump

14. 1813–1814, under Madison

15. 1981–1989, under Reagan

Answer on page 349

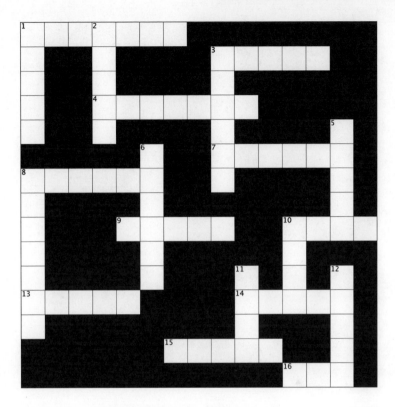

ACROSS

1. City buried in 79 BCE
3. Zip around town on one of these, maybe
4. Italian region famous for art, wine, and landscapes
7. ____ Terre, group of five picturesque towns on the Italian Riviera
8. Sweet treats for a hot day
9. You need a peel and a very hot oven to make one
10. Galileo's birthplace
13. Milan Opera ____
14. Tuscan city with a famous horse race
15. Place to see a famous shroud
16. With white and green, the colors of the Italian flag

DOWN

1. Sauce with basil and pine nuts
2. Orzo, linguine, or orecchiette
3. City with canals
5. With his brother Romulus, fabled to have founded Rome
6. Island off the southern tip of Italy
8. Italian dumplings traditionally made from potatoes
10. Vatican City's most famous resident
11. ____ Spumanti
12. Most famous resident of the Accademia Gallery in Florence

Answer on page 349

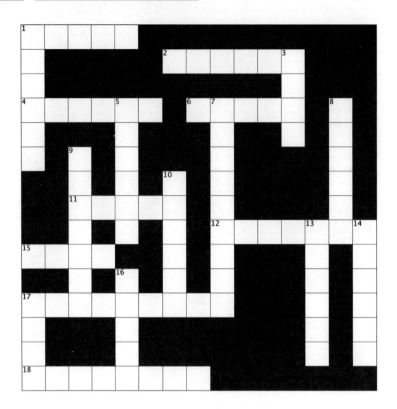

ACROSS
1. Activist Ida B.
2. Jane who founded Hull House
4. With 6-Across, location of America's first women's rights convention
6. See 4-Across
11. With 17-Down, organizer of the Silent Sentinels
12. Pickets
15. See 18-Across
17. British activist Emmeline
18. With 15-Across, early Quaker suffragist

DOWN
1. President Woodrow
3. Clothing item associated with suffragists
5. _____ Chapman Catt
7. Constitutional change
8. Surname of suffragist sisters
9. Elizabeth Cady _____
10. Activist Helen
13. Type of strike
14. Anthony who briefly appeared on a $1 coin
16. Color of the suffrage movement
17. See 11-Across

Answer on page 349

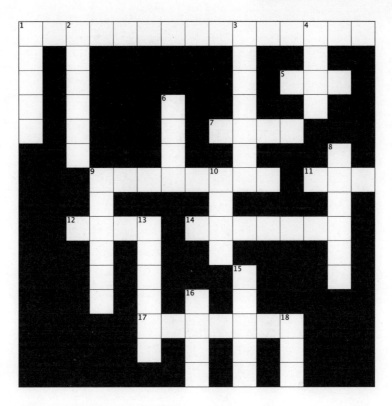

ACROSS

1. Kubrick film with Joker and Pyle (1987)

5. With 6-Down, WWII film clocking in at almost five hours long (1981)

7. 'The ____ Hunter,' film involving Russian roulette (1978)

9. 'Inglourious ____,' quirkily spelled Tarantino film (2009)

11. It can precede 'Horse' (2011) or follow 'Invisible' (2012)

12. '____ with the Wind' (1939)

14. Revolutionary War film with Gibson and Ledger, with 'The' (2000)

17. First in a trilogy of Vietnam war films (1986)

DOWN

1. 'All Quiet on the Western ____' (1930)

2. 'The Hurt ____,' film about a bomb disposal squad in Iraq (2009)

3. Gulf War film that takes its name from a slang term for Marines (2005)

4. Eponymous river in a 1957 film

6. See 5-Across

8. General played by George C. Scott (1969)

9. 'Da 5 ____,' Spike Lee film about Vietnam vets on a mission (2020)

10. Private who needed saving in a 1998 film

13. 1963 film about a POW camp breakout

15. Civil War film about the 54th Massachusetts Infantry Regiment (1989)

16. 'Black ____ Down,' 2001 film about a military raid in Somalia

18. 'Apocalypse ____,' 1979 film loosely based on 'Heart of Darkness'

Answer on page 350

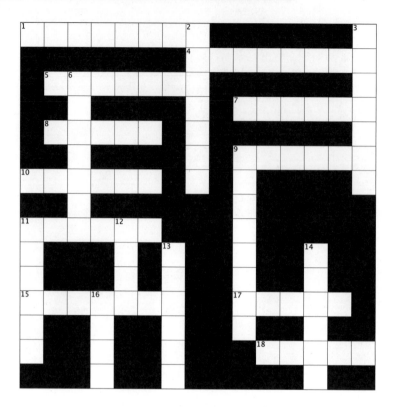

ACROSS

1. He became the world's heavyweight boxing champ in '52
4. Famous pianist and entertainer
5. Salk, Pasteur, and Corbett have all developed one
7. Cuban leader
8. Organized crime syndicate
9. Illegal payments for radio broadcasts
10. He was elected in '80
11. Star of 'On the Waterfront'
15. Its capital is Beirut
17. Most addictive form of cocaine
18. Thermonuclear weapon

DOWN

2. It was integrated by James Meredith
3. 'On the Road' author
6. Site of the Montgomery bus boycotts
9. Music genre with the Ramones and Bikini Kill
11. City with a noted wall
12. Star of 'Rebel Without a Cause'
13. '59 Best Picture winner
14. Artificial fiber
16. Virus destigmatized by Diana

Answer on page 350

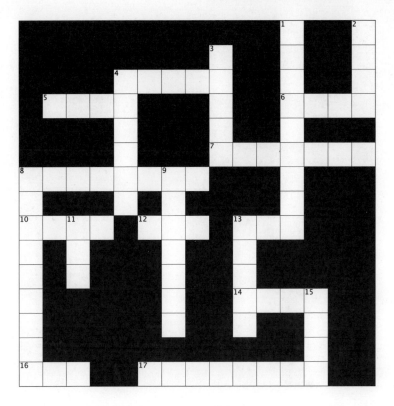

ACROSS

4. Wind _____
5. Chunks of falling ice
6. What a thermometer measures
7. _____ Alley, a Midwestern area prone to extreme weather
8. Degree of moisture in the air
10. '_____, _____, go away'
12. Star that's about eight light-minutes from us
13. Common London weather
14. Frozen precipitation
16. Central part of 8-Down
17. Storm with heavy 14-Across

DOWN

1. Electricity generated during a storm
2. Big blast of 15-Down
3. Sort of rain, sort of snow
4. Cirrus and nimbus
8. Katrina or Andrew, for example
9. Sound that accompanies 1-Down
11. It can form in sheets
13. It'll kill your plants
15. Movement of air

Answer on page 350

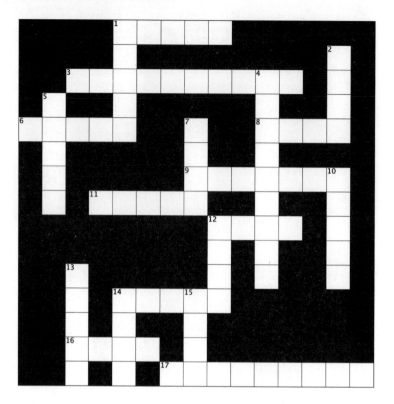

ACROSS

1. A woman getting married

3. One who strews petals

6. A man getting married

8. Traditional wedding dessert

9. Canopy used in Jewish weddings

11. Bridal color, usually

12. A 1-Across might cover her face or hair with one

14. Jewelry that couples exchange

16. '_____ is all you need'

17. British term for a bachelor party

DOWN

1. It's traditionally jumped over in African weddings

2. Guests may throw this at the couple as they depart

4. The post-ceremony party

5. It may have a bustle or a train

7. Material for a 5-Down, maybe

10. Temporary skin staining common in Indian weddings, also known as mehndi

12. Promises the couple makes to each other

13. A wedding processional may come down this

14. What guests are asked to do beforehand

15. It's traditional for a guest to bring one

Answer on page 350

ACROSS

1. She played Dorothy

5. 17-Across, for one

7. 'That's a horse of a different ____!'

8. Em's relationship to Dorothy

9. Mode of transportation for the Wizard

11. 2003 musical based on the film's antagonist

14. Winged animals

15. What the Scarecrow seeks

17. She arrives in a giant bubble

18. '____ and tigers and bears, oh my!'

19. Dorothy's surname

DOWN

2. 'Over the ____'

3. Natural disaster that transports Dorothy to Oz

4. He was played by a Cairn terrier named Terry

6. He rusts when he cries

10. Gemstone that the Wizard's palace is named for

12. Pay no attention to the man behind this

13. '____! The Witch Is Dead'

14. One of many that Dorothy meets upon arriving in Oz

16. Soporific flowers

Answer on page 350

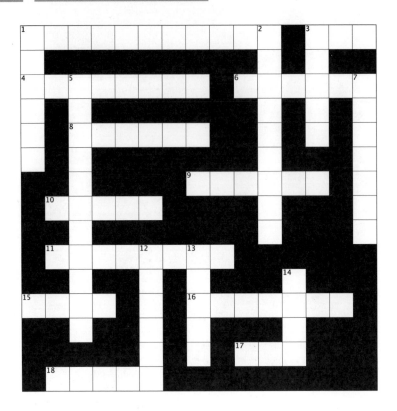

ACROSS

1. 1838 Dickens novel adapted into a 1960 musical
3. 10-Across narrator
4. 'The _____ [8-Across],' Dickens' first novel
6. 'Little _____' (1857)
8. See 4-Across
9. Format in which Dickens published many of his novels
10. '_____ Expectations' (1861)
11. 'Nicholas _____' (1839)
15. 'Is Little _____ dead?'
16. Country where much Dickens literature is set
17. 'The _____ Curiosity Shop' (1841)
18. Gang leader in 1-Across

DOWN

1. 1-Across, 3-Across, or 15-Across
2. 'A Tale of _____' (1859)
3. One of two main settings in 2-Down
5. 'David _____,' Dickens' autobiographical novel
7. Character who says 'God bless us, every one!'
12. The other setting of 2-Down
13. '_____ House' (1853)
14. '_____ Times' (1854)

Answer on page 350

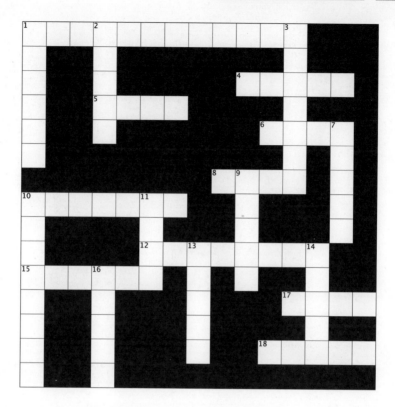

ACROSS

1. Someone with great aim
4. Wild West greeting
5. Bill with a namesake Wyoming town
6. Buffalo _____
8. Calamity _____
10. Butch _____
12. Pests or nuisances
15. Job tending cattle
17. Gold _____
18. Animal hunted to near-extinction

DOWN

1. Establishment with swinging doors, maybe
2. Large farm where cattle are raised
3. Animal skin that hasn't been tanned
7. Rope for restraining cattle
9. _____ Oakley
10. Folk hero and frontiersman
11. First name of 10-Down
13. Not my first _____
14. They're worn on boots
16. _____ the Kid

Answer on page 351

ACROSS

1. Pooh's smartest friend
3. Burrowing creature
5. Creatures that Pooh sees in nightmares
10. See 4-Down
12. Appropriately, Tigger is this sort of animal
14. Pooh's gloomy friend
15. Pooh's house
16. President who's often lampooned with an image of Pooh
18. Kanga's son
19. 'Oh ____!' (9-Down's catchphrase)

DOWN

2. Creatures that Pooh sees in nightmares
4. With 10-Across, Pooh's human friend
6. Author A. A.
7. ____ Wood, home to Pooh and his friends
8. Pooh's favorite food
9. Best friend of Pooh
11. 14-Across's species
13. Character based not on a stuffed plaything but on a live animal
15. 'The ____ of Pooh'
17. Color of Pooh's shirt

Answer on page 351

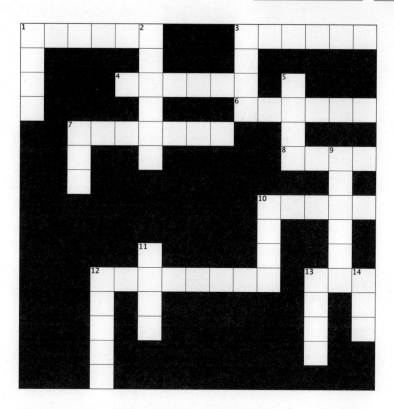

ACROSS
1. Hand protectors
3. Wintertime tool
4. Drop below 32 degrees Fahrenheit
6. Gray and cold
7. Bedding material in the winter, maybe
8. Gradually warm
10. Post-snowball fight beverage
12. Strong winter storm
13. Winter activity

DOWN
1. Sky color in winter, maybe
2. Season to look forward to
3. Toboggan
5. You'll want to have this on in your house
7. Winter malady
9. Waterproof jacket
10. Winter woe
11. Something built to stay warm
12. Foot protectors
13. Frozen precipitation
14. Salt target

Answer on page 351

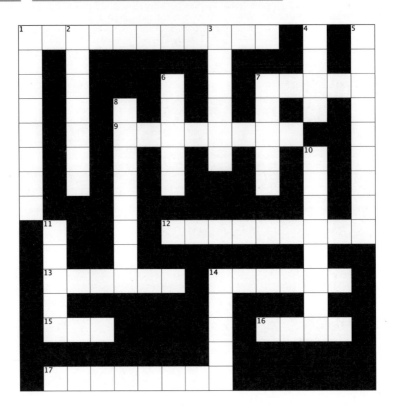

ACROSS

1. 2019 retelling of an 1868 novel
7. '____ is Burning'
9. '____ Psycho'
12. What you might be in Seattle
13. See 4-Down
14. '____ Woman,' superhero film
15. She directed David and Carmen in 11-Down
16. '____ in Translation'
17. 'A League of ____'

DOWN

1. 2017 film that opens with Saoirse Ronan throwing herself from a moving car
2. '____ Are All Right'
3. With 'The,' film with Neo and Trinity
4. With 13-Across, first Best Picture directed by a woman
5. '____ at Ridgemont High'
6. She directed Emma, Timothy, and Laura in 1-Across
7. With 'The,' film for which Anna Paquin won an Oscar at 11 years old
8. Horror film in which the antagonist wears a top hat
10. 1995 film retelling of a Jane Austen novel
11. 2014 historical drama
14. 'Promising Young ____,' #MeToo thriller/romcom

Answer on page 351

ACROSS

1. Kendrick, Gunn, or Wintour
2. Harlow, Seberg, or Smart
4. Breslin, Adams, or Disney
5. Reynolds, Harry, or Gibson
7. Fitzgerald, Baker, or Emhoff
10. Dern, Bush, or Linney
12. Pickford, Berry, or Steenburgen
13. Whitman, March, or Ryan
14. Hunt, Mirren, or Keller
15. Washington, Stewart, or Graham
17. Duke, Ridley, or Duck

DOWN

1. Peet, Bynes, or Gorman
2. Roberts, Louis-Dreyfus, or Child
3. Kerrigan, Pelosi, or Cartwright
6. Banks, McGovern, or Taylor
7. Bronte, Blunt, or Mortimer
8. Walters, Tandy, or Alba
9. Waters, Munro, or Cooper
11. McAdams, Weisz, or Maddow
16. Adams, Carter, or Heckerling

Answer on page 351

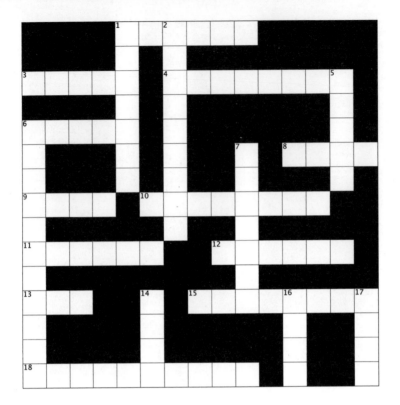

ACROSS

1. Insufferable know-it-all
3. Religious
4. Kids' hopping game
6. Shoddy or inferior
8. Things that go _____ in the night
9. Break of day
10. Insect, or 2017 film starring Saoirse Ronan
11. 'I Wandered _____ as a Cloud'
12. Untamed
13. Poem of praise
15. Dreadfully cold
18. Where the basement is

DOWN

1. Thumbtack
2. Black-and-white firehouse dog
5. Dust and dirt
6. Unfeeling
7. Accept or support
14. You might need one if you're stuck on one of these answers
16. Madcap, wild
17. Pregnant people often have one of these

Answer on page 351

ACROSS
1. Kenya
5. South Korea
7. Indonesia
9. South Africa (one of three)
10. Peru
13. Belarus
14. Egypt
16. Poland
17. Japan
18. Norway

DOWN
2. China
3. Spain
4. Bulgaria
6. Vietnam
8. Afghanistan
9. Venezuela
11. Ghana
12. Latvia
13. Russia
15. France

Answer on page 352

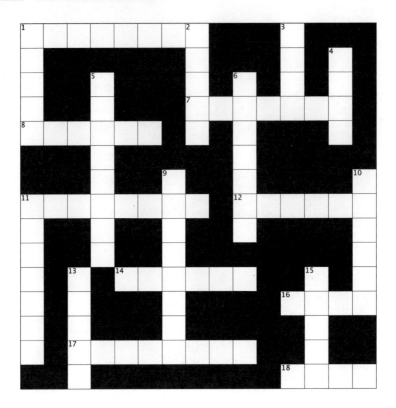

ACROSS

1. Poetic-sounding Irish town
7. Canadian city where the Expos used to play
8. City with a famous opera house
11. Capital of Hungary
12. Pakistan's second-largest city
14. Italian city with canals
16. South Sudan's capital
17. In Maori, it's called Tamaki Makaurau
18. Peruvian city that shares its name (but not its pronunciation) with a bean

DOWN

1. Biggest city in Nigeria
2. The cultural capital of Japan
3. Beethoven's birthplace
4. French city known for its cuisine
5. Hometown of Pablo Neruda
6. Libyan capital
9. Home to the Hagia Sophia
10. Global hub for diplomacy and banking
11. Capital of Iraq
13. World's highest city
15. Middle Eastern city known for shopping and nightlife

Answer on page 352

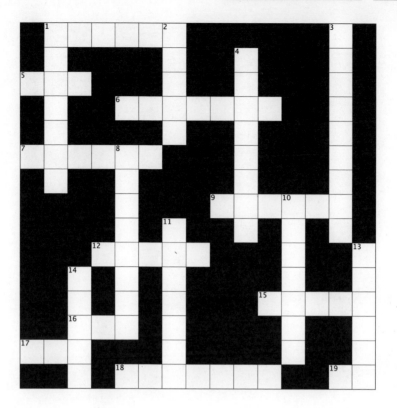

ACROSS

1. Jacinda of New Zealand
5. Theresa of the UK
6. Ellen Johnson of Liberia
7. Willy of Germany
9. Angela of Germany
12. Vladimir of Russia (b. 1952)
15. Vladimir of Russia (b. 1870)
16. Shinzo of Japan
17. Ki-moon of South Korea
18. Nelson of South Africa
19. Jinping of China

DOWN

1. Kemal of Turkey
2. Jawaharlal of India
3. Winston of the UK
4. Margaret of the UK
8. Charles of France
10. John F. of the USA
11. Abraham of the USA
13. Mahatma of India
14. U of Burma

Answer on page 352

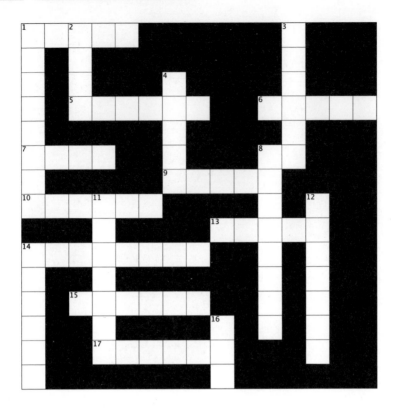

ACROSS

1. Its three principal gods are Brahma, Vishnu, and Shiva
5. Christian resurrection holiday
6. Religion that celebrates Samhain and Beltane
7. Islamic worship leader
8. In 1-Across, sacred chant
9. Ritual feast in Judaism
10. Muslim house of worship
13. Middle Eastern religion established by Baha'u'llah
14. Belief system associated with Anton LaVey
15. Jewish denomination that emphasizes the evolving nature of the faith
17. One of two main branches of Islam

DOWN

1. Nontheistic movement centered on value inherent in all people
2. Growing response to the question, 'What religion are you?'
3. Chinese philosophy
4. In Christianity, the son of God
8. Religious term for strict adherence to principles of faith
11. They're also known as Friends
12. Transcendent state in Buddhism
14. Practitioners of this religion might have a household shrine
16. Buddhist sect

Answer on page 352

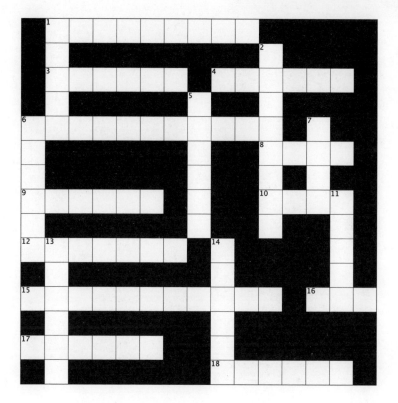

ACROSS
1. Wartime president
3. Brutal Soviet leader
4. Machine used to encode Nazi communications
6. Hawaii base bombed in 1941
8. Germany, Italy, and Japan
9. USA, the UK, the Soviet Union, and others
10. June 6, 1944
12. Wartime evacuation recreated in a 2017 film
15. Soldiers who used Native American language to communicate in code
16. _____ Man, bomb code name
17. Type of bombs dropped on Hiroshima and Nagasaki
18. Major target of the Blitz

DOWN
1. Fictional riveter
2. Type of attacks carried out by planes
5. Country occupied by Germany
6. First country invaded by Germany
7. Iwo _____
11. Conference held in 1945 to discuss postwar strategy
13. German submarines
14. Holocaust survivor Elie

Answer on page 352

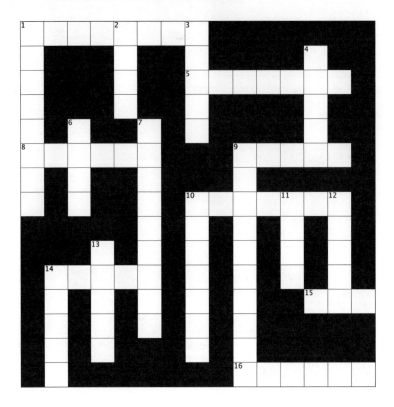

ACROSS

1. 2000 Spinelli novel about nonconformity

5. 'A _____ in Time' (1962)

8. 'The _____ [10-Across],' Pullman novel that's first in a series of three

9. Its protagonist is Stanley Yelnats

10. See 8-Across

14. 'The _____ in Our Stars' (2012)

15. 'My Louisiana _____' (1998)

16. Green _____, home to Marilla and Matthew

DOWN

1. J.D. who wrote 'The Catcher in the Rye'

2. 'The Hate U _____,' 2017 novel about police brutality

3. 'The Giver' author

4. Author of 'Forever' and 'Blubber'

6. With 7-Down, 'Cinderella' retelling

7. See 6-Down

9. The first of seven novels in the Tillerman Cycle

10. 'The Hunger Games' author

11. Title character in books featuring 16-Across

12. 1999 novel about sexual assault and trauma

13. Marcus who wrote 'The Book Thief'

14. 'Lord of the _____' (1954)

Answer on page 352

ANSWERS

1. CHILDREN'S TOYS

AMERICANGIRL LIT
SLINKY YOYO
GAMEBOY
TROLLS
PLAYDOH KIDS
POKEMON JENGA
HEAD
HOTWHEELS
POLLYPOCKET

2. 2010s SLANG

THIRSTY LIT
THROW
MOOD
EXTRA FLEX
DEAD
FINST SLAPS
STAN SALTY
BAE KAREN

3. 2021 BEST PICTURE OSCAR NOMINEES

PROMISING
SEVEN
MINARI
FATHER
MANK META
NOMADLAND
ASL
FER ZHAO
FINCHER

4. A CUP OF JOE

STARBUCKS DECAF
LATTE
POUROVER
ROAST ICED
JAVA MOCHA
FLATWHITE
BLACK

5. A DAY AT THE RENAISSANCE FAIRE

FALCON
MEAD
JOUSTING
DRAGONS
KINGS
QUEEN
WIZARD
KNAVE MUSIC
MUDWRESTLING

6. A GALAXY FAR, FAR AWAY

FORCE
YODA
SKYWALKER
HAN
JEDI DROIDS
LEIA SOL
WOKS ENDOR
HOTH FINN

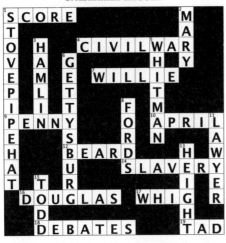

13. ACTRESSES BY LAST NAME

WASHINGTON
FISHER
THOMPSON BATES
ANDREWS PORTMAN
HATHAWAY
STREEP
OHARA
MOSS
NEWTON

14. AFTERNOON TEA

MILK CHAMOMILE
MATCHA
ICED
KOMBUCHA WATER
TURKEY
HERBAL
OOLONG
EARL GREY
INFUSER
STEEPING
COSY
GREEN

15. AHOY THERE!

STARBOARD
TACK
BRIG
HELM
FATHOM
SOS
PORT ANCHOR
GALLEY
GANGWAY
RUDDER

16. ALASKA AND HAWAII

ANCHORAGE
INUIT
ALEUT
JUNEAU
HILO
SITKA
SPAM OBAMA
LEI
KAMEHAMEHA

17. ALICE IN WONDERLAND

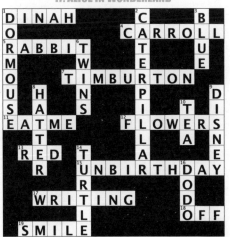

DINAH
CARROLL
RABBIT
TIMBURTON
EATME FLOWERS
RED
UNBIRTHDAY
WRITING
OFF
SMILE

18. AMERICAN FOOTBALL

HAILMARY
REF
SAFETY TACKLE
SACK CUP
AUDIBLE
KICKER
HELMET
BLITZ
RUSH
TOUCHDOWN
SUPERBOWL

19. AMERICAN LANDMARKS

Across and down grid filled with:
FAITHFUL, BELL, MCHENRY, KITTY, TIMESSQUARE, SIGN, ALAMO, OLE, CRAZYHORSE, FREEDOM, ROCKETY, LINCOLN, MYSTIC, TRAIL, ROBUNBURG, MCCALLTRA, MONUMENT

20. ANIMALS OF AFRICA

CROCODILE, BUSHBABY, PANGOLIN, ASP, BABOON, GIRAFFE, RHINO, ELEPHANTS, SNAKE, CHEETAH, HYENA, HIPP, MAN, LION, FROG, ORYX

21. ANIMATED MOVIES

ANASTASIA, TOTORO, SHREK, SPIRITEDAWAY, TIME, ICE, PRINCE, CORALINE, TOASTER, PAGEMASTER, BALTO, STRONG, HEAVEN, TRIVALLY

22. ARRESTED DEVELOPMENT

MAEBY, STEVE, MARTA, TOBIAS, KITTY, ALIA, STAIR, TOUCHING, BANANASTAND, CAR, ANNUSVEAL, BUSTER, ARMY

23. ARTISTS BY ART

HOPPER, CASSATT, MONET, KLIMT, ROCKWELL, MAGRITTE, SEURAT, MAPPLETHORPE, HARING, PICASSO, BANKSY, DUCHAMP

24. AT THE BEACH

FISHING, UMBRELLA, FRISBEE, SHELLS, SUN, CRAB, WAVES, SAIL, ROCKS, HAT, OCEAN, KITE, SURFING, SANDCASTLE, BOARDWALK, SWIMMING

25. AT THE CASINO

26. AT THE DELI

27. AT THE GYM

28. AT THE OFFICE

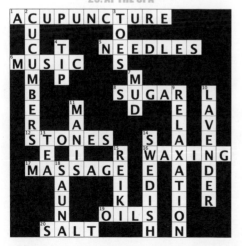

29. AT THE SPA

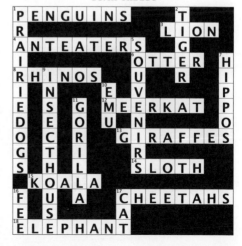

30. AT THE ZOO

31. AUTOMAKERS

32. AUTUMN

33. BABY ANIMALS

34. BACK TO TITANIC

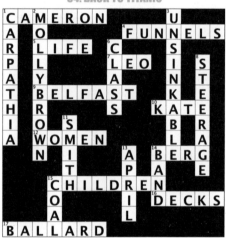

35. BANNED AND CHALLENGED BOOKS

36. BARACK OBAMA

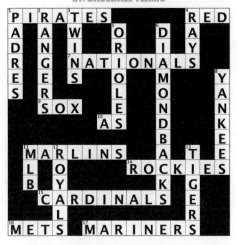

43. BEST PICTURE WINNERS

44. BLACK WRITERS

45. BOARD GAMES

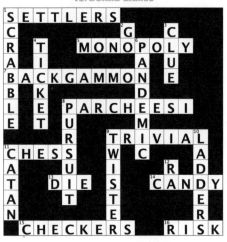

46. BOB MARLEY

47. BODIES OF WATER

48. BOND...JAMES BOND

49. BOY BANDS

50. BREAKING BAD

51. BRINGING UP BABY

52. BUON APPETITO!

53. BUSY AS A BEE

54. CAMPING AND HIKING

55. CAN YOU TELL ME HOW TO GET TO SESAME STREET?

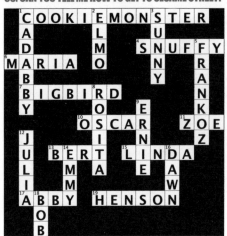

56. CAT FANCY

57. CEREAL KILLER

58. CHEERS!

59. CHILDREN OF CELEBRITIES

60. CHINA

61. CHI-TOWN

LAKESHOREDRIVE · COOK · OHARE · SEARS · WINDY · BEAN · CLOUDGATE · HYDE · FIELD · SOX · BEARS · MICHIGAN · WHITE · CUBS · DEEPDISH · FERRIS · FIRE · HOME

62. CHRISTMAS MOVIES

LOVEACTUALLY · LIFE · CHARLIE · HOME · MUPPET · SANTA · RUDOLPH · NIGHTMARE · BROWN · MIRACLE · HAROLD · JINGLE

63. CIRCUS CIRCUS

CIRQUEDUSOLEIL · CAGE · BIGAPPLE · SIDESHOW · RINGMASTER · MIME · UNICYCLE · HORSE · TIGER · ACROBATS · LIONTAMER · BARNUM · TENT · TRAPEZE

64. CIVIL RIGHTS IN AMERICA

JIMCROW · BLM · HAMPTON · EMMETT · RUSTIN · NAACP · BROWN · LEWIS · SELMA · KING · SITIN · SUNDAY

65. CLASSIC HOLLYWOOD ACTORS

GUINNESS · HEPBURN · LEIGH · WAYNE · KELLY · BURTON · BRANDO · CLIFT · DAY · REYNOLDS · GABLE · STEWART · MONROE · HAYWORTH · TAYLOR · BACALL · NOVAK · BOGART

66. COME FLY WITH ME

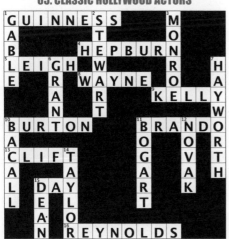

TURBULENCE · CHECK · BAGGAGE · TERMINAL · LAYOVER · DRINKS · GATE · JETWAY · EXIT · SAFETY · TAKEOFF · DEPARTURE · SEATBELT · RUNWAY · TICKET · AISLE

67. COMEDY HOUR

Across/Down answers shown in grid:
CROSS, GAFFIGAN, OLIVER, DAVID, GADSBY, CARLIN, OSWALT, PRYOR, CHAPPELLE, WONG, NOTARO, HEDBERG, HICKS, HOHNG, COOK, REEARIL, JOON, CENA, FRYY

68. CRUISIN'

CARNIVAL, BUFFET, THEATER, ISLAND, DECKS, BALCONY, CAPTAIN, EMBARK, DISNEY, PORT, BOOZE, LIFE, CASINO, TOURISTS, BOAT, STATEROOM, POOL, RIGGING, BENDER, TAN

69. CRYPTOZOOLOGY

BIGFOOT, LOCH, FAKE, CHUPACABRA, TOY, YETI, NESS, MOTHMAN, SEA, CHESSIE, VIDEO, WILDMAN, FOOTPRINTS, APE, HOAX, SASQUATCH, MONSTER, CRYPTID, HORN

70. DEATH BY CHOCOLATE

MILKSHAKE, TEMPERING, NIB, SYRUP, COCOA, BUTTER, WHITE, BAKING, SUGAR, CACAO, SPRINKLES, MAYANS, GANACHE, MOLD, HERSHEY, DARK

71. DESERT STORM

SAHARA, CANYON, COYOTE, HOWL, GOBI, JAV, CACTUS, SNAKE, DUNES, HEAT, DRY, SCORPION, SAGUARO, ANTARCTICA, ARID, MOJAVE, RAIN

72. DINOSAUR WORLD

PREDATOR, LIZARD, FOOTPRINTS, NECK, BIRDS, METEOR, SKELETON, TREX, HORN, PALEONTOLOGIST, RAPTOR, EXTINCT, FOSSIL, SPINES, PROLITE, BONE, PARK, TOOTH

73. DISNEY CHARACTERS

74. DON'T BUG ME

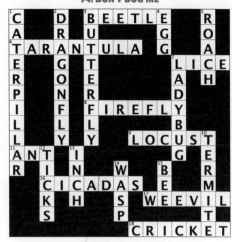

75. DOWN UNDER

76. DRIVE MY CAR

77. DYSTOPIAS

78. EAT YOUR VEGETABLES

79. ELVIS PRESLEY

80. EPONYMOUS FOODS

81. EXTINCT ANIMALS

82. FAMOUS BASEBALL PLAYERS

83. FAMOUS CHEFS

84. FAMOUS OLYMPIANS

85. FARMERS' MARKET

86. FAST FOOD NATION

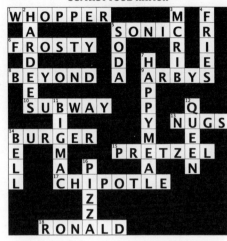

87. FAUNA DOWN UNDER

88. FICTIONAL PETS BY OWNER

89. FILM DIRECTORS

90. FILMS OF THE 1980S

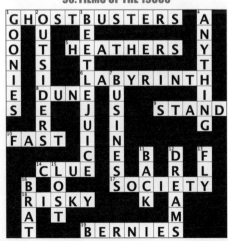

91. FOLK HORROR

92. FOODS AROUND THE WORLD

93. F-WORDS

94. GAME OF THRONES

95. GAME SHOWS

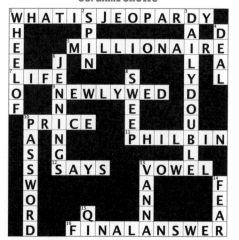

96. GANGSTER CINEMA

97. GEMSTONES

98. GIRL GROUPS

99. GIVE MY REGARDS TO BROADWAY

100. GOING NUTS

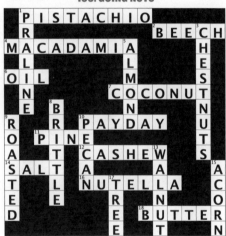

101. GOING TO THE DOGS

102. INVENTED BY ACCIDENT

103. GONE FISHIN'

104. GOOD NIGHT, SLEEP TIGHT

105. GRAB A SLICE

106. GREEK MYTHOLOGY

107. GRIN AND BEAR IT

108. GROUPS OF ANIMALS

109. GYMNASTICS

110. HALLOWEEN NIGHT

111. HAPPY THANKSGIVING!

112. HATS OFF

113. HERBS AND SPICES

114. HIGH SCHOOL MOVIES AND TV

115. HIGH SCHOOL READING LIST

116. HISTORIC FIRSTS

117. HORNS AND WOODWINDS

118. I FEEL THE EARTH MOVE

119. I NEED A HERO

120. IMAGINARY PLACES

121. IN LIVING COLOR

CHROME · WHITE · ONE · PRIMARY · PURPLE · SECONDARY · PINK · COLOR · ORANGE · SPECTRUM · RED · DENIM · WHEEL · TAN · LIGHT · GREEN · BLUE · BONE · YELLOW

122. IN THE GARDEN

FLOWERS · SHRUBS · FERTILIZER · SQUIRREL · SHOVEL · PERENNIALS · HELBER · WEEDS · ANNUAL · MOWER · RAKE · MULCH · WATERINGCAN · WHEELBARROW · WORMS · HERB · THORNS · ROSES · POTS · ARIL · SEEDS

123. IN THE JEWELRY BOX

GEM · BRACELET · CLASP · CHAIN · EARRINGS · LINKS · PACE · NECKLACE · RINGS · PENDANT · DOGTAGS · SIGNET · CLIP · STUD · BANGLES · SILVER · CUFF · AMULET · BROOCH · HOOP · FRIENDSHIP

124. IN THE KITCHEN

MICROWAVE · DISHWASHER · STOVE · FREEZER · COOKBOOKS · OVEN · COUNTER · BOWL · TAP · SINK · FRIDGE · ICE · SPATULA · JAR · MITT · LIST · TOASTER · MIXER · RAGS · TRAY · CRISPER

125. IN THE PINK

CHERRYBLOSSOMS · COTTON · SALMON · TAIL · SHRIMP · FIT · CANDY · LYCHEE · TONGUE · FLAMINGO · ADILLAC · TS · PIG · ROSE · PANTHER · LIPPER · SLIP · RADISH · SALT · RIBBONS · MEAT

126. IN THE RAINFOREST

JAGUAR · FUNGI · JUNGLE · GORILLA · RAIN · FROG · GREEN · SNAKE · LOG · FALL · MOSS · SLOTH · EEL · CHIMP · AMAZON · PIRANHA · CANOPY · PARROT · BOA · MOSQUITO · VINE

127. INDIA

BOLLYWOOD, RICE, SHIVA, NEW DELHI, SARI, GANDHI, MAHAL, YOGA, CRICKET, MUMBAI, JAIPUR, IDLI

128. INDIAN CUISINE

MASSAMAN, SOUP, SAMOSA, PANEER, CURRY, LASSI, KHEER, BIRYANI, DAL, MANGO, CHUTNEY, ONION, RICE, VINDALOO

129. INTERNATIONAL LANDMARKS

INCAS, OPERA HOUSE, ROME, SIGN, EIFFEL, TAJ, ANGOR, EASTER, GOLDEN, ULURU

130. ISLAND HOPPING

MAJORCA, BERMUDA, AUSTRALIA, IRE, SRI LANKA, SICILY, FIJI, HAITI, BALI, HAWAII, BAFFIN

131. IT'S RAINING ON PROM NIGHT

GO STAG, DINNER, LIMOUSINE, KING AND QUEEN, PUNCH, CORSAGE, CURFEW, UPDO, TEACHERS

132. IT'S THE MUPPET SHOW!

CHRISTMAS, BUNSEN, GONZO, RATT, BEAKER, ISLAND, ROWLF, ELECTRIC, CAP, MAYHEM

324

133. JAPAN

134. JOHN HUGHES FILMS

135. JUST DESSERTS

136. JUST LIKE MAGIC

137. KIDDIE TV

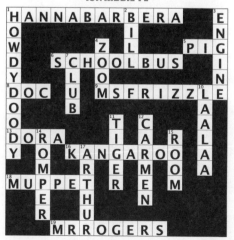

138. LAUNDRY DAY

139. LET'S GET BRUNCH

140. LET'S GET SUSHI

141. LET'S GO BOWLING

142. LET'S GO TO FLORIDA

143. LET'S GRAB A BEER

144. LET'S PLAY CHESS

145. LET'S PLAY MONOPOLY

CAR
COMMUNITY
RENT
PARK
ELECTRIC
MF
UNCLE
BOARDWALK
WATER
LUXURY
ORANGE
CHANCE
VENTNOR
CHEST
SCOTTIE
DEEDS
PARKING

146. LEWIS AND CLARK

PACIFIC
PURCHASE
LOUIS
GID
YORK
DOG
SHOSHONE
SEAMAN
MERIWETHER
JEFFERSON
LAKOTA
OREGON
FRANCE
BUFFALO
MY
LOUISIANA
FORT
ONE

147. LGBTQ+ FILMS

BROKEBACK
BIRDCAGE
MOONLIGHT
DESERT
M
L
CHEERLEADER
FOO
LOVE
FAVOURITE
VACATION
ANGRY
CAROL
MAMA
KISSING
GAME
GIRL
INCH
BLUE

148. LGBTQ+ HISTORY

ACTUP
JOHNSON
SOCIETY
IM
FLAG
ELLEN
LARAMIE
RUSTIN
PINK
TURING
KINSEY
WINDSOR
BOSTON
PRIDE
STONEWALL

149. LOONEY TUNES

THATSALLFOLKS
TWEETY
BLANC
WILEE
TEXAVERY
BUGS
WAC
YOSEMITESAM
FUDD
TAZ
PORKY
DAFFYDUCK
MARS
CARROT
PEPELEPEW

150. MAKE ME OVER

POWDER
PUFF
SEPHORA
PRIMER
FOUNDATION
MAC
LIPSTICK
CONCEAL
SPF
GLOSS
ACNE
PENCIL
MASCARA
BLUSH
BRUSH
BRONZER

151. MAKIN' BREAD

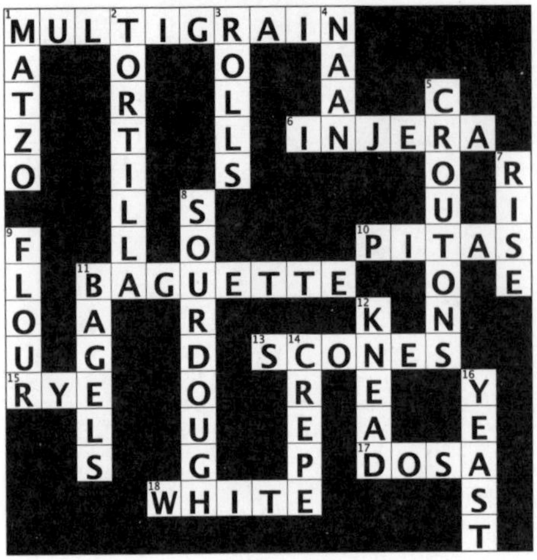
1 MULTIGRAIN
6 INJERA
10 PITAS
11 BAGUETTE
13 SCONES
15 RYE
17 DOSA
18 WHITE
1 MATZO
2 TORTILLA
3 ROLLS
4 NAAN
5 CROUTONS
7 RISE
8 SOURDOUGH
9 FLOUR
11 BAGELS
12 KNEAD
14 CREPE
16 YEAST

152. MARINE MAMMALS

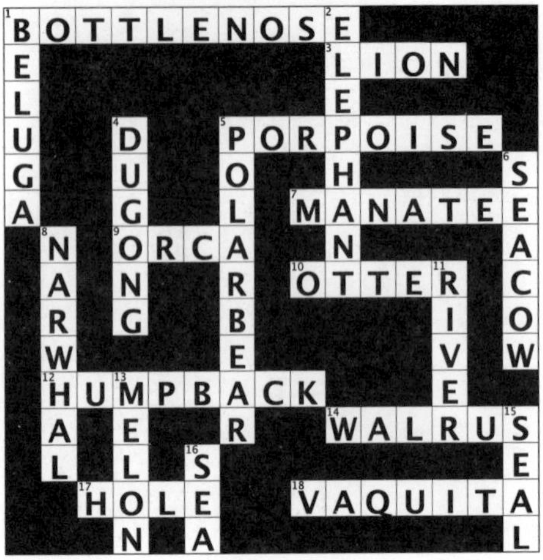
1 BOTTLENOSE
3 LION
5 PORPOISE
7 MANATEE
9 ORCA
10 OTTER
12 HUMPBACK
14 WALRUS
17 HOLE
18 VAQUITA
1 BELUGA
2 ELEPHANT
4 DUGONG
5 POLARBEAR
6 SEACOW
8 NARWHAL
11 RIVER
13 MELON
16 SEA
15 SEAL

153. MARVEL MOVIES

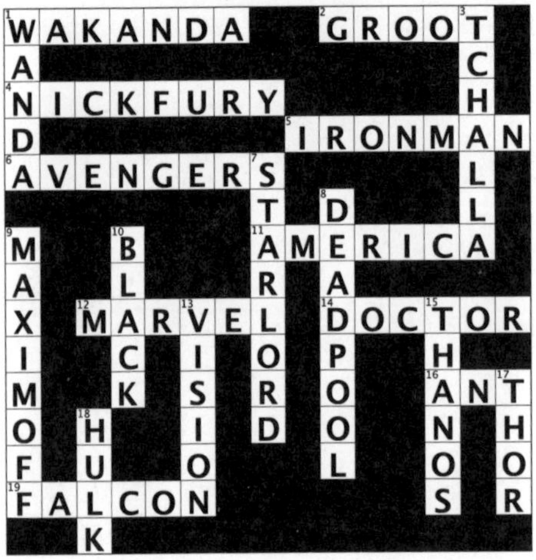
1 WAKANDA
2 GROOT
4 NICKFURY
5 IRONMAN
6 AVENGERS
11 AMERICA
12 MARVEL
14 DOCTOR
16 ANT
19 FALCON
1 WANDA
3 TCHALLA
7 STARLORD
8 DEADPOOL
9 MAXIMOFF
10 BLACK
13 VISION
15 THANOS
17 THOR
18 HULK

154. MEN'S NAMES

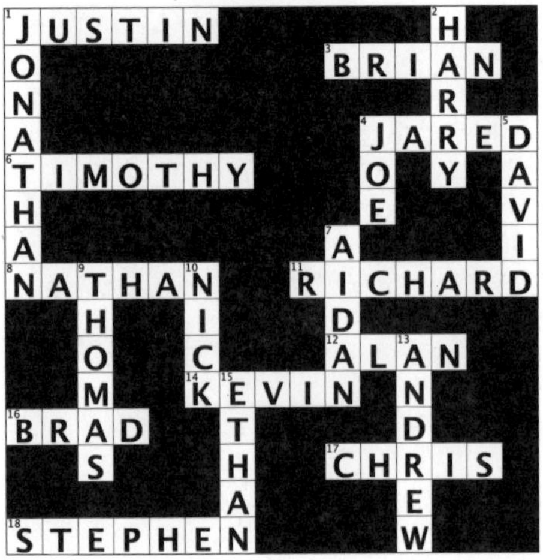
1 JUSTIN
3 BRIAN
4 JARED
6 TIMOTHY
8 NATHAN
11 RICHARD
12 ALAN
14 KEVIN
16 BRAD
17 CHRIS
18 STEPHEN
1 JONATHAN
2 HARRY
4 JOE
5 DAVID
7 AIDAN
9 THOMAS
10 NICK
13 ANDREW
15 ETHAN

155. MERRY CHRISTMAS!

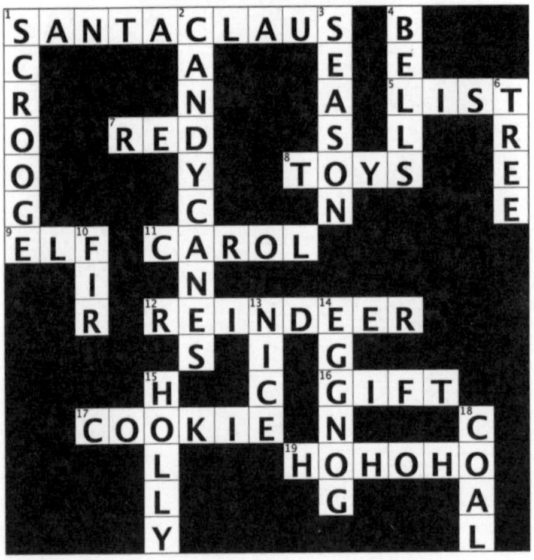
1 SANTACLAUS
5 LIST
7 RED
8 TOYS
9 ELF
11 CAROL
12 REINDEER
16 GIFT
17 COOKIE
19 HOHOHO
1 SCROOGE
2 CANDYCANES
3 SEASON
4 BELLS
6 TREE
10 FIR
13 ICICLE
14 EGGNOG
15 HOLLY
18 COAL

156. MONEY, MONEY, MONEY

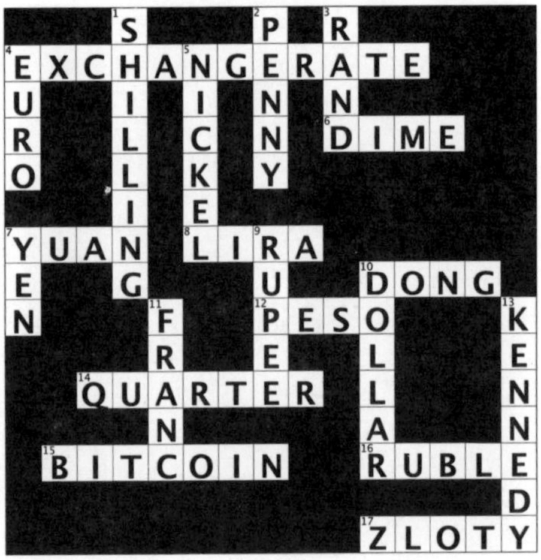
4 EXCHANGERATE
6 DIME
7 YUAN
8 LIRA
10 DONG
12 PESO
14 QUARTER
15 BITCOIN
16 RUBLE
17 ZLOTY
1 SHILLING
2 PENNY
3 RAND
4 EURO
5 NICKEL
7 YEN
9 RUPEE
10 DOLLAR
11 FRANC
13 KENNEDY

157. MOUNT EVEREST

158. MOVIE MUSICALS

159. MOVIE VILLAINS

160. MOVIES BASED ON BOOKS

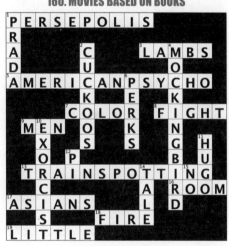

161. MOVIES BY QUOTE

162. NATIONAL PARKS

163. NBA TEAMS

KNICKS W
PACERS IZARD
SUNS LIPPERS
SIXERS NE
HORNETS CELTICS
HEAT NUGGETS MAV
RAPTORS BUCKS BULL
CAVALIERS LAKERS

164. NEW ORLEANS

BEIGNETS VODO
BAYOU
LOUIS MONDE
BEADS OYSTERS
TAROT
GUMBO GRAS YAT
ZYDECO

165. NOTED LGBTQ+ CELEBS

SONTAG
BUTTIGIEG
WILDE
LILNASX
RUPAUL
MILK
PAGE
COOPER
MADDOW REED

166. NOW WE'RE COOKING

BROIL
GAS BLANCH FONDUE
STEW
SIMMER SAUTE
MICROWAVE TANDOOR
BRAISE
OVEN
FRY

167. OH, BABY!

CSECTION
MIDWIFE
DOULA WOMB
HEAD
TWIN
LABOR ICE
NURSERY EGGS
CRAMPS

168. OLYMPIC CITIES

LONDON MOSCOW
LAKEPLACID
SEOUL ROME MELBOURNE
ATLANTA RIO STLOUI
SOCHI
BERLIN
ATHENS
HELSINKI

169. ON THE FARM

SCARECROW, SOWS, COWS, OATS, SILO, SOIL, ROOST, GOATS, LAMBS, PIGS, MILKING, HARVEST, HENS, WHEAT, EWES, BARN, EGGS, GRAINS, KIDS

170. ON THE GRIDIRON

FOOTBALL TEAM, FALCONS, BILLS, LIONS, NFL, GIANTS, EAGLES, TITANS, CARDINALS, SAINTS, SEAHAWKS, STEELERS, TEXANS, RAVENS, COLTS, BEARS, BUCS, RAIDERS, JETS, RAMS

171. ONE-HIT WONDERS

MMMBOP, MAMBO, MCFERRIN, MEN, FUNKYTOWN, LOVE, TUBTHUMPING, SOFTCELL, FALCO, VANILLA, NENA, MYSHARONA, AFROMAN, ROBIN, WAIT, DUTCHIE, RAIN, TONI, WHEATUS

172. OUR FEATHERED FRIENDS

CHICK, PIGEON, CUCKOO, EAGLE, CARDINAL, OWL, FINCH, EGGS, FLIGHT, SPARROW, JAY, DUCK, STORK, ROBIN, CROW, ORIOLE, MOLT, NEST

173. OUR SOLAR SYSTEM

MERCURY, GRAVITY, MARS, GIANT, WATER, SATURN, URANUS, EARTH, HOME, JUPITER, NEPTUNE, PLANETS, PLUTO, SUN, ECLIPSE, RED, TRITON, PHOBOS, RINGS

174. PARIS, JE T'AIME

CROISSANT, TOWER, DAME, CATHEDRAL, NOTRE, MUSEUM, MOULIN, MACARONS, AMI, BOUQUETTE, CHAMPAGNE, IRON, ROUGE, MONA, CREPE, BRIE, MARGUERITTE, TRIOMPHE, SEINE, LISA

175. PARKS AND RECREATION

```
P A W N E E          S   M
E         A P R I L   E   O
R   A   G     N   A   B E N
D   F   L   D O N N A   A L
    F   E     I   S     L I
    L   T     A   T     I S
    E   O     N   I     S A
  T O M       A   A
J A M M       D I A N E
E   I         U     T
R I C H       K     I
R   H     M O U S E R A T
Y   A         T   M
    E         A   M
  L I T E R A L L Y
```

176. PASSING FADS

```
P O K E M O N
O     A       S                S
G     C   T B                  K
S     T A M A G O T C H I       I
A     R   E       H I          R
A   P E T       F U A          T
N   N         B Y O           S
G U I T A R H E R O
R     B       B       R I N G
Y     E     Y O Y O C
B E A N I E         K
I   B   L           K
R   B   M       F R I S B E E
D   I   H O O P
S   E   S
```

177. PLAYING PERCUSSION

```
        M A R I M B A
        A     A
T R I A N G L E
        L   T A I K O
M O O N L     C         S
    K I T     A         T
A       J S   S N A R E E
N   H I H A T   C O W B E L L
G       N Y     O     U
G O N G D R U M N     M
    I   L R     G     B
    E       B   O     I
                A
  W A S H B O A R D
```

178. POETS BY POEM

```
S I L V E R S T E I N       A     F
A         P L A T H   G I N S B E R G
P         H     U       H       O
P H O     G O R M A N   I       S
O         H     H   E L I O T   T
B U R N S       E   T   N
L       A       D A N T E     T
A   K E A T S       O   R I C H
K   E           U   N   U   H
E   U           D   D   O
N   P O E   W H I T M A N   A
            S               S
```

179. PORTMANTEAUS

```
    F   B R O N Y   B L O G
    O   R           E     E
    R   E       L I G E R R
B O T O X I T   C O S P L A Y M
A   N   S       A   B   A   A
C   I   T       S   R   D   N
N   G           T   A   O   D
E   H     B         D   R   E
  T W E R K     M
  B     U   S   O
V I T A M I N   I T C O
  O     C   S M O G   D
  P     H       E     L
B I T   O   P O R T M A N T E A U
```

180. POTPOURRI

```
A T W O O D             W
    H       C H E E S E E
P S I       A         A
  T O B L E R O N E   T
  E       E   A       H
  W A T E R F A L L S E
  A   M   E       T   R
L A K E M I L Y   C I C A D A
I   E   L   E   A K   N
N O R A Y   A D Y L   E
D   W       D   E E
S   F R O S T Y G R I E F
A   U               S
Y E L L O W C A R D
```

181. POTPOURRI II

JOHNOLIVER · BLUSH · JAKARTA · KURDS · DAMASCUS · CAVITY · BAM · ASTAIRE · USHER · WINERY · ISHIGURO · SPYCRAFT · GREEK · LIBRARY · DOLL

182. POTPOURRI III

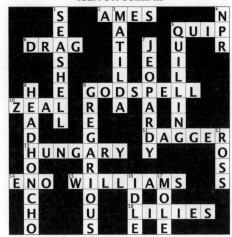

AMES · QUIP · DRAG · SEASHELL · GODSPELL · ZEAL · DAGGER · HUNGARY · ENO · WILLIAMS · LILIES

183. POTPOURRI IV

ROCKYHORROR · BLIMP · PICTURESHOW · FACETIME · CNOTE · BEYHIVE · AMERICA · BALL · ABASH · COUSIN · NERDY · CHEERS

184. POTPOURRI V

BILLS · POKERFACE · BATHE · GREY · OWEN · MATT · UNCANNYVALLEY · ACEOFBASE · TAYLOR · SWIFT

185. POTPOURRI VI

OCCAM · SOUTHPARK · LIMBS · FLORIDA · HELIO · EARLYBIRD · VILE · CHEF · ROSARY · EMILY · NOMADE · PEPPER

186. PRESIDENTS

BUCHANAN · MONROE · BIDEN · WASHINGTON · JACKSON · PIERCE · HOOVER · OBAMA · COOLIDGE · TAFT · ARTHUR · NIXON · REAGAN · POLK

187. PRIMATES

KINGKONG
ORANGUTAN
AYES · GIBBON · CHIMP
HAM
MAMMALS
HUMANS
LUCY · LEMURS
TOOLS
PLANET

188. PUT ON YOUR DANCING SHOES

CANCAN
TAP
WALTZ · BALLET · POINTE
TWERK · STEP
LEOTARD
SWING
HORA
REEL
CONGA

189. RAISE A GLASS

MOJITO
CUBALIBRE
MIMOSA
MARTINI
SANGRIA
EGGNOG
COSMO · TEAL
RYE

190. REPTILES

CHAMELEON
GECKO
SCALES
GILA
COBRA · KOMODO
DINOSAURS
DRAGON
TUATARA
TORTOISE · TURTLE

191. RIDING LESSONS

ENGLISH
TAIL · CANTER
CURRYCOMB
WALK
SADDLE
SPURS
DRESSAGE
REINS
MANE

192. RODENTS

CHINCHILLA
MARMOTS
TEETH
GROUNDHOG
PORCUPINE
AGOUTI
BEAVER
GOPHER

193. ROM-COMS

194. ROMEO AND JULIET

195. SAT WORDS

196. SATURDAY NIGHT LIVE

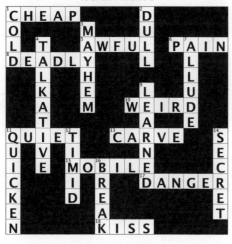

197. SAY CHEESE

198. SCHITT'S CREEK

199. SCHOOL DAYS

200. SCHOOL OF ROCK

201. SEAFOOD SALAD

202. RISE AND SHINE

203. SEATTLE

204. SETTING THE TABLE

205. SMART COOKIES

206. SOCCER

207. SODA POP

208. SONGS NAMED AFTER WOMEN

209. SPACE EXPLORATION

210. SPACE MOVIES

211. SPAIN

Across/Down entries include: STEAK, MANCHEGO, PAMPLONA, PAELLA, SIESTA, GAUDI, FLAMENCO, TOMATO, CHURRO, BULLS, ALHAMBRA, CERVANTES

212. SPIELBERG FILMS

Across/Down entries include: RAIDERS, PRIVATE, CATCHME, TERMINAL, RYAN, SIDE, WAR, MUNICH, SCHINDLER, LINCOLN, HOOK

213. SPOKEN IN

Across/Down entries include: ENGLISH, URDU, MANDARIN, POLISH, THAI, TAGALOG, CZECH, GERMAN, MALAY, LAO, FRENCH

214. SPOOKY STORIES

Across/Down entries include: JAWS, BLATTY, SCARYSTORIES, IAM, FRANKENSTEIN, POE, RICE, HOUSE, REBECCA, LOTTERY, LEGEND, DEAD

215. SPORTS MOVIES

Across/Down entries include: MIRACLE, TONYA, DURHAM, BULL, ROCKY, MONEYBALL, LEAGUE, REMEMBER, ALI, COOL, SUNDAY

216. STATE BIRDS

Across/Down entries include: TURKEY, QUAIL, ROBIN, LOON, FALCON, PELICAN, REDFINCH, BUNTING, BLUEBIRD, CARDINAL, WREN, ORIOLE, DOVE, GULL

338

217. STATE CAPITALS

JACKSON · STPAUL · JUNEAU · CONCORD · NASHVILLE · LITTLE · OLYMPIA · SALEM · DESMOINES · ROCK · MADISON · AUGUSTA · ALBANY · DENVER · BOISE · ANNAPOLIS · SLC · CITY · HELENA

218. STATE FLOWERS

BLUEBONNET · BITTER · SUSAN · DOGWOOD · PEACH · MAYFLOWER · PEONY · SAGE · IRIS · YUCCA · SEGO · BLACK · BREY · ROSE · MAGNOLIA · VIOLET · CHEROKEE

219. STATE NICKNAMES

PELICAN · OCEAN · PEACH · BAY · NATURAL · GARDEN · SUNSHINE · FIRST · GOLDEN · SILVER · HAWKEYE · BEEHIVE · EMPIRE · SNOWM · KEYSTONE · LONESTAR · PINE

220. STATES BY MOTTO

MINNESOTA · OHIO · ALASKA · TEXAS · ALABAMA · CALIFORNIA · NEVADA · IDAHO · LOUISIANA · VIRGINIA · MAINE · FLORIDA · OREGON · HAWAII · GEORGIA · ARIZ · WISCONSIN

221. STEPHEN KING

REDEMPTION · CUJO · CARRIE · RICHARD · LOVE · INSTAND · STAND · DOCTOR · SHINING · BAG · GREEN · CHRISTINE · MISERY · CLOWN · SEMATARY · MILE

222. STEPPIN' OUT

FLIPFLOPS · FLATS · CLOGS · PUMPS · LOAFERS · SANDALS · TAP · SKATES · STILETTO · BOOT · BROGUES · HEELYS · CROCS · SADDLESHOES · SLIPPERS

339

223. SUGAR, SUGAR

224. SUPER NINTENDO

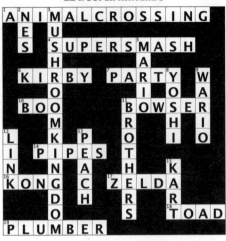

225. SWIMMING AND DIVING

226. TAKE ME OUT TO THE BALL GAME

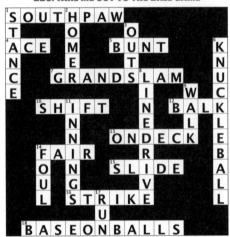

227. TAKE YOUR MEDICINE

228. TAYLOR SWIFT

229. THE 1950S

230. THE 1960S

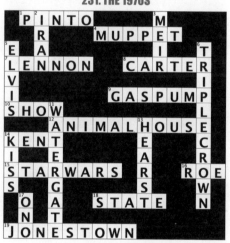

231. THE 1970S

232. THE 1980S

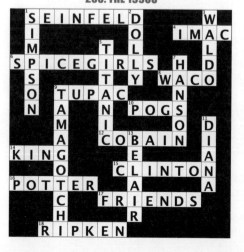

233. THE 1990S

234. THE 2000S

235. THE 2010S

236. THE AFRICAN CONTINENT

237. THE BIG APPLE

238. THE BIG BLUE SEA

239. THE BOY WHO LIVED

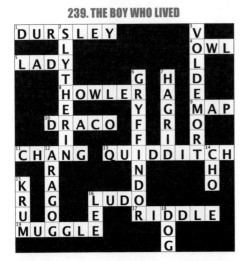

240. THE BRITISH ROYAL FAMILY

241. THE CITY OF ANGELS

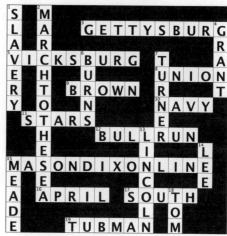

242. THE CIVIL WAR

243. THE COUNTY FAIR

244. THE DISTRICT OF COLUMBIA

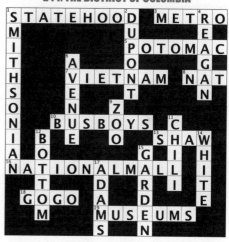

245. "THE EARTH LAUGHS IN FLOWERS"

246. THE ELEMENTS

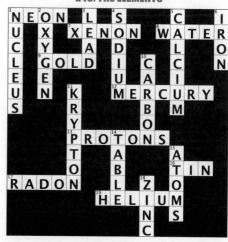

247. THE FAB FOUR

248. THE FILMS OF STANLEY KUBRICK

249. THE FINAL FRONTIER

250. THE FOURTH OF JULY

251. THE HORROR, THE HORROR!

252. THE HUMAN BODY

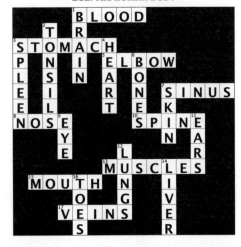

253. THE LONE STAR STATE

254. THE LORD OF THE RINGS

255. THE MEDITERRANEAN

256. THE MOON LANDING

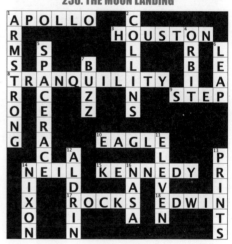

257. THE MUSIC OF ABBA

258. THE OFFICE

259. THE OLD COLLEGE TRY

260. THE OREGON TRAIL

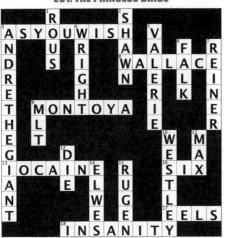

261. THE PRINCESS BRIDE

262. THE REVOLUTIONARY WAR

263. THE SUPREME COURT

264. THE US PRESIDENCY

265. THE WILD BLUE YONDER

266. THE WONDERFUL WORLD OF DISNEY

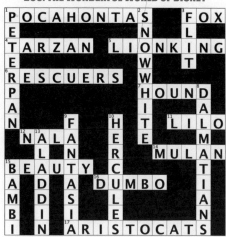

267. THE WORLD OF ALFRED HITCHCOCK

268. THE WORLD OF BEVERLY CLEARY

269. THE WORLD OF PIXAR

270. THE WORLD OF SHAKESPEARE

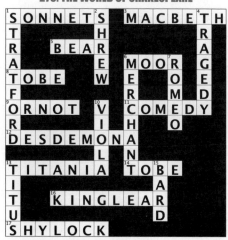

271. THE WORLD OF WINE

272. THE WORLD WIDE WEB

273. THE ZODIAC

274. TOM HANKS MOVIES

275. TREE HUGGER

276. TUTTI FRUTTI

277. TV FAMILIES

278. TYPES OF DOCTORS

279. VAMPIRES!

280. VICE PRESIDENTS

281. VIVA L'ITALIA!

282. VOTES FOR WOMEN

283. WAR MOVIES

284. WE DIDN'T START THE FIRE

285. WEATHER OR NOT

286. WEDDING BELLS

287. WE'RE OFF TO SEE THE WIZARD

288. WHAT THE DICKENS

289. WILD WILD WEST

Across/Down grid words: SHARPSHOOTER, HOWDY, CODY, BILL, JANE, LASSO, CASSIDY, VARMINTS, COWBOY, RUSH, BISON, SALOON, CROCKETT, BILLY, HANCOCK, HIDEOUT, RODEO, MOE, SPUR, HUNDREDACRE...

290. WINNIE THE POOH

OWL, GOPHER, OOZ, CHEFFALUMPS, CHRISTOPHER, PIGLET, ROBIN, HONEY, HUNDREDACRE, TIGER, RABBIT, EEYORE, KANGA, TREE, EXIT, ROO, DEAR

291. WINTERTIME

GLOVES, SHOVEL, GRAY, FREEZE, DREARY, FLANNEL, THAW, SLEIGH, COCOA, COLD, FLAG, FLU, BLIZZARD, SKI, BOOTS, FIRE, SNOW, ICE

292. WOMEN BEHIND THE CAMERA

LITTLEWOMEN, HUG, FAST, LADYBIRD, PARIS, THEKIDS, GRETA, AMERICAN, BIGBADOO, SLEEPLESS, SELMA, LOCKER, WONDER, AVA, WOMAN, LOST, CLUELESS, TIME, THEIROWN

293. WOMEN'S NAMES

ANNA, JEAN, NANCY, AMANDA, ABIGAIL, JULIE, DEBBIE, ELLA, JESSICA, LIZ, LAURA, ALICE, MARY, MEG, HELEN, MARTHA, AMY, DAISY

294. WORDS COINED BY SHAKESPEARE

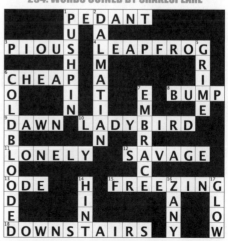

PEDANT, PIOUS, LEAPFROG, PUSH, ANIMATE, GRIPE, CHEAP, EMBER, BUMP, DAWN, LADYBIRD, LONELY, SAVAGE, ODE, FREEZING, HINT, DOWNSTAIRS, LOW, COLDBLOODED, ZANY

351

295. WORLD CAPITALS

296. WORLD CITIES

297. WORLD LEADERS

298. WORLD RELIGIONS

299. WORLD WAR II

300. YOUNG ADULT FICTION

Brimming with creative inspiration, how-to projects, and useful information to enrich your everyday life, Quarto Knows is a favorite destination for those pursuing their interests and passions. Visit our site and dig deeper with our books into your area of interest: Quarto Creates, Quarto Cooks, Quarto Homes, Quarto Lives, Quarto Drives, Quarto Explores, Quarto Gifts, or Quarto Kids.

First published in 2021 by Chartwell Books,
an imprint of The Quarto Group,
142 West 36th Street, 4th Floor,
New York, NY 10018 USA
T (212) 779-4972 F (212) 779-6058
www.QuartoKnows.com

10 9 8 7 6 5 4 3 2 1

Chartwell titles are also available at discount for retail, wholesale, promotional, and bulk purchase. For details, contact the Special Sales Manager by email at specialsales@quarto.com or by mail at The Quarto Group, Attn: Special Sales Manager, 100 Cummings Center Suite 265D, Beverly, MA 01915, USA.

ISBN: 978-0-7858-4011-4

Publisher: Rage Kindelsperger
Creative Director: Laura Drew
Managing Editor: Cara Donaldson
Puzzle Editor: Rebecca Falcon
Cover Design: Beth Middleworth
Interior Design: Danielle Smith-Boldt

Printed in China